A OMI SCHNEIDER BOOK

Highlighting the lives and experiences of marginalized communities, the select titles of this imprint draw from sociology, anthropology, law, and history, as well as from the traditions of journalism and advocacy, to reassess mainstream history and promote unconventional thinking about contemporary social and political issues. Their authors share the passion, commitment, and creativity of Executive Editor Naomi Schneider.

UBERLAND

The publisher and the University of California Press Foundation
gratefully acknowledge the generous support of the
Barbara S. Isgur Endowment Fund in Public Affairs.

UBERLAND

HOW ALGORITHMS ARE REWRITING THE RULES OF WORK

ALEX ROSENBLAT

UNIVERSITY OF CALIFORNIA PRESS

University of California Press, one of the most
distinguished university presses in the United States,
enriches lives around the world by advancing scholarship
in the humanities, social sciences, and natural sciences.
Its activities are supported by the UC Press Foundation
and by philanthropic contributions from individuals
and institutions. For more information, visit
www.ucpress.edu.

University of California Press
Oakland, California

Library of Congress Cataloging-in-Publication Data

Names: Rosenblat, Alex, 1987– author.
Title: Uberland : how algorithms are rewriting the rules
    of work / Alex Rosenblat.
Description: Oakland, California : University of
    California Press, [2018] | Includes bibliographical
    references and index. |
Identifiers: LCCN 2018023686 (print) | LCCN 2018025474
    (ebook) | ISBN 9780520970632 (e-book) |
    ISBN 9780520298576 (cloth : alk. paper)
Subjects: LCSH: Uber (Firm) | Ridesharing—United
    States.
Classification: LCC HE5620.R53 (ebook) | LCC HE5620.
    R53 R67 2018 (print) | DDC 388.4/13212—dc23
LC record available at https://lccn.loc.gov/2018023686

Manufactured in the United States of America

26 25 24 23 22 21 20 19 18
10 9 8 7 6 5 4 3 2 1

CONTENTS

ACKNOWLEDGMENTS

She's great at making humongous Uber stories, but what does
that have to do with making breakfast?

> Raphael, age eight, at seven o'clock in the morning

That's just the outcome. What's the reason?

> Aron, age five, past bedtime (He asked why he
> had to go to bed and was warned he would get
> into trouble if he didn't.)

I owe special thanks to my family, my mentors, colleagues, and friends. This book also takes special inspiration from my grandfather, Ernie Rosenblat, a trucker who was always on the road, and my grandmother, Molly Rosenblat, who was very glad to see him at the end of each week.

No one has engaged more with my day-to-day discoveries in Uberland than Adam. His excitement and curiosity buoyed my own, and he gave vision and moral fortitude to a project of critical inquiry. He is also a devoted parent and husband, a doctor, and a health technology entrepreneur, and he cooks almost all of our family meals.

danah boyd is infinite in her friendship and brilliant in her mentorship. She instantly understands and appreciates the observations I can make in the world. With her unique ability to identify what people are capable of becoming, she created opportunities for me that I couldn't see myself. I am grateful to her beyond measure.

To Yossi Farren, who's been reading and supporting my work since before I knew I was doing it.

I am always grateful to Beverly and Ed, from whom I got my adventurous spirit and my educational opportunities. To Randy, who discouraged me from overworking. And to Carly, who read and shared everything I worked on.

I owe special thanks to Patrick Davison and Jeremy Durant for their editorial contributions. Patrick was invaluable to this book and all the research publications that inform it. He's a clean and insightful academic thinker, a compassionate human, and a brilliant editor whose structural mind helped scaffold the details and analyses of driver stories. I set two goals for the writing process when I started this book: to write it quickly and to make it accessible. Jeremy Durant was indispensable to both. He helped me sharpen and organize my ideas. His keen attention to wordiness saved me from academic tangents, except where I overruled his advice. True to his word, he made my book a priority at all hours of the day and night as deadlines neared. He is more than a talented editor—he is a great friend.

I'm also grateful to David Lyon, Annette Burfoot, and David Murakami Wood, who first gave me confidence to pursue sociological work. And to Ruth Donsky, my first teacher.

To Natasha Singer, Anne L. Washington, Tom Igoe, and Jessica Bruder, whose brilliance and kindness were deeply encouraging to me as I wrote this book.

To Labor Tech, a group of scholars organized by Winifred Poster, who, along with Michael Palm, offered generous feedback on my manuscript. To Frank Pasquale, who has a rare ability to detect and draw intellectual connections across different fields of research and to connect scholars accordingly.

To Stacy Abder, who patiently explained to me how things work while she was busily taking care of business. To Janet Haven, who demonstrates leadership through stewardship. To Sam Hinds Garcia, who commands respect for everyone she works with. And to Irene Chung, whose quiet competence, visible empathy, and talent for making everything both more functional and more beautiful brightened the Data & Society office for everyone who passed through it.

To Daniel Grushkin, for giving me his time and attention to help me see the bigger picture when I reached stumbling blocks. And to the Digital Cultures Research Lab at the University of Lüneburg, which offered me a fellowship and provided an ideal writer's retreat with wonderful colleagues at a pivotal time.

I owe thanks to so many people who helped me as I pursued the research and asked a lot of questions about technology, security, labor, media, and computer science, and these include Michelle Miller, Surya Mattu, Tamara Kneese, Finn Brunton, Christo Wilson, Caroline Jack, and Martin Shelton. And to my brilliant coworkers and colleagues whom I worked with at different stages of my interdisciplinary scholarship, including Luke Stark, Alexandra Mateescu, Julia Ticona, Ryan Calo, Tim Hwang, and many more.

And of course, I owe special thanks to the publishing team that made this book happen, including Lisa Adams and Naomi Schneider. Microsoft Research, the Open Society Foundations, the John D. and Catherine T. MacArthur Foundation, and the Robert Wood Johnson Foundation have my deepest thanks for their generosity as funders for this research and for their interest in the social impact of technology on work.

INTRODUCTION

*Using an App to Go to Work—Uber as
a Symbol of the New Economy*

Freddy, a driver with both Uber and Lyft, pulls into the parking lot when he comes to pick me up, giving me a moment to search out his large sedan on a bright day in Atlanta, Georgia. With more than three years of vagrant sociology research under my belt, I've learned to hop into cars on busy streets as soon as I recognize the vehicle's license plate from my smartphone screen. His Chevrolet Impala is spacious, and I'm struck by the instrumental jazz on the car radio, which reassures me like a lightweight fleece on a foggy day. Most drivers stick to pop music when I'm in the car, perhaps because of the color of my skin. And I've heard some drivers suggest they get higher ratings from black passengers if they play Cardi B. or other rap music. I guess Freddy just enjoys jazz.

Freddy tells me he's a twelve-year veteran of the army, having left around 1989, just before the Gulf War. I explain to him that I'm not just another passenger; I'm a researcher studying how Uber and technology affect work. As I ask him basic questions, he tells me that he also works full time as the manager of a fast-food restaurant in a nearby city. When he has time off from his primary job, he commutes three hours into Atlanta to take ridehail jobs. During his vacation period, he spends about four days working ridehail jobs, heads home for a day or two and then returns to the lineup of drivers waiting for ride requests in the airport parking lot. "We have a quale [queue], a place where all the Uber and Lyft drivers park, and I stay there." His sister lives not too far away, and that's where he showers.

When I ask him where he sleeps in between driving shifts, he nods to the front passenger seat and exclaims, "You're sitting in my bed!" With a reassuring smile, he adds that he's not the only one who does it—men and women from outside the city are catching up on sleep in the airport parking lot.[1] Sometimes he works fourteen to sixteen hours in a single day, and the next day he'll do eight hours, depending on how he feels. He aims to average two hundred dollars a day, and on this trip he's proud to be earning "double money"—his vacation pay from his fast-food job supplements whatever he makes driving. "During the vacation period, I really had nothing to do," he says, "and I'm a people person. I love meeting new people."

As in the case of many of the people I've met during my research, driving is a second job for Freddy, and he genuinely enjoys the social connection he gains from conversations with passengers. Taking mental notes as I ride with him, I notice an open pack of Newport cigarettes that sits neatly on a little shelf near the gear shift, and a frayed brown wallet below. After hundreds of Uber rides, I've learned that the minimal personal effects that drivers leave scattered in their cars can provide revealing windows into their lives. Most keep their valuables out of sight, except for the phones and charging wires they use to manage their ridehail work. Freddy's own phone is mounted on the windshield, but I notice that its charging cord runs down and partly obscures a business card tucked into a crevice beneath his wallet: "Learn how 1000's are earning FREE GOLD while being paid a weekly massive RESIDUAL INCOME."

The promise of free gold is perhaps a fitting symbol for the gap between hype and reality in Uberland. A culture of shaky and insecure work in precarious times shapes the dynamics of driving for Uber,[2] even though drivers do not individually perceive their employment as being precarious. As a near-geriatric migratory driver, Freddy illustrates the "fool's gold" of Uber's rhetoric. Contrary to the company's marketing, he isn't "sharing" his spare asset and time with his riders: he is working hard to make ends meet. Uber claims drivers can earn upward of ninety thousand dollars per year doing ridehail work,[3] but Freddy's situation is a far cry from the picture of middle-class comfort promoted by the company.

Uber rose to prominence as an employer by providing the masses with low-barrier-to-entry employment opportunities—with little more than a car and a background check, anybody could be on the road driving as much or as little as he or she wanted. At its core, Uber does one thing really well: it organizes work for drivers and rides for passengers through a smartphone app. When it comes to marketing, Uber paints itself as the whole package for would-be drivers, pulling off a clever doublespeak. On one hand, it promises drivers freedom, flexibility, and independence. It tells them that they are entrepreneurs who can "be your own boss."[4] For legal purposes, Uber classifies them as independent contractors, meaning they are largely excluded from the employment and labor law protections to which employees are entitled.[5]

Yet on the other hand, Uber leverages significant control over how drivers behave on the job. Rather than supervising its hundreds of thousands of drivers with human supervisors, the company has built a ridehail platform on a system of algorithms that serves as a virtual "automated manager."[6] Freed from the necessity of layers of real bosses, algorithms manage drivers directly according to the rules that Uber lays out. But it's not as glamorous as it might sound at first. As entrepreneurs, drivers theoretically set their own hours, accept or decline passengers freely, set their pay rates, and build client lists. Some of that is true for Uber drivers. Drivers benefit from flexible hours, but Uber's promotional offers can effectively create shift work for drivers who need the money. The company may deactivate drivers who try to build their own client lists, and many drivers with whom I broach this subject say they don't even bother trying because they feel safer knowing they are covered by Uber's insurance policy (which offers $1 million in auto liability insurance per accident if one occurs between the time a driver accepts a trip and the trip's completion).[7] They are penalized if they decline passengers, but Uber doesn't actually give them the information they need to assess whether a ride is profitable in advance. And Uber perennially, and unilaterally, changes their pay rates, usually by cutting them. Drivers are supposedly free and independent, but Uber's rules, enforced by these algorithmic managers, significantly limit the opportunities for entrepreneurial decision making available to them. Drivers have noticed the tension between the promise of freedom and the reality of invasive algorithmic management. In fact, this tension is the basis of legal claims that drivers should not be classified as independent contractors.[8]

One of the fascinating aspects of Uber's approach is that according to the company, its drivers are not workers at all—they are "consumers" of Uber's technology services, just as passengers are. In 2013, a group of drivers and lawyers filed a class-action misclassification lawsuit, alleging that Uber was not justified in classifying drivers as independent contractors; they argued that Uber treats drivers like employees.[9] In a January 2015 court hearing of the case, Uber's lawyer explained that the company's drivers are actually customers of its software. "Fundamentally, the commercial relationship between these drivers and transportation providers and Uber is one where they are our customer, where we license to them our software, and we receive a fee for doing that."[10] If we follow this logic to its natural conclusion, the company doesn't have any worker problems, despite mounting lawsuits, protests, and conflicts with drivers across the country.[11]

This is a book about how Uber created a fundamental cultural shift in what it means to be employed. It is also a book about technology ideology—the stories Uber tells us about users, and the stories we tell each other about the role of technology in our lives. It's a tale of how a small start-up in Silicon Valley put algorithms in charge of managing hundreds of thousands of people in the United States and Canada. By

2018, Uber employed 3 million active drivers globally. This book traces the story of how the company crafted a narrative that defined workers first as working-class entrepreneurs, then as customers, because redefining traditional categories was a clever way of pursuing its own growth. *Uberland* also exposes how Uber has utilized self-serving arguments to advance its own interests.

For example, Uber self-identifies as a technology company, not a transportation company. As federal judge Edward M. Chen articulated in the same lawsuit where Uber argued that drivers are actually customers, this technology-exceptionalism reasoning is "fatally flawed." Uber may use software for the mechanics of its business, but it is substantively in the business of arranging transportation. Judge Chen writes, "Uber does not sell software; it sells rides. Uber is no more a "technology company" than Yellow Cab is a "technology company" because it uses CB radios to dispatch taxi cabs."[12] But by self-identifying as a technology company, Uber has proceeded to argue elsewhere that it isn't covered under the Americans with Disabilities Act (ADA) because it's not a transportation company. Therefore, by their argument, Uber is not legally obliged to provide wheelchair-accessible services for disabled passengers under the ADA, unlike its competitors in the *transportation* business.[13] Uber has continued to flourish as a technology company despite misgivings about its rhetoric, though not without certain pitfalls.

More often, Uber's arguments about its identity or its actions are dressed up in morally persuasive causes that appear to promote the interests of drivers, passengers, civil rights activists, regulators, cities, and the public at large. These alliances each contain a grain of truth, but they mask much more than they reveal. Under our noses, the company has ushered in a wave of changes touching most aspects of society, be it family life or childcare arrangements, worker conditions or management practices, commuting patterns or urban planning, or racial equality campaigns and labor rights initiatives. Uber's wide-ranging impacts have not just upset the status quo across society but have also created a future of uncertain implications. The company has harnessed technology to create an entirely new business logic for employment, like Napster did for music and Facebook did for journalism.[14] Uber is a symbol of the New Economy, a powerful case study illustrating how digital culture is changing the nature of work.[15]

RIDING IN CARS WITH "ENTREPRENEURS"

For nearly four years, my job has mainly been to ride around in cars with strange men (and sometimes women).[16] Studying Uber drivers from mid-2014 through the winter of 2018, I've crossed more than twenty-five cities and traversed more than five thousand miles in cars in the United States and Canada, from Juneau to Montreal. In the traditions of multisite ethnography and immersive journalism, I've observed the culture of work in Uberland in more than a dozen major cities,[17] like New York and Atlanta. I've had one-off rides and short conversations with ridehail drivers in other cities, like Bozeman, Montana, and with taxi drivers, such as in "pre-Uber" cities like Vancouver, British Columbia, and Winnipeg, Manitoba.[18] Once in a while, I've conducted phone interviews with drivers in cities I haven't been to, like Baton Rouge, Louisiana; Houston, Texas; and Raleigh, North Carolina. In some places where Uber was illegal, I observed and interviewed drivers while they worked underground, and I returned to observe after the company came out in the open. In all, I have conducted interviews with 125 drivers who work for ridehail companies, as well as some taxi drivers, in cars, on the phone, through Skype, and occasionally in online chats. I have also made observations by riding along with over 400 drivers in cars. Hundreds of rides later, the treacly scent of air fresheners I inhale on each trip still makes my eyes water.

The stories that these ridehail drivers share with me remain etched in my mind. Manoj is an Uber driver in Montreal who started driving for the company while it was still operating illegally. He explains to me why, back then, he was unfazed by the risks of attack by taxi drivers or censure from the transportation police. "I cross many countries' borders, illegal," he says with a crackle in his voice as he shares his life story with me. Both quiet and brazen, he isn't afraid to break the rules. A Hindu religious minority in his native Bangladesh, he left for the Soviet Union as an economic migrant to find work. He continued through the former Czechoslovakia, burrowed under electrified fences to cross through East Germany to Frankfurt, and found asylum in Canada after his refugee claim in Germany was rejected. Although Manoj was indifferent to the prospect of driving illegally, Uber finally obtained legal permits to operate in Montreal in October 2016,[19] where Manoj continues to drive for the company.

Nathan, a researcher during the AIDS epidemic who now works as a psychotherapist, started driving for Lyft (Uber's smaller-twin competitor) in Los Angeles to find emotional relief in the less-pressing needs of his passengers. He read reports of Uber's shadier practices, and he tells me it gave him pause as he wondered if he might be treated in a similar way at Lyft. Karen, who had long worked in the service industry in New Orleans, liked driving for Uber, in part because of the flexible schedule: if her son were to have a sudden episode of his chronic medical condition, she could stop working at the drop of a hat. Meanwhile, Hukam, who studied mechanical engineering in India, used his immigration work permit to drive part time for a taxi company in Winnipeg, after completing graduate studies in Canada. Anticipating Uber's impending arrival in the city, he observes, "Definitely the taxi business will go low for some time. Because it's new, people will love to try the Uber." Upon reflection, he says he may try driving for Uber, but he will wait and see.

My rides across cities and across the continent have reinforced the idea, for me, that Uberland is an array of contrasts. Some drivers sign up because they need extra cash on the side; others do it as their full-time job. Many resort to it as a stopgap solution when businesses fail or unemployment strikes; others take up ridehail work for the fun of it. Some are trying it out to pad their savings; others have little choice, putting in fourteen-hour days just to feed their families. Some tell me that they do it simply to get out of the house and experience a sense of human connection; others are desperate to find a way out of Uber. Former taxi drivers, chauffeurs, and truck drivers are part of the Uber workforce, but others have no primary occupational identity as drivers, even as they drive for both Uber and Lyft.

Their stories are all too often tales of folks on the margins, of workers in transition, of people who are part of a new wave of social progress that we are still trying to comprehend. Uber drivers frequently make the headlines as part of larger societal discussions about the future of work, and as part of a growing nervousness that technological advancement threatens to automate all of us out of jobs. But beyond this simplistic narrative, I've found that drivers are barely treated as workers at all. Given that Uber treats its workers as "consumers" of "algorithmic technology," and promotes them as self-employed entrepreneurs, a thorny, uncharted, and uncomfortable question must be answered: *If you use an app to go to work, should society consider you a consumer, an entrepreneur, or a worker?*

Why does it matter? Consider government benefit programs. In 2014, attorneys with Philadelphia Legal Assistance noticed a rash of frustrated unemployment claims. Pennsylvania has a robust unemployment system: even those with part-time employment are eligible for benefits. But the recently unemployed who began driving for Uber to try and make ends meet? That's independent contractor work—*self-employment*, not part-time employment—and so their unemployment benefits were jeopardized.[20]

Or consider immigration status. Ibrahim, an Uber driver I chatted with in Montreal, immigrated to Canada from Libya. He was caught in bureaucratic limbo when he tried to sponsor his wife so she could join him, because he could not provide the necessary proof of employment. Uber was operating in Montreal without a proper permit (as it does in many places before it becomes legitimate), so immigration authorities had trouble recognizing his job. Ibrahim assures me the authorities made accommodations for his case after his wife got pregnant.

There is a real argument to be made that Uber provides employment to its drivers, but Uber's "consumer" spin provides a simple out for the company. I interviewed Kofi in the fall of 2017. He drives for Uber and Lyft in Washington, DC, and he was formerly an assistant attorney for the government in his country of origin, Ethiopia. He responded to the provocation that drivers are actually consumers by accusing ridehail companies of operating in bad faith. He said, "The motive is to exclude the drivers from being in a worker or an employer relationship, or something like that. I will take it as more than a technology." By claiming to operate in a world of consumption rather than in a world of labor, Uber excuses itself from a series of obligations that it finds inconvenient. Kofi also objected to the idea that drivers have full autonomy to make entrepreneurial decisions; he cited the disciplinary actions that ridehail platforms take against drivers as evidence of the invisible authority they lord over their drivers (even while the company claims not to be an employer).

Kofi's criticisms highlight the fact that Uber confuses categories such as innovation and lawlessness, work and consumption, algorithms and managers, neutrality and control, sharing and employment. It does so with practical insistence on questionable facts, spinning tales about its business that directly contradict its actual operations. And the story doesn't stop when the ride ends: Uber's dealings with its drivers also reveal a much larger narrative about how technology is destabilizing and redefining relationships across society. By muddying the bright red lines that define traditionally distinct roles, like those of worker, entrepreneur, and consumer, Uber rewrites the rules of work surrounding algorithmic technology.

HOW I BECAME AN UBER SLEUTH

My quest to understand the inner workings of ridehailing has taken me into many worlds. I've encountered many of the major characters of Uberland over the years, including critics and advocates of the Uber model, Uber employees seeking to improve the Uber driver experience, industry researchers, labor advocates, venture capitalists, civil rights groups, senators, regulators, students, and members of organizations from the World Bank, in my various capacities as an expert, a researcher, a writer, a passenger, and simply as a person who is of interest, or interested. Along the way, I've interviewed a handful of industry experts and one of Uber's cofounders, all of whom helped fill out some of the contours of Uberland. In this book, I endeavor to include the wide variety of experiences and observations I informally accumulated as a longtime observer in the gig economy, in addition to my formal ethnographic fieldwork. This work principally explores Uber in its immediate American backyard as a brainchild of Silicon Valley, though it is a global phenomenon.

One perk of my position as an outsider to the company but an insider in Uberland is that I detect early warning signs, like fractures of discontent, before they hit the front pages of newspapers or even the company's internal eyes and ears. Uber is so decentralized in its driver operations that sometimes I obtain information that directly contradicts what the company says from its headquarters, perhaps because various outposts of Uber's operations just do things differently. I think of the screenshots I capture from forums as digital muckraking, using proof of drivers' experiences to expose the difficult conditions of ride-hail labor platforms—similar to photojournalist Jacob Riis's use of photography to expose the squalid living conditions of New York City slums.[21] *Uberland* is a written account of what I have seen, read, heard, and experienced among drivers online and offline and how their stories reflect the impact of technology on society.

My intense curiosity about even the most seemingly routine aspects of driving for Uber churns against my efforts to be unobtrusive as an ethnographer, but I hope my hunger for information isn't too sharply apparent in my interactions with drivers. Some of the more harrowing stories they confide wrap around me like an iron lung, controlling my breathing and bringing the immediacy of their experience into sustained focus. Sometimes I get the feeling of whiplash, jumping from certain cities where Uber's arrival is exciting and imminent to others where the company is the subject of sustained protest. I have begun to measure my travels not according to the calendar but according to the most mundane features of the Uber cars I ride in: the absence of a phone holster or dashcam, for example, becomes a "tell" of which stage of the driver experience a particular driver, or city, is at. As I make observations in ride after ride, I draw on the rich scholarship around me to shape my ethnographic observations into more scholarly analysis. I'm so immersed in Uberland that I retell parts and parodies of the Uber experience in bedtime stories for my family.

MEET THE DRIVERS

Many of the drivers I meet (and whom you'll meet, too, throughout this book) are transplants from other states or provinces or even other countries. In Orlando, I met a group of drivers from New Jersey and New York. They moved to find affordable suburban homes with amenities and the possibility of a man cave. In French-speaking Quebec and nearby Ottawa, I met drivers from Francophone African and Caribbean countries, like Algeria, Senegal, the Congo, and Haiti. On the West Coast of the United States, I learned that many came from South America—Argentina, Bolivia, or Brazil. In New York, I meet many drivers from Pakistan and Bangladesh.

One dynamic that I frequently noticed in the cities I visited in the United States is that drivers who immigrated are sometimes hesitant to say where they are from, perhaps because it makes them more prone to discrimination, to claims that they do not belong in America. I spoke to a few from Muslim-majority countries, like Iraq or Egypt, who referred vaguely to "the Middle East." I often break the ice by confiding that I'm from somewhere else too—an immigrant from Canada. In the United States, many of the immigrants I met proudly announced that they were "American": being American is a desirable social status. In select cities, like Atlanta or New Orleans, a lot of the drivers I met were local, born and raised there or nearby. In the Canadian context, which I'm more familiar with, drivers were more comfortable saying where they came from, perhaps because Canadians celebrate a "mosaic" model of cultural belonging. (In either country, however, the question "Where are you from?" can be an affront: the people inquiring position themselves as entitled to knowledge of your ethnic background, or they might be asking as a derisive comment on your place in the race ladder—or both).

Other cultural quirks stood out to me as I parachuted into different cities. In Salt Lake City, where half the population is Mormon,[22] many drivers told me, unprompted and often with a familiar apologetic note, "I'm not Mormon," as a means of introducing themselves as transplants. In Washington, DC, the previous occupations of drivers are striking: former political analysts at embassies and former interpreters in Afghanistan for the U.S. military are among them. In DC, I notice that you're allowed to ask people what they do for work, but if they are vague about it, you're not supposed to ask further (presumably) because they might work for one of the various government agencies, like the CIA. This cagey dynamic permeates my discussions with drivers, and I modify my style by talking more about what I do before I ask drivers about their work.

Drivers often demonstrate their awareness of their city's local culture by reciting common refrains. Ali, who moved to Montreal from Libya, punctuated some of his observations about driving for Uber in Montreal with the commonly accepted truth that "in Quebec, there are two seasons: winter and construction." In several cities, including Dallas, Salt Lake City, and Atlanta, drivers described their connection to driving for Uber within the context of a flourishing local technology scene or, as in Charleston, South Carolina, a revival of the city's industries and downtown core. However, in New York City, where Uber has operated since 2011, drivers tend to compare Uber to the taxi industry (which has deep roots in the city) rather than linking it to the rise of technology jobs. In New Orleans, drivers embrace the central role that the service industry occupies in the city's economy, and Uber is an additional layer of that service industry. Drivers in New Orleans treated me as a peer, both in my capacity as a passenger and when I approached them as a researcher. They pointed out restaurants they had tried recently, or planned to go to, and made authoritative recommendations. In contrast, there might be a wide class divide between the restaurants that drivers and passengers in New York City can afford to dine at. All of these factors affected the dynamics of my interactions with drivers, and they gave me a sense of regional differences in Uberland.

Most of the drivers I've spoken with have found work with both Uber and Lyft where both are available. Strategically, I used multiple ridehail apps to speak with Uber drivers, which generally works because drivers often start with Uber before they go on to work for additional ridehail employers. Because Uber is a dominant market player, even drivers who have never worked for the company have some knowledge of it or experiences with it. I have also spoken with or interviewed some taxi drivers, especially in cities that are "pre-Uber." For years, I have also kept up with many online forums for Uber drivers. Toward the end of 2017, the forums I followed had about three hundred thousand members collectively. I've spent hours nearly every single day for years reading the text of drivers' forum posts about their experiences, from anxieties and advice to warnings against passenger scams (like passengers who cancel a trip midway to their destination to try and score a free ride). These daily check-ins not only reveal the minutia of driving work but also give me an emotional connection to Uber's dispersed workforce. I have developed an intuition about Uber's relationship to its drivers from spending so much time on the forums, much as historians develop intuition about archival sources they spend a lot of time reading.

At times, however, I feel less like a historian and more like a moving target. Trying to study an international corporation—known for its ability to harvest data—has put me in the shoes of an almost-spy. I use an assortment of diversions to cover my tracks. To prevent Uber (and, to some extent, Lyft) from pinpointing the drivers I've interviewed, I hail rides from multiple accounts and phones, even purposely leaving highly identifiable trails of my movements among drivers and cities on some accounts and services to obscure my forays into the field through alternate accounts and services in case I am being tracked. And not every ride involves an interview. In addition to being concerned about driver confidentiality, I operate with the general assumption that I am being surveilled. This is not just a misguided sense of paranoia: Uber demonstrated to a female journalist, Johana Bhuiyan, that they were tracking her whereabouts.[23] They also threatened the family of another female journalist, Sarah Lacy, and floated the idea of launching a million-dollar campaign to silence her.[24]

Although drivers from all around the world form groups online—some smaller, some larger—I primarily follow national and regional groups in the United States and Canada. By the time this book was nearing completion, I was following driver groups and chat boards with memberships that, though they range in size, together comprise about three hundred thousand members. Some have fewer than twenty members, while other memberships hover around sixteen thousand; most of them are English-language forums, and select ones are primarily for French- or Spanish-speaking drivers. (I can more or less keep up with the French ones, with some help from translation services, but I mostly note screenshots of the Uber app in languages I am less familiar with.) Many forums function as virtual watercoolers,[25] although only a portion of those are highly active, and some forums are much more dynamic than others. An important side effect of this intersection of technology-mediated work and the social features that develop externally to it is that drivers are constantly comparing notes and identifying discrepancies in company practices and policies. This tension is somewhat inherent to technology-driven work on platforms, because Silicon Valley companies like Uber and Facebook are constantly experimenting on their users to assess the effectiveness of different practices. However, because drivers don't really expect to be the subjects of A/B testing, such as when the company tests one version of an app feature or pricing on some drivers and another version on other drivers to evaluate which one performs better: the experimental practices that might work on everyday consumers on the Internet have different consequences in the workplace at Uber. Drivers can lose trust in their employer when they are subjected to iterative features and wage experiments.

MY RELATIONSHIP WITH UBER

Every so often, I'm asked what Uber thinks of my research or if I've had contact with them while researching their practices. For the duration of the fieldwork that this book relies on, I had sporadic communications with the company in an official capacity and a handful of meetings off the books. Most of the employees I have met appear to be, above all, *excited* by the challenges and promises they work toward. My first memorable encounter with a senior Uber employee was at a gathering of labor and technology scholars and advocates shortly after I published the article on Uber's "phantom cabs" (see chapter 3), which had gone viral.[26] Halfway through the group gathering, after the lunch period, an Uber representative invited me to sit with them and made reference to my "research" with the slight affectation of a person making air quotes. (The lightly dismissive tone of Uber's representatives has often spurred me to vindicate my findings with even *more* research and publications.) On at least three subsequent occasions—and probably more by the time this book comes out—I have asked former and active senior Uber employees for their thoughts on some of my research findings. My conversations have included pointed questions about the possibility that Uber was engaging in automated, low-level wage theft, at scale, for its drivers, through the technical design and affordances of its driver app. (They denied any intentional wage theft, but they did offer to investigate my findings with their internal teams.)

I am grateful for the doors they left open so that I could understand and address the implications of my findings with them outside of the public relations machine. Speaking with them didn't change my findings, but it did inform my sense of their logic and frameworks and made me cognizant of gaps or limits in my own thinking or approach. Occasionally, I've run into senior Uber and Lyft employees at conferences and at hosted meetings that address the future of work. When we've sat down to chat, we've sifted through the details and debated the far-reaching implications of the rise of ridehail work. Meetings such as these have made it clear that there are unresolved tensions in how we understand the future of work: some thinkers study macroeconomic trends, others focus on the law, and some, like me, emphasize the social and cultural dynamics at stake.

When I was visiting San Francisco in 2016, I arranged a meeting with a senior Uber employee, one of a handful of senior employees I would meet over the years. Like everyone who entered their headquarters, I was prompted to sign a nondisclosure agreement (NDA) at the electronic check-in kiosk of their San Francisco headquarters. I refused, and the secretary communicated this fact to the person I was coming to meet. We went to a "non-NDA café" across the street instead. I jokingly asked if they brought all of their non-NDA'ers to this café, and this person replied that this situation had never happened before. A non-NDA, neighborhood café became the template setting for my future meetings with specific Uber employees. On two occasions, the next senior employee I met brought along additional witnesses, junior employees, to observe and participate in the conversations. This move simultaneously suggested that our meeting was a teachable moment and that the witnesses made these informal meetings a little more official. On another occasion, in the spring of 2016, I presented a paper alongside my coauthor, legal scholar Ryan Calo, entitled "The Taking Economy: Uber, Information, and Power" at the biggest conference of technology and privacy-law scholars in the United States. Our session was presided over by an active commissioner for the Federal Trade Commission. Uber sent one of their lawyers to listen, and she sat quietly while a packed room of leading scholars vocally piled onto the challenges we raised in our paper. Around that time, Uber also assigned two policy employees to communicate with me more consistently, and these two have been remarkably responsive to the queries and concerns that I have raised (or blogged about). Outside of official channels, I have had limited encounters with Uber stakeholders, including one of Uber's cofounders. He and I bonded over a common interest in the ripple effects of technology and inequity on society, and in the regional differences evident in the impact of Uber's business model.

Outside of my communications with Uber's senior employees, Uber's PR reps remained in touch with me or made themselves available for me to contact. After I published the article discussing Uber's misleading "phantom cabs" phenomenon, their senior PR rep insisted it was false and tried to persuade me to take it back. Uber widely repeated this message to the media—that my finding was wrong—before adjusting the company's statement, affirming that my finding was true but stating that they had good reasons to hide the true locations of, and misrepresent the number of, cars in the street through the passenger app. I later learned that the senior PR rep who contacted me had departed from Uber. This became a pattern. I did not have a consistent point person to speak with among the communications or policy staff until the two employees mentioned above were finally assigned as my "handlers." This inconsistency may have resulted partly from the fact that, in several cases, Uber employees sought new employment within months of their contact with me.

One of the oddest moments on my research journey was when Uber tried to hire me. On a rare sunny day in rainy Vancouver in the spring of 2017, I looked at my email inbox and found two adjacent messages. One was from a book publisher offering me a contract. The other, sitting beneath it, was a job offer from Uber, or the beginnings of one. This moment says a lot about what happens to experts: once they know enough to be a threat, the companies they study will try to absorb them. I was sorely tempted, and even waited for a phone conversation with the senior employee who offered to hire me, before accepting the book offer I had been seeking. At that point, I had spent over three years studying this behemoth through the experiences of its drivers. I was hungry to learn how the people building the company in senior management understood the same dynamics I was seeing from the outside. That conversation was delayed, which was fateful timing: I accepted the book offer.

I continued conversations with some of Uber's senior employees on what this sort of job could look like, but I held firm on one point: full independence to write. I'm not a purist, but my intellectual curiosity about information, coupled with my sense of fear and risk, convinced me that whatever insights I had would be quashed if I did not have the freedom to publish. As my mentor advised me when I called her from San Francisco's busy airport to get her thoughts, you can't study the company you work for. While writing this book, I occasionally had Uber's senior employees in mind, many of whom have voracious intellectual appetites of their own. I think they will find this book interesting; while undoubtedly they will disagree with some of it, they may find it reveals certain insights that they sensed but hadn't necessarily seen from the perspective of the drivers.

LET'S TAKE A RIDE

As a technology company in the ridehail business, Uber has an employment model that is changing the nature of work. The company promised to leverage its technology to provide mass entrepreneurship to independent workers. At Uber, algorithms manage how much drivers are paid, where and when they work, and the eligibility requirements for their employment. But the power of algorithmic management is obscured from view, hidden within the black box of the app's design. While speaking with hundreds of drivers, culling thousands of forum posts online, and working together with scholars across disciplines to suss out the implications of what I've observed, I've found that the technology practices Uber implements (such as algorithms) significantly shape and control how drivers behave at work. This finding is a lightning rod in debates over whether drivers are misclassified as independent contractors rather than as employees, but this book is not focused on questions of labor history or labor law.

Instead, *Uberland* is an exploration of how Uber and other corporate giants in Silicon Valley are redefining everything we know about work in the twenty-first century through subtle changes ushered in by technology. Chapter 1 traces the rise of Uber in the context of a new sharing economy. In the midst of declining economic conditions and class mobility at the end of the first decade of the twenty-first century, technological innovations sparked the rise of companies like Uber, TaskRabbit, and Airbnb, sparking rapid changes for American workers in the process.

Against this backdrop, chapter 2 explores Uber's success in constructing a mass workforce by examining the kinds of workers who decide to drive with the platform and exploring their motivation. Given that each group of drivers—full-timers, part-timers, and hobbyists—has unique needs, Uber has found ways to divide and conquer by pitting drivers against each other.

Chapter 3 then examines the storytelling that Uber relies upon to expand its empire. Entrepreneurship has a noble heritage in the United States, a fact that Uber makes use of when recruiting its drivers. Despite the company's grandiose promises, however, the experience that Uber delivers to its drivers is a far cry from actual entrepreneurship. Uber's pay structure, information asymmetries, and management controls are indicators that ridehail work is not the entrepreneurial endeavor the company makes it out to be.

A lingering question—can we trust Uber to be a fair and honest broker?—is the subject of chapter 4. When we think about tech-mediated transactions, the technology part sounds pretty neutral—it's just an engine that works behind the scenes. But in the age of Uber, "technology" isn't as innocent as it sounds. Uber's algorithms aren't neutral: they broker transactions according to a set of company rules that may have built-in biases in favor of the company's own bottom line.

Based on reports, leaks, studies, and firsthand accounts of drivers and passengers, we know that Uber collects a vast amount of information (ranging from the battery level on a user's device to the likelihood that a client is willing to pay a higher rate), potentially using these data points to play both drivers and passengers. Chapter 5 builds on questions of fairness by exploring some of the tools Uber uses to rule by algorithm, including the rating system and a seemingly robotic customer service system.

Uber is more than just a ridehail company. Like other Silicon Valley companies with global aspirations, such as Google or Facebook, Uber crafts public policy initiatives to brand its business operations with positive social contributions to society. Uber has actively enhanced its brand on the public stage by, for example, supporting criminal justice reform or allying with Mothers Against Drunk Driving. Going beyond drivers and passengers, chapter 6 explores the alliances Uber makes between competing stakeholders to accomplish its goals, and what emerges is often a form of doublespeak. On the one hand, Uber tells cities that it creates the equivalent of full-time jobs, and on the other hand, it argues that drivers are ineligible for many of the employment rights associated with full-time work, like the minimum wage. There is often a vast gap in Uberland between high-level debates about Uber's impact on society and the downstream effects of its alliances on drivers. Nonetheless, drivers can become unwitting participants in the battle lines that Uber draws for its competing stakeholders.

Finally, a brief conclusion chapter examines Uber in light of the social changes it has sparked and accelerated. Increasingly, we must come to grips with the reality that as platform companies experiment on us, they may also be exploiting us. This may already trouble users of consumer platforms like Google or Facebook, but the stakes are higher when workers rely on platforms like Uber for their livelihoods. These parallels also demonstrate that even if Uber were to disappear tomorrow, it would leave behind a legacy of important shifts that will shape the worlds of labor, technology, and law for years to come. In that sense, although Uber is the primary focus of this book, it is representative of what is happening in the larger society as well.

CHAPTER ONE

DRIVING AS GLAMOROUS LABOR

How Uber Uses the Myths of
the Sharing Economy

In the spring of 2010, Uber launched the first beta version of its now-famous smartphone app. It promised to revolutionize transportation. Uber offered anyone with a car a new way to earn extra income through casual jobs as a driver. Meanwhile, anyone needing a ride could now benefit from an affordable, on-demand chauffeur service to get around. The Uber platform allows users to seamlessly connect passengers and drivers: it calculates the rates, transmits credit card information, and maintains quality ratings for drivers and riders alike.

As a company, Uber has unquestionably changed the way people get around hundreds of cities across the world. It has become a symbol of the New Economy and, for some, the future of work. Uber advertises that its drivers are entrepreneurs who can, with flexible schedules, make middle-class incomes even in an unstable economy. But do these assertions hold up to scrutiny, or is the company playing us with false claims?

THE GREAT RECESSION AND THE SHARING ECONOMY

Before we can understand how Uber treats its drivers, it's necessary to take a step back. Uber's employment model was born in the so-called sharing economy,[1] a social technology movement that capitalized on the economic instability of the Great Recession to sell a narrative.[2] Between 2007 and 2009, the Great Recession and collapse of the sub-prime mortgage markets ravaged American households with waves of foreclosures. The collapse of financial markets challenged societal confidence in American institutions, like banking and governance,[3] while an exodus of former homeowners shut down neighborhoods and led to urban blight in cities like Detroit and Cleveland.[4] Job losses increased suddenly,[5] and national unemployment climbed to 10 percent in October 2009.[6] This instability sharpened the economic consequences of prolonged joblessness for white-collar workers, who comprised 60 percent of the labor force; by 2009, they accounted for nearly half of the long-term unemployed.[7] Still, the greatest job losses from the Great Recession were concentrated in blue-collar industries among workers under thirty.[8] Although the Great Recession officially ended in June 2009, its impact on unemployment persisted well into the economic recovery.[9]

This context helps explain why sharing-economy companies with roots in Silicon Valley, like Uber, so often frame their technologies as powerful engines of job creation. In the media and in some academic debates, the future of work is framed as the threat of a robot coming for your job. While society may benefit from automated work, the fear is that these benefits will not be distributed equally: jobless futures imply some will get left behind. This threat is not an inherent characteristic of technology but, rather, comes from the current American economic climate. As Philip Alston, a poverty investigator from the United Nations, observed at the end of 2017, "The reality is that the United States now has probably the lowest degree of social mobility among all the rich countries. And if you are born poor, guess where you're going to end up—poor."[10] When technology innovators use "job creation" language, they engage in virtue-signaling: the implication is that not only do they deserve credit for producing large economic gains for society,[11] but also they should be shielded from harsh criticism for their methods because the end result is positive.

The sharing economy promised to save the day for a population shaken by the Great Recession: using technology, millions of people across society would now be able to efficiently pool and share their limited resources. The seeds of Uber took root in a climate of profound economic uncertainty. After the recession hit in 2007, shockwaves of economic downturn rippled across the globe: Greece's government tumbled into insolvency, while in Iceland, bankers were frog-marched to jail for burdening the country with a private banking debt seven times its annual GDP. In the aftermath, the front pages of newspapers regularly featured Middle Eastern and African refugees drowning as they tried to reach Europe, compounding a sense of economic urgency in the United States with global humanitarian concerns arising from geopolitical conflict. The collapse of Wall Street was a reminder that no empire, not even the American kingdom of financiers, is absolute. At the World Bank and the International Monetary Fund, leading economists began to rewrite their theories with a new focus on income equality, replacing earlier ideas that had emphasized growth above all else.[12]

Back in the United States, victims of the Great Recession began to push back against the corporations and practices that had caused the crisis. The City of Baltimore, the State of Illinois, and the Pennsylvania Human Rights Commission, among other, bigger victims of foreclosures, sued the notorious lending institutions whose high-risk lending fueled the Great Recession—institutions like Wells Fargo—and settled for hundreds of millions.[13] Predatory lending practices targeted racial minorities during the subprime boom, highlighting the role of finance in social injustice. Emergent social movements that advocate for social equity, like Occupy Wall Street, organized activists with a common desire to re-center society around a moral economy.

While Occupy Wall Street activists formed a tent city in Zuccotti Park on Wall Street, members of Black Lives Matter were staging protests across the country to advocate a political agenda that could address the root causes of inequality.[14] Soon, more voices joined the chorus, this time from the top. Facebook cofounder and philanthropist Chris

Hughes dedicated his intellectual thought leadership to promoting a universal basic income,[15] and Mark Zuckerberg, his former roommate, mentioned it in the commencement speech he gave at Harvard.[16] This quasi-moral solution to income inequality—and to expanding the definition of equality for this generation—finds its strongest American proponents in Silicon Valley. Home to the billion-dollar titans of industry, who form a slightly reluctant political elite in the New Economy, Silicon Valley and the culture of technology radiate influence across the business, political, and media culture of major American cities. And Silicon Valley has a strong stake in national debates over whether automation technology, such as self-driving cars, will take all our jobs. Universal basic income is one form of "automation alimony" that is proposed to relieve the rising inequality often attributed to automation.

It was in this economic and cultural climate that the buzz around "the sharing economy" began. Its promise was seductively simple. The sharing economy was a social technology movement designed to use tech to share resources more efficiently—a true "commonwealth" aimed at remedying some of the insecurity fostered by the Great Recession. The sharing economy was built atop earlier cultural conversations, like those about rental commerce, car-sharing, and cooperative housing. Technology could connect those who possessed underutilized assets, skills, or time with potential consumers, a form of commerce that reduced the costs of ownership and more efficiently distributed goods and services.[17] For struggling millennials displaced by the recession, this new model provided a hopeful new paradigm for earning income. As Robin Chase, cofounder of the car-sharing service Zipcar,[18] wrote in 2015, "In the new collaborative economy, sharing and networking assets, like platforms, car seats and bedrooms, will always deliver more value faster."[19]

Critics, like scholar Nick Srnicek, countered the idea that the sharing economy was anything novel, branding it as a mere reiteration of the platform capitalism of the 1970s.[20] Arguing that platform capitalism will hasten the end of work, Srnicek advocates a future of different possibilities.[21] Meanwhile, culture scholar-activist Trebor Scholz sees platform cooperativism as a viable way of redistributing corporate profits of platforms like Uber to workers. The disparity between billion-dollar tech giants and the rest of society makes it easy for critics of capitalism to shout from the rooftops, and by the mid-2010s they weren't alone. The question that academics, policy makers, labor advocates, and others were asking outright, with greater insistence, by the end of 2017 was blunt: Why aren't wages growing in America?[22]

Against this contentious backdrop, ridehailing platforms began promoting themselves as a pathway to the middle class for anyone who wanted to drive. Uber quickly became the poster child for the sharing economy, advertising itself as "a smartphone app that connects riders and drivers at the touch of a button." Founded in March 2009 in San Francisco, the company grew quickly by hiring decentralized staff in each new city or region. These new staff were empowered to establish Uber's operations with lightning speed, like a vast network of start-ups. By the middle of 2017, the company operated in over 630 cities worldwide, and it had provided 5 billion rides to passengers.[23] By March 2018, it had 3 million active drivers worldwide.[24] More importantly though, Uber offered its drivers a job with personal autonomy and a path to a middle-class life, even as that middle class was shrinking.[25] Meanwhile, as early as 2014, Uber announced that the median income of its drivers was a little more than ninety thousand dollars per year in New York City and over seventy-four thousand dollars in San Francisco.[26]

Arguably, the chief accomplishment of technology in the sharing economy has been the creation of robust platforms for serving temporary jobs to a flexible workforce that cycles through a variety of part-time or precarious and temporary jobs to make ends meet. Of course, gig work predates the technological framework that the sharing economy draws on as one of its distinguishing characteristics.[27] Economists Lawrence F. Katz and Alan Krueger argue that the percentage of workers employed in gig work climbed from 10.07 percent in February 2005 to 15.8 percent in late 2015, a decade later.[28] (Although growth in this area is high, the exact measures of the gig economy are unknown: the Bureau of Labor Statistics did make plans to conduct a 2017 survey of contingent workers, though their efforts are still pending as this book goes to press.)[29]

The prevalence of temp, gig, and contingent work is summed up by a *Wall Street Journal* headline at the end of 2017 announcing, "Some of the World's Largest Employers No Longer Sell Things, They Rent Workers."[30] Highlighting how three out of five of the biggest employers in the United States distribute contract labor, the article describes how they operate like temp agencies. Uber shows us how a company can organize masses of *people* through technology into discrete units who are available on demand to take passengers from point A to point B— until the drivers opt to log out. That same technology fundamentally alters labor relations as well: drivers are billed as consumers of Uber's connective technology, rather than as workers.

To join the Uber driver workforce, prospective drivers download the Uber driver app onto their mobile smartphones. They then take their Uber-eligible vehicles to local mechanics to be certified as in good working order and upload their driver's license numbers and auto insurance policy numbers to their accounts on Uber's website or through the app (drivers I speak with rarely obtain commercial insurance, unless they are obliged to by regulatory requirements). Then, after consenting to a background check that takes under a week in many places, they're ready to go. In other words, barriers to entry are very few. Part of what makes platforms so valuable is their ability to provide jobs to anyone and everyone in a decentralized workforce. As economic sociologist Vili Lehdonvirta observes:

> Piece rates are a substitute for more direct managerial control. Employers who pay hourly rates are pickier about whom they accept into their ranks in the first place, whereas one of the strengths of these platforms is that essentially anyone can sign up and start working right away with minimal hurdles. And workers who are paid on an hourly basis usually cannot take breaks quite as easily as pieceworkers. This low entry barrier and potential for almost minute-by-minute flexibility are genuine features of platform-based piecework, and some workers value them.[31]

Uber's platform manifests a profound tension: the company seeks to standardize work for the masses through algorithmic management while, at the same time, distancing itself from responsibility for workers.

The popularity of Uber among passengers has been central to public support for the sharing economy. Bolstered by popular opinion, tech and labor advocates take to the media to discuss how employment through an app is the future of work, a gangway of progressive opportunity off the sinking ship of the post–Great Recession economy. Perhaps underscoring Uber's shiny prospects as a new player in the labor market, economists have noted that after the job losses of the Great Recession, "recovery job gains came largely from new establishments entering the economy."[32] Sharing-economy employment is often concentrated in the service industry: jobs like delivering passengers, food, or laundry cannot easily be offshored or automated (yet).

With the example of Uber's success, countless other firms began following suit. It seemed that every new company, from domestic cleaning platforms like Handy to the multi-industry temping platform Fiverr, wanted to idolatrously claim their service as the "Uber for X."[33] Many of these imitators went belly-up, including Prim, for on-demand laundry services; HomeJoy, a home-cleaning marketplace; Tutorspree, for tutoring; and SideCar, a direct Uber competitor.[34] Nevertheless, Uber inspired a variety of companies across industries, including nursing, trucking, and others, to think about how technology can be used to create efficient on-demand services by organizing independent providers and consumers through a digital platform. Defining the sharing economy is like trying to nail Jell-O to a wall. It is a haze of converging ideas with popular appeal. Will employers across industries adopt sharing technology to manage their workforces?

The sharing economy grew much more quickly than anyone imagined it would. A Pew Research Center survey published in November 2016 shows that 8 percent of American adults earned money from an online employment platform in the previous year across industries such as ridehailing, online tasks, or cleaning/laundry.[35] Rounds and rounds of venture capital funding bolstered Uber and Airbnb, the two most successful companies to emerge from the sharing-economy period. Both companies became "unicorns," a term for start-ups that reach billion-dollar valuations. In 2016, Uber reached a $68 billion valuation, while Airbnb was valued at $30 billion,[36] less than a decade after their beginnings in 2009 and 2008, respectively. By July 2017, the Oxford Internet Institute's iLabour Project published a report finding that the online sharing economy, which includes clerical and data entry services for jobs posted online, had grown 26 percent in the previous year.[37]

But as the sharing economy has grown, things have gotten complicated. Increasingly, the "sharing economy" has been identified as an intensification of the "gig economy," as people have become suspicious of the way that words like *sharing* euphemistically describe precarious, part-time, and piecework employment.[38] Scholars, as well as media outlets like the *New York Times* and *Buzzfeed*, have moved to rechristen "ridesharing" as "ridehailing" in an attempt to ease the contradiction between altruism and employment. The sharing-economy language has long been both expansive and imprecise, recasting service industry and white-collar jobs alike in the amorphous terms of digital culture and the New Economy.

The sharing economy has also made for odd bedfellows: hopeful, left-leaning advocates of cooperative housing and bike-sharing found themselves allying with industry tech positivists (those who believe that technology will inevitably lead to continual social progress). As sharing technology has taken on a more significant role in society, other civil society actors have chosen to become stakeholders in Uber's future developments. The National Association for the Advancement of Colored People allied with Uber to provide employment for drivers with nonviolent criminal records,[39] and Mothers Against Drunk Driving promoted Uber to reduce drunk driving through ridehailing.[40] (Later, when the working conditions of drivers proved wanting, civil rights advocates were effectively pitted against labor rights advocates through Uber's clever maneuvering, though they might otherwise have found common ground in protecting the rights of vulnerable groups.)

While conversations about the role of Uber in society have their place, the commotion in Uberland may be fairly incidental to the lives and work of many drivers. In Montreal, I met Adnan, a Syrian immigrant to Canada. As I listened to him speak, I absorbed the drama of his life stories. Adnan recounted how he retrieved his pregnant daughter from the war zone of Syria by renting three guys with kalashnikovs to steal over the mountains from Lebanon with him, driven by a man who wore night-vision goggles. Adnan used to work in the entertainment business in Syria, and he developed many contacts among famous actors there who would be hired or invited to attend events for high-level government officials. They alerted him early on to the fact that it was going to get really bad. He started preparing to leave before the conflicts in Syria exploded into a full-out civil war. In 2012, he took his eldest daughter to visit Syria, and she stayed behind to get married. When she got pregnant, she wanted to find a safe haven; Adnan came to her rescue. Adnan drove for Uber in Montreal because, as he described, the manager at his previous job didn't like him. He said driving for Uber is good in a pinch because it's flexible, but he didn't earn enough to make it his livelihood. Luckily, his wife had a steady job as an accountant, through which he maintained his health benefits.

As the gig economy continues to grow, it functions sometimes as a social safety net for workers with high income volatility or gaps in employment, even outside the United States.[41] This is partly why sharing technology has been reframed as an engine of economic populism. Uber's influence on the future of work is compounded by the company's outsized valuation, upward of $70 billion through 2017,[42] and the oversized influence of Silicon Valley in the world. Uber's valuation as a private company is not set in stone: at the end of 2015, the company's investors valued it at $62.5 billion; in 2016, the high point for Uber's valuation was $68 billion;[43] a consortium led by SoftBank invested in the company at the end of 2017 with the understanding that it was valued at $48 billion;[44] and Alphabet obtained shares in Uber in February 2018 on the basis of a $72 billion valuation.[45] The company's value will be determined more concretely after an initial public offering, but the multibillion-dollar question of Uber's worth is part of what propels Uber to the front pages of the news. The company's place on the world stage is fairly irrelevant in contrast to the upheavals that a driver like Adnan has chronicled in his own life. At times, it can feel like the politics of Uber are dwarfed by the lived realities of its drivers. How does a question about whether the sharing economy is really about sharing compare with rifles and night-vision goggles? But this view mistakes exactly how incendiary Uber is. Uber is not incidentally political, nor are the company's politics limited to the features of its app or its driver policies. Everywhere Uber has set up operations, it has disrupted the structure of everyday life, ranging from that of communities to transportation industries. So much of what allows Uber to play us all is the fact that it has such a wide variety of stakeholders who have uneven investments in its methods, or its success, including drivers, civil rights groups, nonprofits that support girls who code, and regulators. Even when Uber plays only a small role in the lives of some of its drivers, such as Adnan, its politics may affect their working conditions and the risks they incur on the job in far larger ways.

The chapters that follow explore the nuts and bolts of Uber's practices and how these practices impact everyone from passengers and regulators to civil rights activists and other Silicon Valley companies. But first, what about the foundational promises of Uber as a service, a company, and an economic symbol in the United States? Uber's business model and its public image, like those of so many other start-ups and imitators, rely on three poetic fables: the myth of the economic value of "sharing," the myth of technological exceptionalism, and the myth of glamorized millennial labor.

THE MYTH OF SHARING

Uber spins itself as an altruistic company. It identifies as a technology company, not a transportation company, to draw a distinction between the laws that govern the taxi industry and what Uber does. But it is also saying that when work is mediated through a technology platform, labor becomes a type of communion, a message that comes from sharing rhetoric and through driver recruitment ads, such as "Get paid weekly just for helping our community of riders get rides around town." Uber drivers are classified as independent contractors in the eyes of the law and termed "driver-partners" in Uber's official lexicon: these categorizations imply a higher level of autonomy and equity in the company than they have in practice. The company positions drivers as "partners" with messages like "be your own boss" and "get paid in fares for driving on your own schedule." Other digital economy labor platforms, like Amazon's Mechanical Turk, and sharing economy companies like TaskRabbit, call their workers, respectively, "Turkers" and "Taskers" or "Rabbits" and bill them as entrepreneurs or micropreneurs.[46] This careful dance with terminology distances platform employers from the rules and norms of labor law.[47] These new platform companies attempt to align themselves with a lineage of "cooperative commerce"[48] or acts of mutual help and generosity like hitchhiking, carpooling, and couch surfing. But they also identify this image of cooperation with technology as fundamentally a new force in society.

Technology does facilitate access to underutilized resources and secondary markets of redistribution for goods and services,[49] and it extends opportunities by bringing the efficiencies of scale to existing transactional relationships.[50] And stories about what sharing technology can do "play a role in binding together these disparate industries and forms of labor: cheap, convenient, and fast services made possible through the empowerment of entrepreneurial, independent contract workers who benefit from the scaling of these industries via digital platforms," observes researcher Alexandra Mateescu, citing the work of media historian Caroline Jack.[51] But there is a gap between the promise and the realities of work in the sharing economy.

Uber, Airbnb, and other sharing-economy services downplay the amount of work that goes into driving, hosting, and similar kinds of "sharing" labor. Instead, they frame these jobs as a form of social reciprocity—users are simply sharing their homes, cars, tools, skills, or time with other users on the platform. This logic comes from the technology culture at large. As an article of faith, Facebook holds that all 2 billion of its users are a "community." Social software, like Wikipedia, fosters collaborative environments across communities of users who can contribute equitably to a common goal.[52] (Although this is the idea behind collaborative, open-source software projects, there are many examples where this vision of equity doesn't hold true. Women's edits to Wikipedia pages, for example, are rejected or reverted more often than men's edits. Their experiences warn us that not all contributions are treated equally.)[53] When companies like Uber capitalize on and co-opt the goodwill that organizations like the Wikimedia Foundation inspire and put it toward a business model that creates precarious work, they are trading on people's unstated notions and understandings about what collaborative online projects do. In the gig economy model, a top-down hierarchical employer is remade into a platform in the image of open-source software culture, where anyone can contribute or share their code to achieve a superior digital product or service.[54] And it's this very act of sharing that suggests a disruption of role identity, because the line between producers and consumers blurs—some scholars use the term *produsers* for this combined identity.[55] By obscuring the incentives of the market economy, the sharing economy painted a portrait of capitalism that felt community-oriented.

As a job with a low barrier to entry, driving for Uber is cast in this image, as an "open-source" opportunity for drivers to contribute their labor and earn "extra" money. Technology often blurs the line between paid and unpaid labor, in much the same way that women's contributions to work are undervalued. The societal failure to acknowledge some forms of women's work, such as emotional care, as work is premised on the assumption that they like doing it or that it's easy for them and therefore not work. The sharing economy similarly posits that technology makes work different than before: it draws on base assumptions about how things that are socially or community-oriented or involve personal passion are fun and therefore not work either. This technology culture can and does blur categorizations between what counts as labor and what doesn't. For example, Internet blogging created a type of free content contribution that effectively undermined professional journalism and made it a more precarious job by loosening access to information production. Uber trades on our cultural assumptions about technology to frame every driver as his or her own boss, implying that its platform fosters a collaborative and equitable environment without traditional top-down labor or management hierarchies. This is an illusion, but sharing rhetoric does overlay longer histories of contingent work.

The gig-economy job offerings at Uber, TaskRabbit, and Fiverr are a feature of low-wage work already. As sociologist Julia Ticona discussed with me in conversation, for low-wage workers it's not a choice between TaskRabbit or Uber and a forty-hour-a-week job with benefits. It's TaskRabbit or twenty hours a week at McDonald's and the other twenty hours at a friend's hardware store. The blend of formal and informal work blurs all the categories of employment we've held sacred for a long time.[56] Nonetheless, sharing-economy companies have had remarkable success in redefining the nature of work as a technology phenomenon and as a form of "sharing," because technology can be framed as a countersolution to more predatory forms of commerce.

THE MYTH OF TECHNOLOGICAL EXCEPTIONALISM

Taxi drivers have protested that Uber violates the laws that regulate their industry by operating without permits,[57] but Uber maintains that it is not a taxi company—it's a technology company that uses neutral algorithms to merely facilitate connections between consumers and drivers. Meanwhile, the growth of Uber has quickly become a threat to the highly regulated taxi industry's monopoly on chauffeur services. Companies like Uber and Airbnb separate themselves from their predecessors, taxis and hotels, by emphasizing the altruistic premise of their "sharing" platforms. Airbnb argues that it is a technology platform, like Facebook, YouTube, or Google, that connects hosts with guests. In conflicts with Airbnb, the hotel industry alleges that the company operates illegal hotels: hosts rent out their spare rooms or homes to traveling guests but do not have to comply with the safety regulations that govern hotels or bed and breakfasts.[58]

Likewise, Facebook, which is in the business of sharing news, resists being categorized as a media company. A media company can be regulated and held to account for journalistic ethics, editorial responsibilities, and news accuracy (rather than "fake news"). A neutral platform that uses algorithms to spread content or to curate newsfeeds is the product of engineering and automation, and these efface the responsibilities a media company might have under the guise of technological innocence. Scholars[59] and journalists[60] have penned marked retorts to Facebook's arguments, but the logic that Facebook uses is similar to what Uber deploys.

Silicon Valley carries the banner of "technological exceptionalism," the idea that the regulations and laws that apply to their industry competitors or predecessors do not apply to them for the simple reason that they identify primarily as technology companies. These tech giants reason that the technology services they offer to achieve a familiar goal (like moving a passenger from A to B in a taxi) are qualitatively different from the actions that these laws were designed to govern. This effectively renders laws archaic, to some degree, and this pattern among Silicon Valley tech companies is often termed "disruption." Law scholar Julia Tomassetti argues that the sharing economy amounts to regulatory arbitrage (an attempt to circumvent unfavorable regulation).[61]

THE MYTH OF GLAMORIZED MILLENNIAL LABOR

Uber has carefully crafted its recruitment messages to invite potential drivers to work for a global technology company, rather than a newfangled taxi service. Its marketing is almost exclusively organized around the archetypical image of the "millennial." Born between the 1980s and the early twenty-first century, millennials are touted as society's most active technology users, and they often find their work in the on-demand, gig economy. The CEO of Intuit, a company that offers tax accounting software for independent contractors that is particularly popular with Uber drivers, echoed the idea that the gig economy is a millennial phenomenon when he commented, "We know the gig economy is real. It's here. It's a secular trend. It didn't just start with Uber and Lyft. It started years ago. It's a lifestyle choice for millennials."[62] Even though they have been the butt of jokes about their limited employment prospects, millennials are simultaneously credited with access to the boundless opportunities of the Internet.

Digital-culture millennials are typically portrayed on TV shows, such as *Girls,* as living in cities with huge service-industry economies, like New York. The protagonists on *Girls* are primarily young women who demonstrate characteristic millennial "narcissism."[63] These characters are locked into perpetual recreational life choices as they flit between jobs and unhinged romantic prospects. Their intimate lives reflect their neoliberal choices in their careers as they seek self-determination based on their passions, rather than on the stable markers of older notions of adulthood, like marriage or steady employment.[64] Consider a 2017 campaign by Fiverr (see figure 1), a labor platform aimed at freelancers and "lean entrepreneurs" who hire workers in a range of capacities, including programming and tech. Fiverr ads plastered on NYC subways appeared to be aimed at selling a fantasy of glamorized gig economy labor built on cultural images of hardworking but unrooted millennials chasing their dreams.[65] In one such advertisement that I observed, a winsome young woman rests her head in the palm of her hand, but tilts it upward, looking slightly beyond the viewer. The caption reads, "How much did you make for your boss today?" followed by a green Fiverr icon and the Fiverr logo, "In Doers We Trust." Another, in the same subway car, read simply, "Reading about starting your own business is like reading about having sex," followed by the green Fiverr

YOU EAT A COFFEE FOR LUNCH.
YOU FOLLOW THROUGH ON
YOUR FOLLOW THROUGH. SLEEP
DEPRIVATION IS YOUR DRUG OF
CHOICE. YOU MIGHT BE A DOER.

fiverr

IN DOERS WE TRUST

Figure 1. Sample Fiverr advertisement from 2017.

icon and the same logo, "In Doers We Trust." As the title of one *New Yorker* article observed, "The Gig Economy Celebrates Working Yourself to Death."[66] An Uber driver posted a link to this article in a forum with the comment "I'd still rather overwork in the gig economy than be a corporate slave tied to a desk from 9–5." This observation affirms the thrust of the Fiverr ad profiled by the *New Yorker*: a beautiful woman is determined to rise above lesser mortals, who need things like lunch. Her slightly gaunt face and long, unkempt hair glamorize the labor that defines her as a "Doer."

The sharing economy takes gig work traditionally done by pink- and blue-collar workers—including people of color and new immigrants— and bills it as fashionable glamor labor for popular technology companies and on-demand platforms.[67] Labor is glamorized in part because popular technology communications, like social media, romanticize mundane aspects of our lives in general. The digital lives of millennials are held up as evidence of their self-indulgence, flakiness, and access to opportunity: the photos of food, friends, and fashion that they share on Instagram broadcast ideas of affluence and extravagant consumption, irrespective of where they fall on the socioeconomic spectrum. (Of course, it's not just millennials who actively project their status onto social media: swiping through Instagram accounts, Adnan proudly showed me pictures of his two daughters thriving in their new lives. One was living on the other side of the world on an exchange program.) Meanwhile, personal updates and excerpts that millennials post on social networking sites like Facebook and Twitter give the impression that they are always busy being "Doers" of something. Unpredictable, "flexible" labor has become just another part of the way today's economy functions. These realities are not unique to the way that Uber does business: digital life keeps many workers "on" all the time. When Uber, and others, frame gig work as a job for flexible millennial labor, it shapes our expectations of what this job should provide.

By using the image of a millennial to identify who workers are in the gig economy, Uber and other on-demand platforms project a higher social status onto work that has long been associated with lower-status workers. Lower-status work is merely an extension of historical attitudes that identified as second class the traditional jobs of women and minorities. Agricultural laborers and domestic workers, for example, are not protected by minimum wage laws in the United States, a concession that nods to the racialized and gendered labor legacy that includes enslaved African Americans working on plantation farms and women of color providing domestic labor to more affluent households. The gig economy tech-washes this work into something more culturally desirable, but the passion and sharing rhetoric reinforce an older idea that workers in this line of work aren't entitled to a living wage or labor protections. The gig economy is also a social expression of an economic trend in employment. For example, during the recessions of 1982–1983,

1990–1991, and 2007–2009, the loss of stable employment for male bread-winners resulted in more wives entering the workforce or increasing their hours, which economists term the "added worker effect." According to one prominent study, the 2007–2009 Great Recession produced the strongest such effect: perhaps the "need" for extra work has been reframed by the gig economy as a positive opportunity for "extra" income. In effect, the work culture that promotes the idea that everyone should get a side hustle puts a positive sheen on the declining economic prospects of male (and female) breadwinners.

The sharing economy draws on these histories, delegitimizing and feminizing work by pigeonholing sharing-economy jobs as mere side hustles. Even when drivers and other gig economy workers depend on their earnings for major household expenses, like mortgages, college tuition, or medical expenses, the pervasive notion that these are just "side gigs" dismantles expectations about what these jobs should pro-vide. Moreover, women's work in the household (child-rearing, house-work, and so on) has long been considered a social commitment that women make to their families and society, rather than a job that should be compensated with a living wage.[68] The language of "sharing" plays on this idea—that the social good is somehow an acceptable substitute for compensated work. "Sharing" also points to how culturally undesir-able it is to think about gigs as work: it's as though we can't change the conditions of labor, so we change the way we think about it instead.

UBER DOES WORK

Uber has proven to be more than just a successful new service. It has rapidly changed how people experience cities, and even how cities *work*. For cities with a saturated market of drivers, passengers no longer need to plan ahead to craft their itineraries; they can just order an Uber. This simple fact has changed how people date in car-heavy cities like Los Angeles,[69] and how likely they are to get behind the wheel drunk when a sober option is only a tap away. To many, Uber solves a problem. It creates cheap private transportation for people in cities with less reliable public transit options, and it improves the efficiency of private transportation for people in cities where are many public and private options too. The ridehail model brings the benefits of innovative technology to millions of people around the globe, and the effects are felt immediately.

For consumers, Uber's network effects at scale are astonishing. A global traveler can disembark from her flight in a midsized city in the middle of the country, pull out her iPhone, and hail a ride with the touch of a button. Chris Sacca, an Uber investor and venture capitalist, summed up the popular support Uber enjoys in its battles with the taxi industry when he declared in a Pando interview by journalist and Uber critic Sarah Lacy: "Who is happy with their taxi service anywhere in America? Like nowhere." On the topic of taxi service in New York City, where yellow cabs are a prominent form of transportation, Sacca commented, "People choose it as a way to get around that city, but nobody at scale is gonna tell you that they fucking love the New York taxi system." Many consumers witnessed the destruction of oligarchic taxi and hotel institutions by tech companies with the peculiar satisfaction that comes from watching a lot of complacency come crashing down. Uber passengers can watch their driver's car approach on the screen and track its movements by the minute. A text alerts them when the driver has arrived, and after they insert their destination, away they go. They don't have to worry much about being taken for a ride, because the whole trip is monitored: if the trip is inefficient, they can complain to Uber and get their money back. Taking an Uber is usually cheaper than taking a cab, and the level of human interaction is low. Payments are processed by credit card, and up until June 2017, there was no tip button. At the end of the trip, the passenger simply gets out of the car and, later, rates the driver on a scale of one to five stars. Rating systems, combined with other forms of verification and safety mechanisms, facilitate trust among strangers. In this way, gig economy companies like Uber are more mature or evolved than other informal networks of commerce mediated by the Internet, like eBay or Craigslist.[70] Uber has professionalized and scaled these patchwork e-commerce solutions and, with its improvements, set a precedent that other institutions more readily adopt.

THE REALITY OF DRIVER EXPERIENCE

The Great Recession made visible the fact that the institutions we trust, like finance and home ownership, are no longer working. It also underscored the narrowing of established pathways of social mobility, whether as a result of education or career-advancement expectations. Diminishing trust in institutions helped pave the way for Uber's rejection of established norms and laws that govern employment.

Driving for Uber has benefits as well as disadvantages. Michael drives for both Uber and Lyft. To do so, he commutes into Atlanta from Marietta, about an hour away. When I interview him on a mild afternoon in spring 2017, he gestures toward the main highway that runs through the city center, which has collapsed, supposedly because homeless kids set fire to it but possibly because of corruption, according to Michael. The collapse added traffic to the streets, which now slows him down as he ferries passengers around. He started about two months earlier, and this week he's driven every day except for Tuesday. Because he is a divorced dad, flexibility at work is important to him, because it enables him to see his younger children. Similarly, mothers of young children who drive for Uber and Lyft have told me they appreciate their ability to work in their spare hours without killing themselves to arrange childcare during an obligatory shift at Walmart or a similar retail outlet. "I have my sons every other weekend," Michael explains, "so the weekend I don't have them I just work through the week and the weekend, and when I do have them I only work during the week." He appreciates the freedom to set his own schedule: on a long week, he does about seventy hours and doesn't take a day off, while on short weeks it's more like twenty-five to thirty, or thirty to forty, hours. Before Uber and Lyft, he mostly did factory work. "I was working third shift at a manufacturing plant, making tires. I did not like working night shift. I did it for over a year. I just could not get used to it.

My body just could not acclimate. It was horrible, man," he says, energized by the finality of his statement, and by the note of surprise it still brings him. "So I just quit. For the first time in my life, I quit a job with no other job [lined up]. Two days after I quit, I said, 'I'm gonna drive for Uber.' So I started with Uber, I did Uber. Then I said, 'I'm gonna try Lyft, too.' Now I do both of 'em," he drawls, with the confidence of someone announcing matter-of-factly that he works out regularly at the gym.

Michael was ready for a change after his divorce, which took place about a year before we spoke. Not too long ago, he graduated from a for-profit Christian university. He's hoping to get into business with his bachelor's degree in interdisciplinary studies, with concentrations in education, psychology, and mathematics. As we accelerate through an intersection, the car in front of us takes too long, and Michael nearly rear-ends him, but barely a ripple passes through his muscular arm. We're a hairline fracture away from the other car. While my thoughts turn fleetingly to the universal public health insurance I could have back home in Canada and my heart catches in my throat, Michael continues. He's not at all perturbed by our near miss.

"I went through college throughout my adult life," he reflects, "I didn't just go get it. I started when I was twenty-two. I would go to work, and I would have to quit school sometimes and work more hours. It took me about ten years on and off." With three children to raise—a daughter who is eighteen, and two sons, fifteen and ten—going to school full time wasn't an option, though he hopes his kids will go away to college and do it all at once, for the experience. About his degree, he adds, "It hasn't helped me very much yet."

Michael's extended efforts to obtain a degree from a for-profit college give me pause, because it's an indicator that the established paths to middle-class life in America aren't working for him. He's not alone. Poor credentialing systems are a reflection of a poor labor market, observes sociologist Tressie McMillan Cottom. She writes, "We have a labor market where the social contract between workers and the work on which college has previously relied has fundamentally changed and makes more workers vulnerable."[71] The rise of useless college degrees is a clear signal that the established systems of social mobility have failed in America, and the gulf of opportunity is part of what makes jobs in the sharing economy appealing. Technology in the sharing or gig economy is framed as an intervention in the declining pathways toward upward class mobility.

Some drivers—so-called "optimizers" because they find clever ways to maximize their earnings—are making the digital economy work for them by juggling multiple kinds of jobs and opportunities. Ron started driving for Uber and other ridehail companies in New York City and New Jersey over three years ago, after his business as a web host went under. When I first interviewed him in 2015, he and his wife ran an Airbnb to support their growing family. He used a number of strategies to maximize his profits, although he chafed against rules Uber set that kept him from making more informed decisions, such as by hiding the destinations of passengers before he accepted their ride requests.[72] Another optimizer, Nicholas Stewart, is a former high school teacher who quit to drive for Uber and Lyft full time in Atlanta. He'd been driving for four years, though he planned to return to teaching in 2018–2019. When I interviewed him in 2017, he was simultaneously pursuing a PhD at the University of Phoenix online, a for-profit university, and running an Airbnb. He calculated that he would drive for Uber only when prices were surging at a premium of two and a half times the base fares, because then he could make $2.50 per mile—otherwise, it wasn't worth it. At airports, Uber's dispatcher puts drivers into a queue, and they may wait for hours until their number is called. When Nicholas waits in long airport queues, he runs laps around the terminal to keep fit and keeps his phone on him in case his turn in the queue approaches. He is also one of the administrators for a local forum of Atlanta ridehail drivers, where he shares advice about his experiences with other drivers, such as how to do taxes or how to account for expenses.

Not everyone who drives for Uber is working multiple New Economy hustles; how drivers identify with their work often depends on their backgrounds and their motivations. Nicholas identified primarily as a teacher, but former taxi drivers and truckers like Ricardo and Faiq in New York City identify as occupational drivers who just happen to be driving for an app now. Others, like Manoj in Montreal and Karen in New Orleans, put driving for Uber into the same box as other service economy jobs available to them, such as working in the restaurant business. Working in a full-time job with benefits isn't necessarily an option for them. Manoj drives for Uber part time, but he prefers his job at the restaurant because the tips are better. Previously, he worked in a garment factory for twenty-one years in Montreal. Some drivers are doing multiple types of gig work, but they don't see what they do as falling under the rubric of "sharing technology."

In Atlanta, I have the misfortune of experiencing two stressful rides in a row as a participant-observer (I don't interview either driver). In the first, the GPS malfunctions and we ride around for twenty minutes circling my original pickup location. I politely exit the vehicle after the driver begins hinting that he can't keep burning gas. In the spring of 2017 in Atlanta, Uber and Lyft paid drivers $0.12 per minute, much lower than the $0.75 they earn per mile, so drivers made money only on distance travel. On the next trip, the driver is anxious because he has trouble logging out of the Uber driver app when he picks me up via Lyft, and he whizzes past speed limit signs while poking around on his iPhone. If drivers don't log out of, for example, Uber within seconds of accepting a trip with Lyft, they might receive a ride request from Uber's dispatching algorithm that they will be unable to accept, which will negatively affect their ride acceptance rate. The action requires a swift, coordinated hand-to-screen motion across multiple phone screens while continuing to drive. It's common for drivers to work for multiple ridehail apps as they strategize to maximize their income, though competing options are not available in every city.

Empowerment-branding celebrates independent, entrepreneurial workers who can choose between competing employers and log in or log out of work at their discretion; but the reality of working for multiple apps or even just managing one app is often stressful. Tim, who drove for Uber and Lyft in San Francisco when I interviewed him in 2016, told me there are times when he's looking at the road, driving, and then a little ride request pops up on the screen, which he says lasts for only ten to fifteen seconds (technically, Uber tells drivers, they have fifteen seconds to accept the ride). "What if a car is coming or you're about to pull over? You can't have your eye on the clock the whole time or it's a safety hazard." Before Uber introduced a feature where drivers could opt to stop all incoming ride requests, he was exasperated with the bind they put him in: "It could be 2 A.M. and I want to get off because I'm done for the night, or I have to pick up my daughter from the sitter and, just as I'm getting off, another ride comes in." And he might, for example, have spent the whole shift working toward a bonus that requires him to maintain a 90 percent ride acceptance rate; if he misses the ride, he could lose the bonus. The technical difficulties of the app also frustrate him: sometimes he gets ghost requests, where the ride request appears for only a second, before he can respond to it, and then disappears—but it still counts against his ride acceptance rate. In some ways, it's as if drivers have become little more than digital pawns on the chessboard of the sharing economy.

Platforms are preparing people to accept gig work as the new norm for employment. But the Uber-touted promises of freedom and flexibility often fall short. Ricardo was a truck driver before he started driving for Uber.[73] He wants to spend more time with his seven-year-old daughter and less time on the road. During the last nine months he's put in fifty hours a week driving for Uber and other ridehail companies in New York City. Gesturing with evident pride, he says,

> The thing with Uber is you have a home base, so if you have a family, guess what? You be there for the family. The problem is, when you look at Uber's actual busy-hour schedule, there's the morning from 6 to 9 A.M., then the evening 5 to 7 P.M., and then from 9 P.M. to midnight. If you were to look at that and you have kids, and if you follow their busy schedule, you'll never see your kids in the morning. You'll come home at lunchtime to sleep, but you still won't see your kids. You might see your kids if you pick them up from school, but in that time frame, you'll only be able to pick them up, drop them home; then you'll have to leave to get into the city for that busy-hour rush.

For David, driving for Uber and Lyft was a stopgap solution after his job with a local firearms retailer went south. He leased a car through Uber in San Francisco for eight hundred dollars per month, but with low pay and long hours, he struggled to balance it with the demands of his family life. "It was a real strain on my marriage. I worked ten-plus hours a day, six days a week. I didn't spend a Friday night with my wife for almost nine months. I was on the verge of a divorce," he observes soberly. In less than a year, he transitioned to his dream job in a managerial position at a local brewing company.

Michael, who commutes into Atlanta from Marietta, says he keeps all his receipts so he can account for his expenses as an independent contractor. But like many new drivers, he isn't necessarily prepared to account for the full range of his possible expenses, like maintenance, wear and tear on his vehicle, commercial insurance for his vehicle, health insurance for himself, self-employment taxes, and more. "If you drive no peak hours and you drive forty hours a week, you can average twelve to fifteen dollars per hour, before expenses," he calculates—but the only expense he accounts for is gas, a fairly common oversight among new drivers. Many people who start working for Uber are prepared to run errands, but they're not necessarily prepared to run their own business. It can take months for them to figure out what they're actually earning, and in the meantime, new drivers often cite the earnings marketed by Uber and Lyft, like "$30/h," before they become aware of hidden costs.[74] *BuzzFeed* reporter Caroline O'Donavan dove into Uber's own data on its drivers, as well as a previous *BuzzFeed* investigation of drivers' earnings, and estimates that, "for example, a part-time driver of a minivan in Chicago earning an average $15.48 an hour would, based on Uber's model, incur $4.02 an hour in expenses, for a net hourly earning of roughly $11.46 an hour. A full-time driver in Washington, D.C., earning an average $18.21 an hour driving a four-wheel-drive SUV would have expenses of around $5.94 per hour, for net hourly earnings of $12.27."[75] The studies Uber has conducted in collaboration with notable academic economists typically cite drivers' net earnings (after Uber's fees but before costs like depreciation and fuel); the true earnings drivers take home after expenses are often unknown not only to new drivers but to the public and regulators as well.[76] It's complicated to accurately estimate drivers' costs overall, because each driver has specific operational costs that depend on factors like the cost of repairs and maintenance, fuel, depreciation, and the make of their car, among other items.[77]

Over time, many drivers say that it's worth it for them to drive only if they work specifically during "peak hours," such as when surge pricing, Prime Time, hourly guarantees, Quest Rewards, or other variations of incentive pricing are in effect. Adjusting the black sunglasses riding atop his closely shorn hair, Michael continues: "For me, I want more than that eventually, because I put all that money and time into that degree. I really just want to own my own business. I work when I want to work, but it's not the same. They [Uber] get 20 percent, that's their fee, which is not bad, I guess." Michael says they could make it a little easier on drivers by cutting it to 15 percent, but in cities where Uber has been established longer, the commission only goes up, usually to 25 percent and 28 percent for the lowest tier of service, uberX. Michael articulates the desire to truly be his own boss, and he enjoys the independence he has as an Uber driver that he didn't have in his previous job at a factory. He is grateful to have this job during a period of career transition. However, he may yet find himself working against higher commissions and rate cuts that Uber implements unilaterally. When the conditions of work change for Uber drivers, many hew closely to Uber's suggestions to work at particular places at particular times to earn premiums on their pay, effectively giving up some of their independence to work on a schedule that is subject to frequent changes and few guarantees.

The reality of working for Uber aligns more closely to the stories of working- and middle-class people who are often far removed from the millennial model typecast as an avatar of digital-technology culture. Amir, who drives for Uber in Montreal, worked as a chemical engineer in Algiers for twenty-eight years before he emigrated to Canada. His adult son and daughter are both married, and he lives with his son in Gatineau, Quebec, just outside of Ottawa. When he tried to transfer his engineering credentials to Canada, they advised him to return to school. He shrugged slightly as he furrowed the deep wrinkles in his brow, saying, "This is not for a guy like me." For the last year and a half, he's been driving to make a living. For ten to fourteen days at a time, he commutes an hour and a half into Montreal to drive for Uber. During these stints, he rents a home-sharing apartment in D'Iberville, about a twenty-five-minute drive from Montreal's downtown core. When he has a day or two free, he returns to Gatineau to relax and play with his granddaughter. He likes working for Uber, but he is critical of the growing role of technology in daily life. He sees babies playing with their iPads, and he thinks that they look at their mamas and papas with vacant expressions after they have spent time absorbed in their screens.

Uber tells its passengers that they, too, can start driving for Uber through its app, which promotes the idea that riders and drivers are interchangeable. After a passenger requests a ride, the message below their destination address might read, "Join thousands of riders who also drive with Uber," an opportunity, illustrated with the image of an outstretched hand holding a smartphone screen with a large dollar sign on it. That idea appealed to Tadesse, who was a ridehail customer before he began driving for Lyft in Washington, DC, and he's considering Uber as a future option. "I ride all the time because, after I have a few drinks, I don't drive. I just call a Lyft, and I talk to the drivers. Then a few friends start[ed] driving too." For a few weeks, he had nothing to do, so he rented a car to try it out. "Some people like it, some people don't like it. It's fun so far, it's not bad. You have to make a whole lot of runs to make money, and that's why I get a lot of customers, too.... It's cheap. You just have to make more trips to make the same as a taxi driver." The path that led him to this line of work is far removed from the archetypes of *Girls,* but it is part of the immigrant biographies that characterize many drivers in the Uber workforce. Tadesse left Eritrea when he was sixteen because of a brewing civil war. When he moved to the United States, he was completely alone, though he expected his twelve brothers and sisters to join him. Every single one of them perished. As a young immigrant, he enrolled in a computer science degree twenty years ago at a nearby university; but halfway through, he took on work as a taxi driver. As he started to make friends, and then girlfriends, the money drew him away from his studies and into full-time work. Leaving school is a decision he regrets—he cites the absence of mentors who could have guided him into better choices, which is evocative of his lost family. He's had a slew of other jobs since his early days as a taxi driver, including as the manager of a restaurant and bar. "I really don't want to work for anybody else," he says, and he's trying to figure out what he wants to do next. But, he adds, technology has been a boon to him. "If it wasn't for technology, we cannot do this job. With this thing right here"—he points to the GPS navigation system on his Lyft app—"I can go anywhere."

For some time, the sharing economy myths have protected Uber against a truer accounting of the working conditions it creates for drivers: the experiences of Michael, Amir, and Tadesse are a far cry from the company's promise to deliver mass entrepreneurship and a pathway to the middle class through technology. Contrary to the company's rosy rhetoric, their jobs do not carry the signature of sharing-economy altruism. Some drivers are working hard at jobs to support themselves and, often, their families. Others, like Tadesse, are trying it out, and they appreciate the fact that technology opens up new possibilities to them. This new gig marketplace is billed as a natural extension of the technology culture and glamorized labor. But there is a stark gap between the sexy marketing of the sharing economy and the more sober realities of who does this work and why.

CHAPTER TWO

MOTIVATIONS TO DRIVE

How Uber's System Rewards Full-Time and
Recreational Drivers Differently

Shortly before midnight, I stand by the curb next to the airport hotel, a lone traveler, scanning the vacant pickup zone for the Uber driver my phone informs me is on his way. I'm in Montreal, a city where Uber is still illegal yet operates anyway. The wind rips through my thin jacket and kicks up dust from the gray sidewalks around the lobby exit. A couple of taxi drivers are queued to one side. One of them, a man with a cropped beard, shouts at me from a few meters away as I half-turn with my eyes on my smartphone. He asks if I need a ride, and I recognize the question he is really asking as he eyes my phone. Am I waiting for an Uber driver? I turn to face him and shout back that I am waiting for my husband to pick me up. He acquiesces, and jokingly replies that I better wait then. Relieved, I spot an inconspicuous car in the shadows of the hotel entrance with a cowed driver hunched over the wheel under a gray-knit cap, covertly scanning the door for his passenger. I walk over to him and slide into the front passenger seat, trying to signal that I understand the stakes. For the duration of this trip, I am his friend, not his paying passenger. The driver's name is Hari. He presses the "Start Trip" button on the phone balancing on his leg, hidden from the peering eyes of passersby. Once we are on the highway, Hari visibly relaxes; the road away from the city center is clear. Hari drives for Uber to support his wife and four young children while he looks for another job. He finished his studies in electromechanics, but he quit his job after he experienced health problems. While he was at home, sending out his CV (curriculum vitae) for months on end, a friend who drives for Uber called and invited him to join while in career transition.

Uber has ushered in a new era of work through its practice of managing its drivers with algorithms, but the factors that influence how drivers experience their work extend beyond algorithmic management. Regional contexts, drivers' own motivations and experiences of work, and their level of investment in the job all affect the ways they perceive its benefits or drawbacks. Over the last four years in Uberland, I have seen that driving is not the same for everyone, everywhere. There are three important categories of Uber drivers: hobbyists, part-timers, and full-timers. Hobbyists are drivers who, quite simply, don't need the money. Part-timers need the money but don't or can't work full time for a variety of reasons. Finally, full-timers are just that: people whose primary income is driving for Uber, some of whom put in significantly long hours. Most drivers work part time, but a minority are pulling long hours as full-time drivers to earn their livelihoods. The same working conditions can have very different impacts on different categories of drivers.

THE DIVERSE MOTIVATIONS OF
FULL-TIME AND PART-TIME DRIVERS

Lyft had 700,000 active drivers as of November 2017.[1] The same month, Uber had 750,000 active drivers, jumping to 900,000 by March 2018 (though the companies may define *active* differently). Meanwhile, in Canada, Uber has 50,000 active drivers.[2] The term *active drivers* doesn't give a full picture of how many people have experiences as Uber or Lyft drivers. For example, between January 2015 and March 2017, Uber counted 1,877,252 drivers who worked for its uberX and uberPOOL services (which excludes other tiers of service like uberXL, uberBlack, and uberEats) in 196 cities.[3]

As I first described in the *Harvard Business Review*,[4] research has shown that most of these drivers work part time. For example, an analysis by Jonathan Hall, chief economist at Uber, and Princeton economist Alan Krueger published in 2015 found that 51 percent of Uber drivers work one to fifteen hours per week, and 30 percent work sixteen to thirty-four hours per week—while 12 percent work thirty-five to forty-nine hours per week, and 7 percent work fifty hours or more per week.[5] According to Lyft, 78 percent of their drivers in 2015 worked one to fifteen hours per week, and 86 percent of their drivers were either employed full time elsewhere or seeking full-time employment.[6] Across the United States and Europe, other reports have found that independent workers don't rely on platforms like Uber as their primary sources of income.[7] The platform model of gig work comes with high attrition rates for workers, though—one in six online-platform workers is new in any given month, and more than half of participants quit within a year.[8]

The ridehail model is geared to part-time work, according to later reports by Uber and Lyft as well. For example, Lyft surveyed 37,000 drivers and 30,000 passengers in fifty-two major cities. Its results, published in a 2018 report, state that on the national level in the United States, 93 percent of its drivers drive fewer than twenty hours per week, and 93 percent are employed, seeking employment, full-time students, or retired.[9] In February 2018, Uber published a blog post stating that "nearly 60% of U.S. drivers use Uber less than 10 hours a week."[10] Uber confirmed in an email to me that the latter statistic accounted for drivers who drove fewer than ten hours a week in a typical workweek over the previous three months, according to data scientists on Uber's policy team.[11]

However, the Uber and Lyft reports on how much drivers work for either company tell only part of the story: a typical driver I met in New York City worked full time for multiple apps (often two to three), such as some combination of Uber, Lyft, Juno, Via, and Gett. Indeed, a 2016 report by the Office of the Mayor in New York City states that, of taxi and for-hire drivers (which includes ridehail drivers), "about three-quarters of all drivers say that driving a taxi or other for-hire vehicle is their full-time job."[12] Lyft's 2018 report also offers a city-by-city break-down of driver statistics, and it states that in New York City, 91 percent of drivers work fewer than twenty hours per week[13]—but that may simply reflect the fact that drivers who work full time are giving some of their hours to local competitors, like Uber, Juno, or Via. (Among the drivers I meet in my research, most New York City drivers work full time). If each company claims that drivers work an average of 10–20 hours per week, it would indicate that drivers are primarily working part time, such as to supplement their incomes.

While definitive statistics on part-time and full-time drivers are not available, there is nonetheless a divide between drivers who work part time and drivers who work full time. As UCLA law professor Noah Zatz has observed, "A small proportion of drivers are doing most of Uber's work."[14] This creates tension between a minority of full-time drivers and a majority of part-timers who drive for supplemental income or for social reasons. The availability of part-time earners reduces pressure on employers to create more sustainable earning opportunities. The workers who hope to make a living in ridehail work take on the most risk. And the consequences of this model for drivers boil down primarily to the different stakes they have in the system. Steven, an Uber driver in Toronto, Canada, uses his spare Mercedes to drive for uberX as a hobby. As an Uber driver, he delights in socializing on the job, meeting new people from all walks of life, and discovering new neighborhoods. He says, "I'm just retired basically, so I decided to do this as a part-time job. It's for fun, absolutely for fun. I really enjoy it." Steven immigrated to Toronto from South Africa thirty years ago, and he was a successful businessman before he retired to his home in a well-to-do suburb. Like other hobbyists, Steven has spare assets, and he's primarily motivated to work for recreational reasons. Drivers like Steven don't necessarily see themselves as workers. Hobbyist drivers might identify primarily as retired individuals or as professionals in other fields.

The full spectrum of driver motivations complicates how we understand the Uber model more broadly and its impact on the future of work in the near term. Recreational, or hobbyist, drivers, for example, have fewer economic incentives to advocate better pay, and they can take this work more lightly—though most drivers are responsive to the issue of unfairness within Uber's system. And many drivers, whether they drive for Uber or a taxi company, cite a positive social connection they enjoy from meeting new people. Hukam, who drives a taxi part time in Winnipeg, says, "You can meet different people [who] love to share. I met some people from the army, and I asked them about the army—how you do your training, stuff like that, you know. So, you can gain knowledge."

Drivers do not intentionally stratify themselves according to their motivation or investment, because they work as a disaggregated labor force. In the earlier stages of my research, I met some who had never met another ridehail driver. In online forums, drivers commune in large, national groups, and they post their experiences of different cities; however, some smaller, local city groups have also sprouted up. Although driving is clearly not the same for everyone, Uber's business model benefits from having drivers with differential investments in this job: it can depress wages, for example, to meet the needs of the lowest common denominator—part-time earners.[15]

Despite Uber's success, it's important to understand that the company's model effectively pits the most invested drivers against the least-invested drivers (who comprise the majority), even though drivers are often unwitting participants in this model. Drivers work as lone rangers through the use of an app, and they have no official channels of inter-driver communication. Most drivers I meet or observe are not organizing for labor rights advocacy, though some drivers participate in the workplace culture and information-sharing practices that flourish in online forums. However, forums are full of drivers from many regions and, therefore, provide no centralized local basis for worker organization or power.

For people in transition, it's great that there is a job with a low barrier to entry, providing them near-instant income. For full-time drivers, the part-timers function a bit like scabs: occasional drivers are tolerant of working conditions that are anathema to occupational drivers trying to support their families. Indeed, this divide is actively weaponized by Uber to undermine organizing efforts by occupational drivers to improve their working conditions.

In Seattle, for example, unionization efforts are under way to represent ridehail drivers, who are classified as independent contractors. In December 2015, Seattle passed an ordinance allowing drivers to bargain collectively (which was challenged by the Chamber of Commerce and ultimately upheld in federal court).[16] Uber insists that every driver should have a say in that union. Effectively, this would weaken the traction of labor organizers by giving equal weight to a driver who works five hours a week alongside a driver who works fifty-plus hours a week. Ultimately, Seattle's city council proposed that drivers who have made at least fifty-two trips during any three-month period in the preceding twelve months should have a vote on the union agreement, which is inclusive of many part-timers.[17]

Both full-time and part-time drivers work for a variety of reasons: they are in the midst of a career transition, they need to supplement their earnings, or they are seeking a form of recreation. Nearly all drivers value flexibility, because they can log in and log out at will—although promotions, like guaranteed hourly earnings and surge pricing, can re-create the conditions of shift work for drivers seeking to earn a premium by meeting certain additional criteria for when and where they drive. These differences can have significant impacts on drivers' experiences. For example, many drivers, especially recreational hobbyists, cite the social connections they make through Uber and Lyft as a main motivation for working. Both occupational and part-time drivers may also enjoy this aspect of work: some are eager to practice their English as a second language. More rarely, a driver might confide that he is socially anxious, and that driving helps him socialize more easily. ESL practice and social anxiety management are generally some of the "soft" benefits of this work rather than primary motivations for working. Other drivers value a "good bad job" compared to their other, non-Uber options.[18] These diverse motivations and contexts demonstrate why Uber's impact on work is varied; they also help explain why the dissent animating a vocal minority of Uber's drivers isn't shared more widely among the driver workforce.

HOBBYIST WORKERS

Big differences separate those who financially rely on gig work (56 percent of workers surveyed) and "casual" gig workers (42 percent), who report that they could live comfortably without the additional income, according to a Pew Research Center survey published in 2016.[19] But what starts off as supplementary work can turn into a full-time job. David Aguirre, who drives for Uber in Houston, Texas, speaks of a fairly common experience when he says to me, in 2018, "This started as a side job for me, but I started doing it full time in September [2017] when the company I used to work for went out of business." The economic dependencies that drivers bring to this work can evolve over time. And as the Pew survey highlights, gig work (beyond ridehailing) is a necessity for some, but it is recreational for others.[20] The choices of hobbyist drivers comport with some of the cultural claims that the sharing economy makes about work as an altruistic endeavor, but they do not define the full scope of employment for drivers any more than bloggers define the profession of journalism.

While I was working on my computer from a café in Montreal one afternoon, Nathan, a driver in Los Angeles, joined me for an interview by phone during one of his breaks. He is in his late sixties, and he has trained as a licensed clinical social worker; he works in mental health in the Los Angeles area. On weekends, when he's not working at his primary job, he drives six to twelve hours for Lyft. Although the money is a plus, he drives mainly for social reasons and to decompress after the emotionally taxing demands of dealing with patients. He told me, "I deal with PTSD, real serious depression, and long-term anxiety. For me it's kind of nice to go out and just have these more lighthearted interactions with people.... [I]t's a new way of people interacting with each other." Nathan earns about $130 an hour as a psychotherapist, and he initially made $34 an hour driving for Lyft (thanks to incentive pay), though this has dropped over the four months he's been driving, to between $15 and $20 an hour. He told me, "If I didn't like going out to do it, I'd probably stop."

In Charleston, South Carolina, Carol started driving for Uber after her grown son mocked her for buying a brand-new SUV that sat in the driveway. She enjoys learning about new shows and restaurants in town when she drops people at their destinations in the evenings before she heads back to her house outside the city. Like other women drivers I meet on the road, she generally avoids the late-night "vomit shift" for pickups, although she's never had a real problem with the flirtatious young men on the late shift. For her, the benefit of Uber is the chance it affords to learn new things while simultaneously gaining her son's respect. With Uber's flexible model, she can work when she wants to.

Supplemental earners—who are largely retirees, working professionals, and empty nesters—are primarily motivated to work for social reasons. My research suggests that they benefit most clearly from Uber's employment model of independent contract labor, since they gain more opportunities for marginal employment and are less vulnerable to the same business practices (e.g., rate cuts) that prompt strikes and protests by drivers who rely on Uber as a significant source of their household income.

PART-TIME DRIVERS

The majority of Uber's drivers work part time. My research has revealed three common motivations among them for doing this kind of work: it compensates for a career transition, it allows for much-needed flexibility, or it fills the need for a "good bad job."

Drivers Who Value Income during Career Transitions

"I'll say I'm grateful for it," Jake says about working for Uber. "Our business took a hit, and I had to scramble. And it's been paying my mortgage, so, you know, it's great for what it is." Jake was in the high-end nutrition business, and he's been driving part time for the company for about a year in Denver, Colorado. It's often easy to cast the plight of the Uber driver in terms of precarity or exploitation, but that doesn't apply readily to a host of drivers, some of whom promote the value of ridehail work as a remedy for unfortunate circumstances.

Raj has been driving professionally in Toronto for nine years, first as a taxi driver, then as the owner of a for-hire vehicle business, and now for uberSelect, a higher-end service. He admires Uber's technology, but he sees the influx of nonoccupational drivers as a threat to his livelihood: "Competition is always good for everyone; but again, it should be reasonable, not that you just flood the market." With the advent of Uber, he's become anxious about the stability of his income as a professional driver and is looking to change careers. He keeps textbooks under the front passenger seat so that in between rides he can study to become a mortgage broker.[21] In essence, Uber's model opens up employment opportunities for anyone who wants a job, but the conditions Uber sets for this work undermine driving as a viable occupation.

Although this is counterintuitive, unstable work and low retention rates may not signal the need to improve the stability of long-term earning potential for this job or similar work in the broader gig economy. A report in February 2016 by JPMorgan Chase examined payment data from Chase customers who participated in at least one of thirty online platforms. Researchers found that users were active for 56 percent of the time on labor-intensive online platforms like Uber (as opposed to asset-intensive platforms, like Airbnb), and their reliance on it as a secondary source of income did not change over time.[22] This could be because independent workers use their income to cover short-term expenses or to transition to other careers, as Hall and Krueger have argued regarding the high turnover of Uber drivers.[23]

One insight from my research may offer another explanation: some drivers hesitate to commit full time because they consider it a risky proposition, even if they earn more as drivers than they do working at their other jobs.[24] And for some, gig work is a way to smooth over income volatility and unexpected expenses or gaps between jobs. Uber and Lyft send jobs to drivers who log in to work, and drivers are paid on time—weekly or occasionally through instant pay—which is no small thing. As a side gig, it can be used as an additive to, rather than a substitute for, other employment.[25]

Drivers Who Value Flexibility

One of the promises of the gig economy is that workers have more flexibility to work when and as much as they want. That's why many people start driving to earn extra income outside of their day jobs.[26] Drivers for Uber and Lyft cite the flexibility—the freedom to take breaks when they want, pause to run errands, or go home and take a nap in the middle of the day—as one of the most important benefits of this job. As a company, Uber points to the fact that the majority of drivers are part-time earners as proof of the freedom and flexibility that characterize the work of a driver who can log in and log out of work at will.

Raul, a New York Uber and Lyft driver and a former Yellow Cab driver, was working eight to nine hours a day before rate cuts; now he works twelve to fourteen hours. He still values the flexibility that allows him to choose which hours of the day he works. He can go home and nap at three in the afternoon or eat the homemade lunch that his wife prepares. But having the autonomy to choose which fourteen of the twenty-four hours in a day to work doesn't create the sense of freedom implied by "flexibility" rhetoric. Raul used to be home by about six o'clock in the evening, in time to see his children after they finish school, but now he's working until nine to make up for rate cuts. He's looking for a job with a cab company again so he can have more reliable shifts and stable pay.

Most drivers value flexibility in their scheduling, and some use that advantage to work part time for supplementary income. This job, however, isn't sustainable in the long-term as a primary source of income unless drivers hew to the shifting wage incentives Uber provides over time.

Drivers Who Value a "Good Bad Job"

Driving for Uber and Lyft is a "good bad job" for some, especially for those who have a criminal record or limited education.[27] Cody, in his mid-twenties, is a Lyft driver in the Ann Arbor–Detroit area. He tells me that, with only a high school education, he's not eligible for good jobs. "There's not a lot of jobs, unless you're looking at working in a factory for eighty hours a week, that pay better for a high school education," he said. The Pew survey from 2016 found that one in five respondents said they used these digital platforms because job opportunities in their area were limited. Cody's previous job was as a youth counselor, where, on his fourth day, he was punched in the face by the young man he was counseling. For Cody, ridehail work is perceptibly safer than that, and it pays a better hourly wage—he earned a little more than ten dollars an hour at the juvenile detention center, though it also came with benefits. He tries not to think too much about the cost of replacing the benefits he loses as he transitions to ridehail work full time.

DeMonte drives for uberEats—a service Uber operates to deliver food to customers who order from participating restaurants—in Marietta, Georgia, northwest of Atlanta. He has a bachelor of science degree from a nearby university. He graduated five years earlier, and he was working two warehouse jobs when he started with Uber, though one of those was seasonal. He gets health-care benefits from his full-time warehouse job, and he earns between $150 and $175, and sometimes $200, for being logged in to work for about twenty-five hours a week. When I ask DeMonte what he thinks a good job would pay, he takes a long, contemplative pause in a nonstop discussion over the phone before finally exhaling, responding, "Double digits. $10 per hour. I think that'd be real good for the economy." He says he wouldn't do uberEats full time unless the pay was much higher: it's just not enough to support his needs, he says, and he still aspires to use his degree to find a job where he can apply his education in sports management.

For Jin Deng, who formerly worked as a food delivery driver for a restaurant in New Jersey, driving for Uber and Lyft in New York City is a step up, although he's quick to note that he drives because he didn't go to school here and doesn't have enough education to get a better job. Jin Deng was robbed twice in his last job, once with pepper spray that stung his eyes. As we talk, he reaches for the pocket on his cargo shorts, indicating that the thieves missed his wallet when they grabbed his bag of food and the cash he carried to make change for food deliveries. Now he's driving a large Suburban for Uber and Lyft in New York City, and he finds that the cashless exchange of payments facilitated by the apps gives a huge boost to his perceived sense of safety on the job. He invested in a larger vehicle to accommodate his big and growing family: his new baby is five months old, and his wife will go back to work at her job in a nail salon once her parents arrive from China to stay at home with their baby. The safety benefits for Jin Deng outweigh the workplace considerations that cause other drivers to chafe, in part because his alternatives are limited. Similarly, ridehail drivers with stronger occupational identities as drivers often evaluate the differences between Uber, Lyft, and taxi or truck driving with an eye toward the design of ridehail technology. Pierre-Alexandre, who is originally from Haiti, used to drive for Yellow Cab in New York before he started with Uber and Lyft while pursuing his MBA at an online college. During our interview in 2017, he references specific features that improved his sense of security: "The name and the rating—it's like you know who's coming to your car before you even pick them up, you know.... It should be safer. If you want to do something to the driver, you already know that the driver has all of your information, so [*laughs*] it's a done deal right there." He also comments on the role of a partition in taxis, and whether that offers a type of physical safety that ridehail cars lack: "That's not the safest thing—yeah, because you have to open up the partition for some kind of exchange with the passenger," he notes. For Pierre-

Alexandre, the design and affordances of ridehail app technology offer a kind of safety that taxis do not.[28]

Many newer drivers prefer Uber and Lyft to their alternative workplaces, but it is also typical for drivers to overestimate their earnings when they start. Drawn in by company advertising with claims of earnings such as thirty dollars per hour or up to eighty-five thousand dollars per year, drivers may take months to appreciate the type or range of their expenses or their actual earning ability (which sometimes hinges on an ever-changing series of promotional incentives). Uber famously advertised that drivers in New York City have median earnings of ninety thousand dollars per year, and that drivers in San Francisco have median earnings of seventy-four thousand dollars per year. In 2017, Uber was fined $20 million by the Federal Trade Commission for recruiting prospective drivers with exaggerated earnings claims, like the ninety-thousand-dollars-per-year assertion.[29] Looking across other regions, a *Buzzfeed* investigation found that in late 2015, after expenses, Uber drivers made $13.17 per hour in Denver, $10.75 per hour in Houston, and $8.77 per hour in Detroit.[30] Uber drivers in the U.S. take home $10.87 an hour after deducting Uber fees, vehicle expenses, and the mandatory Social Security and Medicare taxes that self-employed drivers must pay, according to an analysis published by economist Lawrence Mishel in May 2018. He notes that this figure doesn't account for the costs of the health or retirement benefits that independent contractors must provide for themselves.[31] In communications with the FTC, Uber's lawyers implied that lazy drivers who choose not to work hard enough are responsible for the gap between advertised and real earnings.[32] However, any claim about hourly earnings is complicated by Uber's dynamic pay incentives, which I discuss later. For some, driving for Uber and Lyft are still better than their alternatives. Dontez, who drives only for Lyft full time, about fifty to sixty hours per week in Atlanta, Georgia, says driving is better than any other job he's had before. Before Lyft, he was working in a warehouse at Walmart. "I'm making more in one week than I made every two weeks," he says in a low mumble.

In the fall of 2016, I hail a ride from an Uber and Lyft driver in Denver to take me to the red rocks (which are really a dusty burnt-orange hue) native to the region. The coordinates of the first destination I choose somewhat randomly take us squarely into the middle of a field. Hesitating to disembark, I ask the driver if he would mind taking me to, well, anywhere else. He suggests a notable concert venue, where nothing lively happens in the morning. The venue is beautiful and distant from the city center, but Denver is basically a series of suburbs roped together by long stretches of road, meaning that getting from place to place can be a good twenty-five-to-forty-minute drive. After I spend a few hours moseying around, I request a ride on the way back, and I am startled when the driver appears to be just minutes away, around the corner, even though we are in the middle of nowhere. He has some trouble finding the exact entrance, but I flag him down after I notice a car making unusual turns near the parking lot.

"Sorry about that, ha," he says, smiling at me with an agreeable chuckle after realizing the passenger doors are locked as I try to get in. Empty Red Bull and Monster cans, and a Dunkin Donuts cup with coffee dregs, rattle around in the console between the two front seats, and he laughs nervously every few minutes to punctuate his sentences. Today is Joshua's first day driving for a ridehail company, and I am his very first passenger. Like Dontez, he used to work at a big-box retail store, but he got tired of it after seven or eight years. "My son is fourteen months old; I can spend more time watching him. I got sick of paying three hundred dollars a week for day care," he acknowledges. His significant other has two jobs, working part time at the same big-box store while also serving as an operational manager at a second big-box retailer. We circle around the entrance a few more times as the GPS directs us to make multiple U-turns onto the same road, while he wonders aloud if we should take a closer look at the map. We pull into a gas station, and I gently intercede when I notice he hasn't yet pressed the "Start Trip" button, which indicates to the app that he has the passenger and is ready to take her to her destination. That explains why it just kept sending us to the pickup spot. On our way, Joshua chats with me about his new job. I ask him why he came out to the middle of nowhere to start his first day of work as a driver, and he tells me that he received a message from his app earlier that morning that this might be a hot spot. That would make sense if it were nighttime, or if a planned concert event were taking place, but I suspect he was dispatched because the profile I use on that account is that of a frequent passenger, and the app may have anticipated I would need a ride on my return trip. A more experienced driver probably would not have followed that prompt, because doing so would accumulate a lot of unpaid "deadhead" miles—the expense of driving without a passenger—with a slim chance of a ride request.

I meet Tanisha, a woman in her twenties, on a bright day in Dallas, Texas, as I make my way over to nearby Fort Worth. She left her job at a call center in Dallas to work for Lyft and Uber in order to get away from the stifling, heavily managed environment of call center work.[33] She was motivated by Uber's siren call to be her own boss. "It is good extra money on the side. Part-time-wise, the most I made was two hundred dollars in one week.... At that time, I was doing at least four to five hours for three or four days," she offers. When I spoke with her, she was starting to experiment with full-time driving, wanting a flexible schedule and more freedom on the job. Many new drivers cite the amounts offered in recruitment ads, like fifteen hundred dollars per week, to explain their earnings, because they are unfamiliar with the totality of their expenses, including depreciation on their vehicles, and Uber's effective commission and other fees deducted from their earnings. After Uber advertised on Craigslist in Dallas in 2015 stating that drivers could earn fifteen dollars per hour, the Federal Trade Commission found that fewer than 30 percent of drivers earned that amount (after averaging out their fares, even when including short-term promotions and incentives).[34] In a forum discussion in the summer of 2017, one driver posted to the group: "Is it possible to make $1,500/week in Chicago on average?" A swarm of drivers responded with incredulity,

Recruitment
ads (fined
$20 mill for
false ads)

positing that it would be possible if they worked seventy hours a week, though others concurred with the statement "Not just NO, but HELL, NO! You might gross that much, but you'll never net that much." Others jumped in and questioned which expenses that $1,500 amount included. The debate highlighted a larger misunderstanding that I consistently find, where drivers struggle to understand both their earning potential and their take-home pay after expenses and taxes.

Some drivers *do* make good money, as they see it, strategizing around pay incentives and bonuses to maintain a higher income, but this is not the routine experience of drivers. For example, in summer 2017, one forum discussion asked drivers to post the most they had ever earned in a week. In two samples, one California driver posted his earnings statement showing $1,212.18 in the fall of 2016 that had been deposited into his account about nine months earlier. Another driver, from Florida, posted an earnings statement showing $1,083.00 from the spring of 2017 and cackled that it was good to drive during spring break. Part of those earnings came from a $150 cleaning fee he received, presumably because a passenger vomited in his car. Other drivers posted higher amounts, but anything significantly higher typically came from a combination of earnings and bonus amounts, including referral fees (earned when a driver shares a "referral code" with another prospective driver to recruit them) that could be very high, up to five hundred dollars.

Drivers have mixed feelings about their job prospects too: in a forum, drivers debated a post from the summer of 2017 about whether you should quit your job to drive for Uber and Lyft full time. It garnered hundreds of likes and comments, covering the map of views drivers have about the different markets. One driver from Los Angeles wrote,

> Driving full time is a nice little fantasy, but reality soon slaps you in the face when you end up living in your car to make ends meet as demand fluctuates. With low demand and thousands of hungry ants on the road, it's not as easy as people say it is. Yeah, all that free time you are supposed to have, well that's bullshit, you work your ass off, drive your car into the ground for

nothing, if you have a job I recommend you keep it. Life on the road isn't all that great as your health starts taking a toll from all the driving you do to survive the dirt cheap, rates of $3 to $5 for the average ride. If living in your car and sleeping in parking garages to make $1,500 a week sounds appealing to you, great, knock yourself out, but it's not that illusion of freedom that you think it is.

Another driver replied, "Your *[sic]* not doing it right it's been my full-time job for over a year." Others weighed in on whether you should quit your job to drive full time, making comments like: "That all depends on the job you are quitting!"

CASE STUDY: DRIVING FULL TIME IN NEW YORK CITY

Broadly speaking, in most cities with less robust regulatory environments, drivers can afford to work part time and may have fewer experiences with occupational driving. In New York City, however, where the barrier to entry is higher, more drivers work full time, and many have backgrounds in the taxi industry. Full-time drivers make significant investments to do this job. Uber's New York workforce reflects the diversity of the city. One driver, a former Tibetan monk, confided that he had to give up on monastic life and join the hustle when he moved to the city. There, unlike in other markets, drivers are regulated by the Taxi and Limousine Commission, and their capital costs to start driving with Uber and Lyft are higher. They need to pass fingerprint-based background checks, get a TLC license and plates, pass tests, take a class, and obtain commercial insurance, all of which comes with a raft of associated fees. As a result, most drivers are invested in working full time, often fifty, sixty, or even seventy hours a week, with only one day off. In other cities, most drivers just use their personal vehicle insurance, and they can be hired and work without any additional regulatory oversight or requirements.

For some drivers, Uber's model is a debt-to-work pipeline: they take out significant auto loans to lease vehicles that meet the requirements

Uber sets.[35] In New York City, many drivers lease vehicles with TLC plates while applying for their own TLC plates or while trying out the work. Faraz, a part-time driver, has been living in New York City for two years, since he emigrated from Pakistan to the United States with his parents. He works in information technology and he's single, but he purchased a five-bedroom house on Long Island from an Italian man who designed it lovingly, with a bathroom in every bedroom. "I like this better than my nine-to-five job," Faraz says, "but moneywise, there's no breaks. I had fun while I did it, but there's no money in this, that's why I will stop." I ask him what his take-home pay is after his expenses, and he exclaims, "Nothing! I get a lot of parking tickets when I'm taking breaks. It's pretty much the bare minimum; I do it for fun, putting in part-time hours." Faraz has been driving for two and a half months, but he's paying $415 per week to rent a four-door sedan with TLC plates to drive for uberX and Lyft, and the TLC insurance costs double his personal insurance. "I'm getting rid of this car as soon as possible," he says with a laugh. Faraz has alternative employment options as well as assets; he's working for money, but his profile is closer to that of a hobbyist. He clearly isn't making much money working part time, given such high up-front costs. Faraz is one of the lucky ones; drivers who take on subprime leasing options can get stuck paying off the debt, and they can't always afford to turn their cars in.[36]

Mehmet, who moved to Long Island, NY, when he emigrated from Turkey seven years earlier, invested in a huge SUV in order to work for Uber and Lyft, big enough to take comfortable naps in, with its three rows of seats that can fold down. Citing traffic and congestion, he remarks, "It's hard to sleep in the street." When we meet in 2017, he mentions that he keeps a small pillow and blanket rolled up in the back, although passengers stole the pillow once. He didn't call the cops because, well, "It's just a small item," he says abashedly. It's one of the frustrating realities of Uberland: it's obviously annoying to have passengers steal your things and to be put in a situation where you are disrespected, but at the same time, it feels silly to call the police over a small pillow. He reported the passengers to Uber, and a customer service representative promised to get it back for him, but of course he never saw it again.

Mehmet commutes an hour and a half into the city from sixty miles away. He waits in the early morning for an airport call to take him into the city so that he doesn't incur the expense of deadhead miles, but the erratic hours can take a significant toll on his sleep habits. "Two days ago I was sleeping in the car at 6 A.M.," he says. "I was trying to get a customer from Long Island to JFK. My app was open, I touched it and accept[ed] the ride, but after [accepting] the ride I don't remember everything. But I passed out, and in the morning I see the voicemail that says, "Man, are you going to come here? I'm waiting fifteen minutes, and I have to get to the airport." I feel so badly because maybe I'm the only driver out there." He felt the social obligation toward his passenger and didn't want to leave him stranded, but the sleep debt of working airport runs early in the morning had caught up with him.

Mehmet used to drive a Toyota Camry for uberX, which he rented for its TLC plates for ten months at $1,600 a month. Later, he upgraded his vehicle, investing $55,000 in a used luxury vehicle, so he could be eligible for the higher uberBlack and uberSUV pay rates. His expenses for work amount to about $2,000 a month. He says that even drivers who bought that type of car new for $60,000 to $70,000 (the range depends on whether the driver has good or bad credit, according to another interviewee) used to make money, before rate cuts that Uber implemented in January 2017. "I'm lazy, I don't work much," he admits, ducking his chin down. With good humor, he continues: "I work 40 to 50 hours a week, but for this job, you have to work six days, twelve hours a day, like the Yellow Cab schedule."

Many drivers enter into risky financial arrangements to lease expensive black cars with TLC plates, and they have to work exceedingly long hours to earn a profit after their car payments. Zahid, who lives in the New York City borough of Queens, has been driving a rented car with TLC plates for a month and a half. After working in a café for several years, he thought, "Let me try Uber, because it's guaranteeing me so much money." He says it pays about $25 to $30 per hour, but that's before expenses. A Toyota Camry costs him $2,000 per month to lease, but he's in the process of financing his own car and getting the TLC plates installed. The high monthly cost of his car rental is common: drivers in New York City routinely cite *weekly* payments in the range of $415 to $500.[37] For comparison's sake, the average *monthly* car lease payment in the United States in 2016 is $412.[38]

Truly, Uber is a godsend to some drivers. Yet it's hard to reconcile the fanfare of the sharing economy that is celebrated by tech positivists with the inescapable sense of trauma associated with what some drivers called "modern-day slavery" at a TLC hearing in the spring of 2017. Other drivers have expressed that sentiment too.[39] At the hearing, drivers were referencing debt-to-work conditions that trap drivers in their working relationship with Uber through Uber-promoted subprime lease agreements. Alison Griswold, a reporter for the online business journal *Quartz*, reported on Uber drivers who were referred by Uber to predatory lenders when they sought car leases. After pneumonia sidelined one driver, he got behind on payments and amassed $1,800 in debt. When he tried to start his engine and get back to work, the car wouldn't start: it had been remotely deactivated by the lessor for missed payments.[40] And it's not just drivers in New York City who are affected by predatory lending. Katie Wells, Kafui Attoh, and Declan Cullen conducted fieldwork with Uber drivers in Washington, DC, and reported,

> Some also end out *[sic]* in deeper financial trouble by leasing cars from Uber's Xchange program. One driver, Joan, got caught in this trap after she hit a pothole and damaged her car's suspension system. She spent nearly all the money she had to get the car fixed. Then, when efforts to repair the vehicle failed, she spent more to lease a car from Uber. While Xchange offers lower credit barriers than traditional lenders, the payments which Uber automatically deducts from drivers' paychecks are high. Joan pays $138, more than the national lease average of $100 per week.[41]

CASE STUDY: DRIVING ILLEGALLY IN MONTREAL

In Montreal, where I speak with drivers in 2016, drivers and passengers have been placed under siege by irate taxi drivers—the legitimate workforce—and they forge a common social bond with Uber as a company. They are allies. Hari (whom I introduced at the opening of this chapter) recalls how one night, a few local taxi drivers were waiting restlessly by their cars, hovering near a woman outside who was staring intently at a black sedan avatar of Hari's car on her iPhone screen. Hari describes the incident in detail:

> After 3:00 in the morning, the taxi drivers say nothing because they are very busy, they are running, okay? At 3:30, all the bars, discos, everything is closed, so then they are free. Then they are starting to give us a problem, you know. That's what happened to me. It was 4 a.m., and they were just turning on the street, doing nothing. The person who called me, they didn't know I was an Uber driver because I was hiding everything. But she was looking at her cell phone, so they said oh, she is waiting for Uber. The moment I came, they came right in front and the back of me.[42]

The taxi drivers surrounded him on all sides until his passenger agreed to go with one of them instead. This is Hari's only source of income, and he tries to mitigate the safety risks with caution and strategies, such as asking all of his passengers to sit in the front seat, like friends.[43] He hunches low in the driver's seat when he's on the job, listening for Uber's instructions from the iPhone balanced on his legs. A clunky, older GPS navigation system sits visibly on the dashboard, partly as a decoy, and partly as backup in case his slick in-app navigation ever cuts out. When he waits for passengers, his fingers fiddle nervously with the radio dials , his way of feigning disinterest toward anyone who might solicit his attention in an obvious way. The performance he has to give to do his work is one of the understated components of this job.

In 2016, Uber was under attack by taxi drivers and the transportation police in Montreal, and many drivers worked strategically to remain hidden in plain sight; some were even hesitant to pay income taxes on their

Uber earnings for fear it was evidence of their illegal activities. Uber's approach is not unique to Montreal. When Uber was still unregulated in New Jersey, a driver in Jersey City wrote to Uber Support to say that New Jersey officers threatened to ticket him if they caught him picking up or dropping off passengers again. He posted Uber's response in a driver forum online in spring 2015: "You should partner with Uber in confidence. Our team has your back 100% and should you ever run into trouble as a result of your use of the Uber app, we will reimburse you for any regulatory citation received as well as provide any necessary legal support."

This type of support fosters an alliance between the company and its drivers, and it is part of the evolutionary stages of being a driver. Uber is a chameleon: it becomes what it needs to be at different times, in different places. When it is new to a city and its legal status is hazy, it builds positive relationships with drivers. After it is legitimate, it starts to renege on that trust in various ways, such as by lowering the rates at which drivers earn their wages. (Government crackdowns on illegal Uber activities are controversial, and they face political and practical challenges. The company is popular with consumers and leverages them into a political base by, for example, urging them to write their local political representatives and ask them to support Uber-friendly legislation.) How drivers experience the company usually depends on what stage Uber is at in their city: for example, while drivers in New York City are protesting rate cuts, drivers in Montreal, a six-hour ride away, tell me that Uber has their back.

Patrice is a Montrealer in his late twenties who drives for Uber. To provide a smooth trip, he uses a phone mount, but when his car is at a standstill in traffic or dropping off a passenger in a crowded area, he lowers his phone from view, glances peripherally out his windows, and checks his rearview mirrors frequently. It's the only time I notice him looking slightly rattled during our interview. When transportation inspectors fine Uber drivers or impound their vehicles for operating illegally, Uber pays their fines and sometimes finds them a replacement rental until their car is released, about fifteen days later. Faced with the prospect that Uber could be kicked out of the province, Patrice observes,

It kind of sucks, because I'm doing something—service that's very well for the community and something that I fairly enjoy, and it gives me some leisure time where I'm able to take my girlfriend to work and pick her up. If Uber decides to—and I know it's not by their choice—to stop in Montreal, it sucks for a lot of people. A lot of people are going to have to change their lifestyle. In the sense of, where are they going to find a little bit of extra cash even just to live off, or I do the extra cash to pay off little bills and to take my girlfriend to dinner. And it kind of sucks if I stop doing that.

Meanwhile, Mehmet, who works in New York City but lives in Long Island, sometimes tries to hide his pickups from the transportation police of Long Island's Nassau County, which has its own Taxi and Limousine Commission, distinct from that of New York City. But if Mehmet is caught working without Nassau County plates, Uber pays his tickets, just as they do for underground drivers in Montreal. When I share stories of Montreal's underground ridehail drivers with Uber and Lyft drivers in Atlanta, several interviewees remark that they used to be illegal at the airport, and they would pretend to be picking up a loved one. In effect, the risks of being a disruptive start-up are transferred from Uber to the drivers and even the passengers who operate underground, who willingly adopt strategies to outwit the consequences.

While Patrice, Hari, and Mehmet hide from local authorities and the legitimate taxi force, other Uber drivers sometimes go "undercover" for personal reasons. For example, Farhad, whom I met in Toronto, works professionally as an accountant but drives for Uber on the side because he has no one to go home to in the evenings. He doesn't want his colleagues to discover his work as an Uber driver, because he worries they would think it meant his accounting practice is suffering.

DIVIDED AND CONQUERED: HOW UBER WINS

Amid deteriorating working conditions, the Uber model does not work well for everyone. In 2017, a *New York Times* report citing internal documents at Uber indicated that "roughly a quarter of its drivers turn over on average every three months," and Alison Griswold estimated in her weekly newsletter *Oversharing* that Uber's one-year retention rate is between 15 percent and 25 percent.[44] The problem of driver churn is complicated by driver motivations, but Uber's employment model relies on a constant influx of new drivers who can be hired quickly to compensate for poor retention rates. By 2018, Uber published a study on the gender pay gap of its workforce indicating that 68 percent of its U.S. drivers have a six-month attrition rate, and the rate of attrition is higher for women than men.[45]

Hobbyists like Nathan from L.A., Carol from Charleston, and Steven from Toronto, who continue to drive despite declining earnings, represent workers who are motivated substantially by nonfinancial values and are usually better positioned to absorb pay cuts. This may contribute to income destabilization for occupational drivers, while permitting greater flexibility for a wider pool of drivers. The range of driver motivations within Uber's labor pool supports the company's business model of employing part-timers as the majority of its drivers and full-timers as the minority of its drivers: part-timers can inadvertently undermine the leverage that full-timers need to advocate better working conditions. Though their motivations can overlap, happy and unhappy drivers are products of a business model that opens up part-time opportunities for many at the expense of a dedicated few.[46]

CHAPTER THREE

THE TECHNOLOGY PITCH

How Uber Creates Entrepreneurship for the Masses

Mariana was fifteen years old when she had her first child as a poor mother in the Dominican Republic. She moved to New York twenty-two years before I met her as a driver in 2018. She raised all four sons in Queens, a borough of New York City. Two of them moved to California to work in technology, and one of them advised her to try Uber. After five months on the job, she was glowing. It was the best job she'd ever had. Her last job was as a caretaker in a childcare center where there were too many children and not too much money, at six hundred dollars a week in cash. "I try it and I love it," she tells me. "After that, my life changed. When after I been working with Uber, Lyft, Juno, I change. Because the money, its amazing schedule, you can have your own schedule, you met many different people, it's amazing." Smiling and speaking loudly, she continues: "I almost is a five-star driver, almost, in my short time. My life change one thousand percent, not one hundred percent." Of her old job as a caretaker, she adds, "I miss the kids but not the money and the job." As a ridehail driver, she says, she takes home about fourteen hundred dollars per week, and if she's working hard on a good week, about two thousand dollars, all before expenses. Compared to her last job, she earns more respect in society as a driver, and it has opened up new opportunities for her in other ways.

"This is the first job that I have what I like. And this job allow me to go to college too. I study to be occupational therapist because it has the same values like this job. Freedom, I meet different people every day, you don't have a boss. It's nice," she affirms. Mariana's happiness speaks to her success with Uber and what it can offer to some drivers, but it's closer to the margins of the Uber driver experience overall.

The company's dramatic rise would not have been possible without the help of *stories*. Uber truly shines when it uses the power of rhetoric to make the case that its sharing technology can create entrepreneurship for everyone. It promises the moon, but drivers are often disappointed by the sober reality of working on the platform. Take Fernando as an example. He joined Uber as a driver in the Boston area in 2014 after seeing recruitment ads offering the chance to earn fifteen hundred dollars a week. He drives for two tiers of Uber service, uberX and uberXL, to support his family. But two years after signing up, as I interview him in Boston in spring 2016, he reflects on a pattern common to drivers: they're initially optimistic and satisfied with their work, particularly in the early stages of the company's growth in their city, but they become distrustful of it over time.

In addition to the flood of new drivers in his market and lower compensation (he notes that his take-home pay from airport trips has fallen, for example), Fernando is also upset about Uber shifting its eligibility requirements for cars—in 2014, he spent $42,000 on an Uber-eligible car (which meant a 2005 or newer model); but in February 2015, Uber began allowing models dating to 2001.[1] "You know how many people went to the dealer and buy *[sic]* new cars?" he asks. He can't afford to stop working for Uber, though he's looking for another job as competition rises and his pay falls owing to rate cuts.[2] He describes Uber's actions as "worse than discrimination," and his voice drops when he describes his sons' disappointment in his situation: his family thought they were getting a pathway to the middle class, and now their father is working hard at a job that is failing him.

For some drivers, this job is a millstone, and for others, it's a life preserver or a stopgap solution to income insecurity. Another Lyft and

Uber driver, Jacob, owned a bagel store, where he would make everything from scratch starting at four in the morning in a wealthy New Jersey town. "I used to own a business," he explains, "and the place next door to me caught on fire and burned my place down." After the fire, his business was closed for eight months, and he's not yet certain if he'll reopen it. For the time being, driving fits his schedule well; his wife is working, and he can pick up the kids from school. Not everyone is equally invested in this work, meaning not everyone is equally harmed by exploitative practices. That said, the mixed experiences of drivers illustrate where grand but illusory promises of entrepreneurship can fall flat.

Just as Uber uses the appeal of entrepreneurship to persuade society that its technology is both empowering and altruistic, Uber leverages the Uber driver and passenger apps to manipulate the user experience for drivers. Technology is far from neutral. But fundamentally, there is a psychological difference in how drivers experience both management and independence when the rules of work are written by an algorithm. By distancing its employment relationship to drivers through the framework of entrepreneurship, Uber masks its own methods and the power of algorithmic management to shape the nature of their work.

Drivers' experiences demonstrate the gap between rhetoric and reality when Uber talks about being a beacon of entrepreneurial opportunity. The image of driver-as-entrepreneur fails for three main reasons: drivers have no control over the rate at which they work; they do not determine which jobs they take while logged in; and they are routinely punished for any attempt to "disrupt" the system that Uber imposes.

THE ALLURE OF ENTREPRENEURSHIP

"In the U.S. especially, there is a strong cultural consensus that people should feel passion for their work, and work hard,"[3] anthropologist Ilana Gershon observes. The idea is that anyone can make it in America, and that if they do, it's because of their own hard work. Uber's employment narrative builds on this cultural consensus and says that

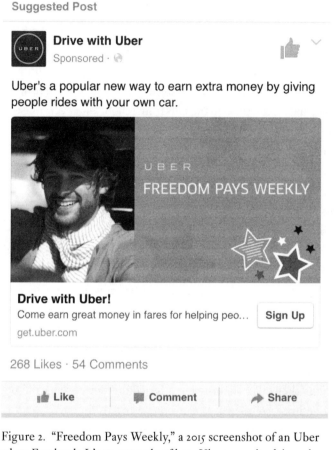

Figure 2. "Freedom Pays Weekly," a 2015 screenshot of an Uber
ad on Facebook. It's an example of how Uber recruits drivers by
appealing to a millennial crowd. (This figure also appears in the
color section following page 116.)

anyone can be an entrepreneur if they partner with Uber. The company's marketing emphasizes the trendy idea of driving for a tech company, which somehow is much more desirable than if the same job were
branded more bluntly as a taxi job for immigrants.

Advertisements for Uber appear in Facebook newsfeeds, emails, on
buses, and in the Uber passenger app, to name a few places. For exam-

ple, the ad "Freedom Pays Weekly" (figure 2), shows us how Uber gentrifies a job typically associated with people of color from immigrant communities in the major metropolitan areas where ridehailing has grown, like New York City, by depicting the driver as a fashionable, white male millennial dressed in soft pink and wearing a scarf. Because the advertisement appears on Facebook, observers can note how people engage with it through "likes" and "comments," which creates a more socially engaging message for the reader, and one that is embedded in digital culture. Next to the "Freedom Pays Weekly" tagline are American flag–themed stars in red, white, and blue. All these features are supposed to signal that Uber truly delivers freedom.

The text of typical Uber recruitment advertisements communicates a similar message about driver independence, accompanied by images of successful, breezy men and women ready to take that next step. Many read like this sample ad: "UBER NEEDS PARTNERS LIKE YOU. Drive with Uber and earn great money as an independent contractor. Get paid weekly just for helping our community of riders get rides around town. Be your own boss and get paid in fares for driving on your own schedule." Another ad shows a stylishly dressed, slim woman wearing sunglasses leaning against a clean, white car, overlooking a relaxing landscape, right beside a form the reader can use to sign up to drive for Uber. A third ad, this one on the back of a New York City bus, encourages taxi drivers to switch to Uber. In blue, medium-sized print, the header reads, "Calling All Cabs," followed by "$5000 GUARANTEED" in large white letters. In the smallest print, a white notice reads, "In Your First Month."

Uber's recruitment methodology boils down to two simple marketing tactics. First, Uber uses the language of self-employment and partnership to promote driving for Uber as an act of entrepreneurship. Then, it proposes entrepreneurship to the masses by projecting images of passionate, flexible millennials onto this work. This is fundamentally a half-truth built on legal fallacies. Uber drivers have filed many employment misclassification lawsuits, contending that Uber's model violates labor law, and the company has settled with the FTC over misleading claims about what drivers can earn.[4] Most drivers desire a certain threshold of independence: even if they don't quite have it as Uber drivers, they are invested in the poetic myth of full independence. In addition, they don't necessarily feel exploited if their entrepreneurial decision-making is limited by Uber's system of algorithmic management. Nonetheless, for a subset of people who are driving for a living, the tensions between the promise of entrepreneurship and the realities of how they are managed eventually emerge. When we look more closely at Uber as an employer, rather than as a company that simply leverages technology to produce entrepreneurship for the masses, it becomes clear that drivers who are successful are simply better at optimizing their take from a system that gamifies work with an ever-changing platter of incentives. By playing society with a false promise about entrepreneurship, Uber's rhetoric blinds us to the constraints that squeeze the independence out of drivers.

The forceful voice that narrates Frank's GPS sounds like the voice of Morgan Freeman, and it startles me when his phone spits out directions in a raspy rumble, occasionally interrupting the flow of our interview. Frank started working for Uber ten months earlier, and Lyft about a month after that. "Specifically for the bonus," he explains. "They [Lyft] were running a $350 bonus, a two-sided bonus. I got my thirty rides in thirty days like I was asked to do, and I got the bonus. My son tried to do the same thing, [but] the bonus went down to $250 the next month, and he was working another job so he didn't make it." He says he'd prefer to work for Uber if they would get little things done, like adding a tip feature to the app. "I get ten times as many calls on Uber as I do Lyft," he says. "And," he adds thoughtfully, "a lot of people I pick up have both apps on their phone—probably 80 percent. I use that opportunity to give them my card with my driver number [promo referral cards] on it so they can get the free rides." I'm meeting with Frank in the late afternoon of a spring day in Dallas, Texas, in 2016, and he moves a few of his belongings out of the front seat so I can sit up there with him. He drives a sedan when we meet, but he has another vehicle too. "It's a 2015 Tahoe; and I have Select status, so it makes more money on

Uber," he explains. The Chevy Tahoe is in the shop, with $5,000 worth of damage from a hailstorm.

Drivers hungry for extra cash are sometimes drawn in with the promise of earning more through promotional opportunities that Uber offers. Referral codes are one way that drivers can make more in ride-hail work: they can refer other drivers to these services, and both of them get a bonus. But this type of maneuvering doesn't always work. Frank explains why his son never managed to get his thirty-ride bonus: "He had too many rides by the same people, the same person. I think I did three with him, and his mom did three with him. The rules—and I didn't read the rules over again—but it's that no more than two rides can be done by the same person," he notes, with the tender admonishment of a father. Referring back to the Chevy, he adds, "My son was driving this one for a while, but now he has another job that doesn't give him the time to drive."

Frank lives in a suburb that boasts a high median income, about twenty-five miles away from Dallas, which he describes as "an upper-middle-class community with a lot of college graduates in most of the town. I been there since '78, thirty-nine years, so I've seen a lot of growth there." He shifts his weight in his low-down seat. "I've done sixty to seventy rides every week for the last month. It's about forty hours a week, is what it is. I was working retail for about four years, and I was getting really tired of it; so I started this part time, and in the first month I grossed over two thousand dollars. And that was part time. So finally I just said, 'You guys can have this retail job back; let someone else beat up their ankles and knees on this concrete floor, and I'm gonna drive.'" He used to work at bars, so he avoids the drunks by driving before 8 P.M. By tracking incentive offers with pay premiums and working with the other factors within his control, Frank tries to maximize the benefits of the job. The relationship between Uber and its drivers becomes inherently adversarial, though without particular animosity: Frank, like many drivers, is always trying to juice the promotions of his employer to get extra money. "The best promotion I participated in was an Uber promotion that said, 'If you can get twenty-five rides by Wednesday, and at least another twenty-five by the end of the week …'" He pauses midthought and mumbles, "And they screwed up the payout on it, but we did get it a week later." In the Uber model of employment, there are no raises for consistent performance, nor are there opportunities for advancement. The only way to make more is to work more, or to hunt for promotional opportunities like Frank does. Piecemeal work, some of it accompanied by promotions, illustrates the limping reality of this type of entrepreneurship. However, for some the steady and reliable fares from Uber beat the realities of unemployment that others face in a precarious job market, such as waiting in line at job fairs with hundreds of applicants for ten or twelve open positions.[5] His passion aside, Frank's middle-class income for the hard work he does stands in stark contrast to the grand narratives of wealth and entrepreneurship that Uber presents.

Another driver, Thomas, lost his job with Uber and Lyft when those companies left Austin, Texas, in the spring of 2016, in a show of protest against regulations passed by the municipal government.[6] In the precise, clipped tones of a native German speaker, Thomas told me in an interview that he invested twenty-five thousand dollars in a vehicle to work for Uber in 2014, and he became a Lyft driver too. After five rate cuts implemented unilaterally by Uber, he'd gone from making $1.90 per mile, for example, with uberX, to merely $1.00 per mile. (Passengers get cheaper trips, and he earns only as much as they are charged.) Once Uber and Lyft had left Austin, he scrambled to find work with local ridehail start-ups. Now, he says, after car payments he barely makes it work. Uber's claim that it provides widespread entrepreneurship opportunities falls flat in light of Frank's short-term gains and Thomas's unemployment after the company left town.

In 2014, Uber's own newsroom stated, "Our powerful technology platform delivers turnkey entrepreneurship to drivers across the country and around the world."[7] The idea that Uber can deliver entrepreneurship to the masses through technology is a compelling anthem for a society eager to reap the benefits of technology that come especially from Silicon Valley kingmakers. Drivers, however, aren't the web 2.0 tech entrepreneurs who emerged from Silicon Valley with a heady array of self-branding marketing skills in the early years of the twenty-first century. They don't game search-engine-optimization results to boost their presence on the Internet, and they don't have Google alerts set to their names to inform them when they are mentioned somewhere (with the possible exception of a few drivers who run forums and blogs). Drivers aren't "happiness engineers" or "code ninjas."[8]

THE LEGEND OF SILICON VALLEY

It shouldn't be surprising that Uber has adopted the myth of tech entrepreneurship: after all, the company was started by such entrepreneurs. Travis Kalanick, the most visible cofounder of Uber, is hailed as one of Silicon Valley's "Great Men." The Great Man theory of success celebrates America's technology founder-heroes for their business acumen and their passion, like Microsoft cofounder Bill Gates and Facebook cofounder Mark Zuckerberg. The Silicon Valley "Great Men" typically celebrated are white men. Equally accomplished founders who are *not* white men tend to get less play—like Yahoo founder Jerry Yang, according to longtime Silicon Valley journalist, Sarah Lacy.[9] The meritocratic theory of success has crossed class lines and entered the culture of work embraced by most people in the United States. Like Frank, they are "doers" and deserve the fruits of their labor. It is the sentiment that animates antigovernment, antitax efforts by the Tea Party, congressional Republicans, and libertarians today, and which prompted Paul Ryan, Speaker of the House of Representatives, to divide the citizens of the United States into givers and takers.[10] This simple story has roots in American history, which celebrates Virginian slave-owners for their business and political acumen, even though it was slaves who bent down to pull up the slave owners' bootstraps. The disparity between founders and workers in the Great Man story of success reveals the gap between theory and reality. For Uber's drivers, information and power asymmetries contradict the claims that drivers are entrepreneurs who make informed decisions about the risks they take on.

The cultural gap between Uber's focus on engineering efforts and the experiences of its drivers cannot be overstated. While Uber hires rarefied artificial-intelligence experts internationally to spearhead self-driving car initiatives, its drivers are still struggling to find places to pee. One passenger recounted an uncomfortable moment when she accidentally dislodged the driver's pee bottle from beneath the passenger front seat, where he had stowed it, and it spilled. They both noticed it, and each decided not to say anything.[11] Peeing into a McDonald's cup or a bottle works for male drivers, though the absence of a dignified place to go the bathroom is a routine problem. But as one driver observed in a forum discussion on the topic, "I don't think I can help you if you're a chick." This was a response to the female driver who had started the thread with the following comment: "I've been driving for a little over two months, and it is a nightmare to work at night because there are no public bathrooms. What do y'all do when you have to pee during the night? Lol." Drivers commonly suggest opening up Google Maps and locating the nearest coffee shop or fast-food joint. Half-jokingly, some post photos of their pee bottles in forums.

Part of what makes Uber so compelling as the future of work is its promise to democratize access to entrepreneurial success. Yet, simultaneously, the Great Man theory de-emphasizes the interdependence between individuals and others—the state, networks, capital, and so on—that can make them successful. The message is that it takes a Steve Jobs or a Travis Kalanick, not a village. The dedication it takes to get your start-up off the ground is not the same dedication it takes to pee into a discarded Coke bottle, but drivers are hustling at every turn. Even if they are ultimately disadvantaged by a capitalist system that places the value of an entrepreneurial "Great Man" in the billions and rewards drivers with diminishing wages, they find dignity in working hard, especially to support their families.

A few drivers have turned their driving experiences into a form of expertise. Randy Lee Shear, for example, has branded himself "Uber Man," and on his Facebook page he lists his occupation as "entrepreneur." He runs a successful forum for drivers from all over the United States, with occasional posts by drivers in Canada and elsewhere. A charismatic presence, he also runs a YouTube channel documenting emergent issues with Uber, Lyft, and other ridehailing companies, as well as describing his experiences as a driver. Harry Campbell runs a blog called *The Rideshare Guy,* but *blog* is an understatement of his business: by the spring of 2017, he had become the voice that represents drivers in the majority of media coverage of Uber issues through his communications with over fifty thousand of them. His team of contributors regularly posts new assessments of how the ridehail business is affecting drivers, and he offers a course titled Maximize Your Rideshare Profits. Leticia Alcala follows these forums 24/7, she says, to emphasize her constant awareness of them, and she runs several Facebook groups, including one for forum administrators and one for women. She became somewhat marginalized as an outspoken female voice in some of the other driver forums, most of which tend to be male-dominated spaces. In response, she decided to set up her own groups.

Most drivers simply drive passengers from A to B for money. Those drivers who become forum brand-builders are exceptions: they monetize their content-production, blogging, and forum administrator roles by, for example, promoting their driver referral codes to different services. Uber, Lyft, and other on-demand companies offer a "commission," or referral bonus, to drivers who spread the word.[12] Their real entrepreneurship is rooted in this secondary monetization of their driver knowledge and skills, rather than in their jobs as drivers. And yet, the rhetoric of entrepreneurship dominates Uber's forays into the American economy. Where driver autonomy becomes most apparent is in the decisions drivers make about their own safety, but when it comes to maximizing their own profits or interests, they often face a greater risk of penalties from the company.

HALFWAY TO THE "ENTREPRENEURIAL" LIFE

DeMonte drives in Marietta, near Atlanta. He delivers food part time for uberEats. A college graduate, he enjoys the flexibility that permits him to work when he wants and to log in and log out at will, but he doesn't feel like an entrepreneur. He adds, though, "It's like trying it out. It's like being halfway to running your own small business." Uber sets the rates and the commissions; it also maintains a policy of blind dispatches, so he can't assess whether it's worthwhile to take a job before he accepts it. Uber also demands high ride-acceptance rates. It suggests how long he should wait at a customer's door (up to ten minutes), but he's not compensated for that time. While driving, he's paid only for the miles he drives from the restaurant to the customer's door. The miles he drives en route to the restaurant to pick up the food don't count, and he was once dispatched to Atlanta, nearly an hour away. On one occasion, an uberEats customer never answered the doorbell. There's a smile in DeMonte's voice as he recounts how he was able to take the food home for himself and his mom to share for dinner, and how he was still paid for the job.

Karen, who drives for Uber in New Orleans (and who used to drive for Lyft, too), drives about twenty-four to thirty-two hours per week to supplement her income. She likes the flexible schedule because it allows her to pick her son up from work sometimes—and attend to him if he has a sudden episode of his chronic medical condition. She's been in the service industry for a long time; handling misbehaving passengers is comparable to dealing with drunks at a club, she tells me. When I interview her in 2017, she says, "I've had a couple of drunks that were just obviously, like, angry drunks, and not necessarily toward me but just in general. I had one guy who was sitting on the phone screaming at somebody, cursing up a storm. I think that's a little bit problematic"—she wavers off briefly before continuing—"when I'm trying to drive. I had one guy that was just, like, cursing at his girlfriend. He was sitting in the front seat and just cursing at his girlfriend in the backseat, and then got rude to me because I wouldn't go through a traffic jam. He started getting rude to me, so I just told him to get out of the car. Those are my worst two experiences, but other than that, I haven't had any problems with anybody." She has the autonomy to make decisions in her own interests when it comes to her security, though not all drivers feel they have the resources to do so. If a passenger refuses to get out, for instance, the situation can escalate.

In 2015, a few years before I interviewed DeMonte from Atlanta or Karen in New Orleans, I conducted a phone interview with Mike, an Uber driver in Savannah, Georgia. He'd been driving for Uber for two to three months when we spoke. When I asked him if he thought driving for Uber was like being an entrepreneur, he paused before answering, "*Entrepreneur* is, I feel like a bit of a stretch. I mean, I feel like the definition of an entrepreneur is, you know, having your own idea and taking off with that. I feel like Uber is just a side gig, not any kind of entrepreneur endeavor. I don't feel like *entrepreneur* is a great classification for drivers, unless you're running a business out of your car. I guess that's something an entrepreneur could do." Many drivers appreciate the independence they have to work when they want and see this as a better opportunity than their previous work provided. And for a few, rare drivers, this job has turned into an entrepreneurial opportunity through blogging. By keeping up with pay incentives and a myriad other factors in this work, many drivers try to be successful at this job; but they don't view their success as entrepreneurial.

In Dallas, uberBlack drivers protested in September 2015 at Uber's local headquarters, taking a stand against a dispatch policy requiring them to accept lower uberX fares; another group did the same in New York City.[13] These drivers felt they were being squeezed, prevented from earning a profitable living by this "bait and switch" maneuver. They had invested in more expensive vehicles so they could drive professionally at a higher-paying tier of service, but the company subsequently pressured them to accept lower-tier fares as well, while also penalizing them for canceling undesirable fares or falling below a

certain ride-acceptance rate.[14] The contrast between drivers who readily accept Uber's policy and those who find the same practice oppressive (like driver-protesters in New York and Dallas) highlights fractures in the popular narrative of who Uber and Lyft drivers are and
what they want. It's easy to get hired, but a lot of drivers quit within the
first few months, or the first year, as they learn more about what driving
for the company is actually like.

Some drivers put up with unprofitable dispatches, believing that
doing so might help position them for much more lucrative trips later
on. Other drivers also explain that Uber's system would be unreliable for
passengers if drivers were free to cherry-pick only the good rides.
Miguel, for example, drives in Montreal, where he emigrated from Gua-
temala forty years ago. He is technically retired with a pension, but he
drives for Uber seven days a week. He also rents out the ground-floor
apartment of his townhouse for additional income. When I meet him in
Montreal on a crisp evening in 2016, he explains, "My wife is working,
my son is working.... [W]e make money, but you have to work hard." To
Miguel, working hard is an important part of his personal identity, even
though he is a retiree in his sixties. In his view, all the money he can
make is worthwhile, even if some jobs are less lucrative than others.

In Montreal (as of April 2017), uberX rates included a base fare of
$1.90, and $0.19 per minute, and $0.79 per kilometer, whereas uberSelect
had a base fare of $4.30, $0.27 per minute, and $1.65 per kilometer (all in
Canadian dollars). Miguel tells me he doesn't mind using his higher-
end, gas-guzzling vehicle, which is eligible for uberSelect, to take
uberX fares that earn money at lower rates.[15] "What I wanna make is
money, my dear. I wanna make money, I don't care," he reasons, adding
that even a few dollars at a time add up. While Miguel is a bit of an
edge case, his sanguine attitude toward the less-than-optimal dispatching and other business practices is a relatively common approach that
drivers take to make sense of the good and bad aspects of this job. Even
so, the Dallas and New York City protests against dispatch policies
show the degree of anger and frustration among Uber drivers.

Uber is dominant, but the experiences of Uber's drivers are not monolithic. Near Orlando, I scan the parking lot next to a swamp with red-faced tour guides from West Virginia who offer boat rides to see alligators in the marshland. Incredibly, a driver arrives to pick me up in a remote area, even though he had to drive for nearly twenty minutes to arrive at my pickup location. That's a lot of deadhead miles. Nor does he know where I'm heading, or whether this ride makes economic sense for him. I ask Jerry why he came, and he says it would be discourteous to leave me stranded—a violation of a culture of hospitality, also found in many other places in the southern United States. In Orlando, which has a car-centric culture, many attractions are a twenty-minute drive away, unlike in the dense, transit-heavy culture of New York City. It's not abnormal to make this kind of trip, but drivers in New York City, and elsewhere, would think twice before burning that much time and gas on a pickup (though many still go through with it). Similarly, Karen in New Orleans is willing to pick up minors (though it's technically against Uber's policy). She's not alone—many drivers accept minors in their cars. Sometimes the parents call Karen and say, "Look, it's my account, but I'm using it to pick up my son." When I interview her, she remarks, "Let me give these people a safe ride home. I don't want to leave anybody stranded." Drivers often fill in gaps in the services Uber provides to its customers, but their decision-making is often mixed with a sense of personal identity and civic duty, rather than driven by entrepreneurialism.

HOW UBER UNDERMINES ITS OWN ENTREPRENEURIAL CLAIMS

Drivers are billed as the boss, but Uber unilaterally sets and changes the rates at which they earn their income. Drivers have barely any bargaining power, and even in rare successful events where driver protests force Uber to back down, their collective action isn't sustained, and the company reverts back to its original plans later.[16] For example, in July 2015, Uber notified drivers in Tulsa, Oklahoma, that uberX prices were being reduced to increase ridership and boost earnings per hour. To support this explanation, Uber showed drivers a graph (a proxy for mathematical and objective proof) of how lowering prices in Austin led to a "huge boost in demand, and partner earnings per hour increased by 25%—that's a lot of extra money!" In reactions that echoed other driver responses to rate decreases in various cities, including Austin, drivers responded with incredulity: they called it "Uber math," "propaganda," and "Orwellian doublespeak." They observed, using simple math, that if they did the same number of rides at the lower rates, they would earn less; and, doing more rides would mean more wear and tear on their vehicles and other higher expenses. Additionally, there is a maximum number of rides drivers can do in any given hour.

Uber was using macroeconomic logic to market its pay cut to drivers. "Partner earnings per hour increased by 25%" (figure 3) refers to an aggregate of drivers, but individual drivers primarily care about their personal take-home pay. These competing macroeconomic and microeconomic logics point to a fundamental disconnect between what's optimal for Uber and what's best for its drivers. This kind of economics debacle isn't unique to Uber: for example, Egypt was able to improve its growth and overall macroeconomic performance in the years right before the 2011 revolution, yet official figures indicated that poverty increased in tandem. At the micro level, households on average were worse off.[17] Competing concepts of inequality can produce similar mixed messaging: wealth inequality might be high, but income inequality can, overall, be low. While this assessment of inequality makes sense to economists, the poverty of this distinction makes it look glaringly suspicious to passive observers, who can see with their own eyes that many people live in poverty while an elite few live very well.[18]

Telling Uber drivers that lowering rates at which they earn their livelihoods will increase their pay (and illustrating this with macroeconomic "proof") is analogous, in my mind, to a situation where one member of a couple has an affair. After it comes to light, the cheating spouse turns to the scorned partner and explains, "But honey, at the

Figure 3. A message Uber sent to a driver. The aesthetic design of the app communication, and the veneer of objectivity provided by a graph, emphasize Uber's authority to make claims based on the data it has. The design also leaves no physical space for negotiation over Uber's message—"lower prices = higher earnings." The message was posted in a forum in 2015. (This figure also appears in the color section following page 116.)

macro level, infidelity is on the decline." Drivers are not reassured by Uber's macro logic, because it is disconnected from how drivers *experience* rate cuts as individuals rather than as abstract members of an average of driver experiences. On the whole, drivers perceive that their pay is lower than what it was for the same amount of work before rates were cut. One might imagine a driver who mutters, "I wish I were paid as a macro worker."[19]

Faiq, an Uber and Lyft driver in New York City who worked as a taxi driver for twenty-seven years before joining Uber, says his biggest concern is depressed wages. "Rate cut actually affects drivers because we don't make enough money nowadays," he explains rapidly, "because we have to work long hours, plus there is a lot of competition and different companies. There is nothing best. Everybody cut the price." It's not only that Uber and its competitors cut prices—it's also *how* changes to the material conditions of their work are communicated that matters. Drivers who don't assent to the perennial changes—by clicking "accept" on a popup listing the new terms of service—can't log in to work (although some drivers report they also receive these new terms via email). As Faiq speaks, I recall an observation made by Jason, a driver from Raleigh: "They keep bonking around with the rates and the different terms of service. You gotta log in, and all of a sudden there's new terms and conditions; and if you don't sign you can't drive. And you're on your phone, trying to read it." As I return my attention to Faiq, he reflects on the positive side, saying, "With Uber, anywhere you go you get a job. *Anywhere.*" There's no shortage of clients, and Uber handles the logistical work of matching a driver with a passenger. In other technology-mediated and freelancer workplaces, workers spend hours and hours just coordinating and messaging back and forth with potential clients.[20] Uber effectively provides platforms for coordinating short-term jobs for a flexible workforce, and drivers trust that the dispatching function generally works (although some have concerns about fairness).

Trusting the technology is not the same as trusting the company overall. According to a 2017 report on Uber by the *New York Times,*

"roughly a quarter of its drivers turn over on average ev
months."[21] Uber's high churn rates may be rooted in the sore feelings
harbored by drivers. Thomas, an Uber and Lyft driver in Austin discussed in a previous section, is jaded by his experience of the repeated
rate cuts that Uber implements. "And every time, they send you an
email, 'Thomas, Good News! We just lowered rates in Austin. Lower
rates equals higher earnings!' ... Every time, I go, like, 'In what parallel
universe?'" Drivers across the country are dismayed by rate cuts, but
it's the arrogance of Uber's messaging that really makes their blood
boil. "I know how much money I used to make, and how many hours I
had to drive for that, what my average was per hour, and what it is now.
They are just driving rates down because they can," Thomas tells me.
"They want to crush the competition [such as Lyft]. They don't care
how much drivers make as long as they can sign up another shmuck.
And they promise the world; and after two or three weeks, [the new
drivers] see it doesn't work, and they drop out. It's kind of hard when
you go from working forty hours to working seventy hours, eighty
hours, just to make ends meet. And that's what I mean when I say they
don't treat their drivers nice."

Many drivers, like Thomas, feel belittled by Uber's messaging,
which adds insult to injury and widens a rift between Uber and its drivers. The antagonism they reveal toward the company speaks a larger
truth about the type of entrepreneurship that characterizes their work:
drivers can play the games that are part of the system by, for example,
tracking pay premiums, but ultimately they have limited information
and limited power to make choices that serve their own interests.

THE ILLUSION OF DRIVER AUTONOMY

The autonomy celebrated by Uber's model stands in stark contrast to the
everyday experiences of its drivers, who are carefully monitored by an
algorithmic boss. Evidence of control is scattered everywhere. The company determines the types of cars that are eligible on its platform, and it

sometimes modifies the list of acceptable types at will; sets and changes the pay rates as it wishes; controls the dispatch; targets drivers unevenly with incentives; retains the full power to suspend or fire drivers without recourse; and mediates and resolves conflicts at its discretion, ranging from issues of passenger disputes to wage theft. An algorithmic manager enacts its policies, penalizes drivers for behaving in a manner unlike what Uber "suggests," and incentivizes them to work at particular places in particular times. This algorithmic boss is qualitatively different from a human manager. When I ask drivers if they are their own boss, they usually pause and remark that it's sort of true, and that they set their own schedule. But an app-employer provides a type of experience that differs from human interactions, and it can be challenging to identify the fault lines of autonomy and control within an automated system.

Uber hides the information that drivers need if they are to make informed economic assessments of the jobs sent to them, such as the destination of the passenger. In addition, Uber tracks their ride acceptance and ride cancellation rates: if drivers' acceptance rates are low or their cancellation rates are high, they risk being suspended or fired from the platform. Uber also enacts policies that, for example, force drivers with higher-end cars (which normally command higher rates per minute and per mile) to accept ride requests from uberX, which has low rates per mile and per minute. Some drivers speculate that Uber's algorithmic dispatcher rewards drivers implicitly for following behavioral prompts (among other factors), although the explicit dispatching rule is that passengers are matched with the nearest driver.[22]

Drivers operate at an informational disadvantage, and so it is harder for them to make full and informed decisions as independent contractors about the work they do. This haze has sparked rampant speculation about what goes on behind the scenes. In the summer of 2017, one driver posted in a forum a sample of this reasoning: "The main way that I feel like an employee these days is [through] the algorithm that pings drivers. Everyone speculates that there are other factors[,] other than being the closest car[,] like: car type, rating, acceptance rate and whether you've been matched with the rider before. The one thing I wish these lawsuits against Uber regarding the employee versus contractor debate would ask for is what is baked into the algorithm. I think we all would find it amazing how Uber is screwing us by the factors they throw in." Another driver agreed, reiterating those factors, and adding, "Yes I know some factors are known to influence this, but I believe those are just the tip of the iceberg, and there is a lot more they can't/won't/shouldn't tell us."

Drivers are often unsure of how Uber's algorithms work because their experiences of them are inconsistent. One recurrent conversational topic in Uber driver forums is whether a ridehail company's algorithmic dispatcher favors some drivers over others depending on factors such as how new they are or whether they are a high-quality driver, based on their ratings. Nathan, whom I introduced in chapter 2, is a Lyft driver who started to question the system after noticing inconsistencies in his own experiences that resembled those of Uber drivers he read about. He observes, "Because I'm 6 months in and they know they've got me hooked. They know I'm going to do X amount of rides or I'm going to spend X amount of time on the roads on the weekends. Is there something built into the algorithm that tells them the kind of driver [I am]?" He describes seeing notifications about high demand in his area but experiencing unfamiliar delays in receiving ride requests now, compared to his first few weeks on the job. He explains, "I feel like something isn't quite kosher. I'm not a person who generally feels the world is working against me in some way, or whatever, so this is not my normal way of thinking, to be suspicious. You know, one of my reasons for doing this is it all seems so fair. Okay, I can jump right in here at sixty-four years of age and go do this, and keep up with a twenty-two- or twenty-three-year-old, [and] it doesn't really matter because, basically, the system is going to guide me to it. That's one thing that attracted me to it, that it's fair. But now it doesn't appear to be so fair."

This sense of unease with the dispatching algorithm is a reflection of the many small ways that drivers' choices are constrained by Uber's authority. As I observed with my colleague Luke Stark, a media studies scholar, in a coauthored paper, "When active Uber drivers receive a ride request through the system, they have about 15 seconds to accept it or reject it. When Uber drivers accept a ride request, they take on the risk that the ride's fare will not be profitable; yet, drivers are not shown destination or fare information before they accept a ride." Jason from Raleigh, North Carolina, who had driven for about a year, said, "You're driving around blind. When it does ping, you might drive fifteen minutes to drive someone half a mile. There's no money in it at that point, especially in my SUV." The "blindness" that Jason describes may also discourage destination-based discrimination,[23] but as Stark and I observed in our research study, drivers absorb the risk and expense of unprofitable dispatches.[24]

I interviewed Jason in 2015, but the sentiment he articulated persisted through 2017. One Utah driver posted the following in a forum in the summer of 2017:

> This is the scam Uber is playing, calling us contractors when we're obviously not. If you're a painting contractor, do you accept a job without knowing what it is or how much it pays? Of course not. But this is exactly what Uber is doing to us. Like telling the painting contractor you have a job for him but he has to accept it before he knows what it is. Paint the whole house for 50 bucks and you the contractor have to supply the paint. You'd tell them to go pound sand, the paint alone costs more than 50 bucks. Then the painting contractor is told he already accepted the job and if he cancels he'll never work in this town again.

A driver I interviewed in 2015 had articulated the same sentiment, characterizing Uber's dispatching policies as unfair. Ron was proudly awaiting the birth of his son and working to save money for his new family; he had recently married a woman who had come from Pakistan to meet him. Ron, who had been driving in New Jersey and New York City for over a year, said, "Show the destination before. If we're independent contractors, we should have the right to refuse. If I look down and it's three in the afternoon, and the guy is going to JFK [a New York City–based airport], I'm not going to take it. When I get to the guy's location, and I get to JFK, I'm not going to make forty dollars for three hours of work.... They tell us it's our choice whether to take a trip or not, so how can they penalize us for that?"[25] The effect of the blind passenger-acceptance rule is that drivers can't assess the economic value of the job before they accept it, which contradicts the idea that they are independent entrepreneurs.

The context of this policy has further implications for Uber's employment relationship with its drivers. If drivers declined trips, even those they deemed unprofitable, they risked dinging their ride-acceptance rate. Before August 2016, when Uber modified its policy,[26] Uber evaluated drivers on the basis of their ride-acceptance rates, their ride-cancellation rates, and their ratings in the five-star rating system. In some cities, if drivers sank below a 90 percent ride-acceptance threshold or exceeded a 5 percent ride-cancellation rate, they risked "deactivation," an Uber word for being temporarily suspended or fired (see figure 4).[27] Under Uber's modified policy, drivers face "time-outs" from the app instead of deactivation, in which they are automatically logged out for a period of time, such as two minutes, ten minutes, or thirty minutes. The takeaway is that even though drivers are still classified as independent contractors, Uber's dispatching practice, app design, and penalty system all shape how they are required to behave at work. In other words, this policy is another potential proof that drivers may be misclassified under labor law.[28] Incidentally, I still occasionally see forum posts from drivers, such as one from spring 2017, long after the policy changed, indicating that a driver's account had been deactivated owing to consistently high cancellation rates.

In August 2017, after Uber launched a program called "180 Days of Change," aimed at improving the driver experience, one driver posted in a regional forum a notice he had received regarding "destination discrimination" (see figure 5)—exactly the type of censure that worried Jose in Los Angeles in the summer of 2016. The driver commented, "Lol I got this in an email and this DOES NOT look like 180 days of change. Maybe if Uber stops hiding the exact addresses of drop off (and even the pickup), maybe people wouldn't have to cancel." He also added,

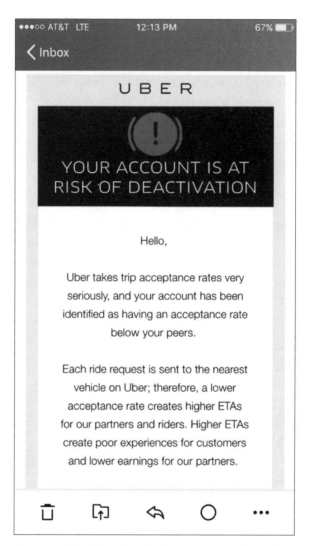

Figure 4. How Uber breaks the news: a sample email that the company sent to warn that a driver's account was at risk of deactivation, on the basis of a trip or ride acceptance rate that was too low. It was posted in a forum in 2016. (This figure also appears in the color section following page 116.)

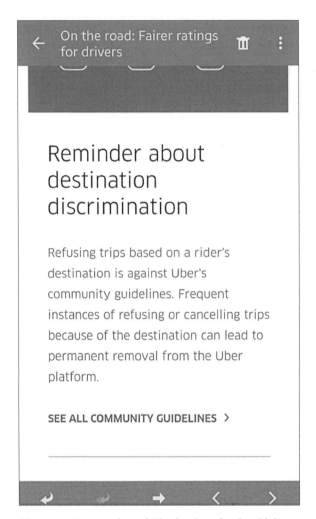

Figure 5. A screenshot of Uber's trip refusal guideline in 2017.

"I personally don't have to cancel because I drive on high surge or higher boost [incentive pay] primarily, but there are way too many drivers on boarded [hired] in areas like LA and SF, NY, etc. to be worried about destination discrimination. What one driver won't do the next will. That's the point of being 'Independent.'"

HOW UBER KEEPS ITS "ENTREPRENEURS" IN LINE

Despite the constraints placed on driver behavior, drivers also game the system to try and earn profitable fares, but they can be penalized for those actions. For example, Uber's algorithmic manager urges drivers to follow its prompts to temporarily relocate and thereby benefit from surge pricing, which is meant to reflect supply and demand: they may garner a pay premium when passenger demand outstrips the local supply of drivers. Drivers, however, may instead be offered "nonsurge" trips once they arrive there, and can be penalized for declining them, after they've absorbed the costs—like gas, time, and lost opportunities—of traveling to the surge zone. In one email a driver received from Uber Support regarding "surge manipulation" (see figure 6), the driver was advised that "a passenger let us know that they felt you unfairly canceled their trip to await for surge to kick in, or that you otherwise unfairly gave preference to surge trips instead of their request." The note went on to say, "Please accept every request that Uber sends your way, and do not cancel trips in the hope that your next dispatch will be a surge trip." In effect, Uber used the promise of surge pricing to shepherd a driver to a particular place at a particular time, and when the driver opted to decline a nonsurge fare in favor of waiting for a more profitable, surge-priced dispatch, he or she was sanctioned by the Uber manager for "surge manipulation." In Uberland, the data that drivers see on their individual screens is deployed to manipulate their behavior, but permitted manipulation is a one-way street.

There are other ways drivers try to game the algorithm, but because Uber controls the interface, their methods may be ineffective. Heather, like many drivers, used the Uber passenger app to track the presence of

From: partnersla@uber.com
To: [driver's email censored]
Subject: Rider Complaint – Surge Manipulation
Date: [Date] [Timestamp]

Hi [driver's name censored],

At Uber, we're committed to supporting our partners by providing them the feedback needed to improve their star ratings. In recent driver surveys, rider feedback was the #1 item drivers requested from us, and we listened! In the past week, we received the below feedback from your riders.

---- Surge Manipulation ----

What does Surge Manipulation mean? A passenger let us know that they felt you unfairly canceled their trip to wait for surge to kick in, or that you otherwise unfairly gave preference to surge trips instead of their request.

How can I improve? Please accept every request that Uber sends your way, and do not cancel trips in the hope that your next dispatch will be a surge trip. If we continue to receive negative feedback from riders that impacts your rating, your account will be reviewed and may be deactivated.

Note: we expect some negative feedback over time for all our partners as this is the nature of the business! If you believe you received this complaint unfairly, please don't worry: as long as this doesn't happen regularly, your account will not be affected. Again, this purpose of this message is to provide you constructive feedback to help you improve.

Hope this helps!

Uber Team

Figure 6. An email Uber sent to a driver about surge manipulation in 2014, transcribed from a screenshot.

competing drivers. At 2 A.M., she was checking out the Uber passenger app while she was sitting at home in a quiet neighborhood outside of the city. She was surprised to see that the app showed several Uber cars clustered outside her door, even though they were, according to the app, seventeen minutes away (see figure 7). The little black sedans represented on the screen of her Uber passenger app were phantoms. I published an article on Uber's phantom cabs, which went viral around the world because, until the user manipulation was revealed, people *believed* that the map represented the accurate location of available drivers. Heather's discovery turned out to be an indicator of a systematic evasion of regulation through a secret tool at Uber termed "Greyball," which was reported in the *New York Times* by Mike Isaac.[29]

In the Greyball program, Uber identifies potential law enforcement and municipal actors by various means, such as through the type of phone or credit card they use, and purposefully misleads them about the presence of Uber vehicles by displaying "ghost," or "phantom," cars in the app, which do not reflect the actual presence of local drivers. In effect, Uber may evade law enforcement's efforts to regulate the activities of its drivers (by ticketing them, for example), especially in cities where Uber operates illegally. When I reported on the presence of phantom cars in the Uber passenger app in 2015,[30] two years before the revelations about Greyball, Uber categorically denied my claim.[31] But the fact is, Uber can use its interface and technical tools to control and manipulate how drivers and passengers interact with its platform.

Similarly, Uber uses its dispatching function as a tool to control its drivers. Drivers may apply to drive for Uber with the intention of working for a particular service tier (because each tier, such as uberX or uberSUV, requires a specific make and model of car), but Uber often pushes drivers to accept dispatches for lower tiers. An uberBlack driver may be dispatched to pick up an uberX customer, who pays the lower uberX rates, even though the driver continues to absorb the cost of operating a higher-end, gas-guzzling vehicle. An uberX driver, likewise, may be dispatched to pick up riders as part of the much-hated

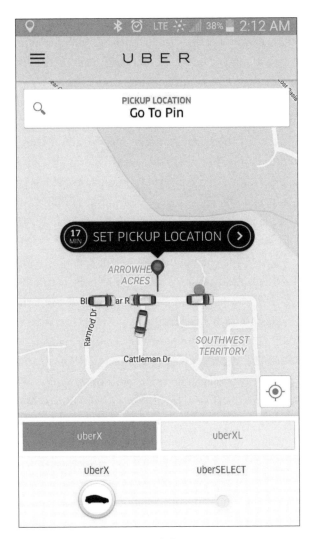

Figure 7. This screenshot of phantom cars was sent to the author in 2015. (This figure also appears in the color section following page 116.)

uberPOOL service, which means he must make multiple pickups and drop-offs and manage passenger group dynamics, too, for about the same cumulative pay as one uberX ride. Echoing many other drivers, one posted the following in a forum: "So much work for a $2.50 fare." Drivers have mixed experiences with "opting out" of dispatches they dislike (see figure 8). One sample post by a driver in a forum online read, "Hey guys, within the last week there was someone who posted a screenshot of a reply from Uber saying they could opt out of Uber pool. Can you please post that again? I am in Seattle market and they [are] saying I cannot opt out.... Request type is being disguised now[;] this is ridiculous!"

In one sample exchange between Uber Support and a driver who wanted to opt out of uberPOOL the company wrote, "There is no *[sic]* currently an option for partners to opt out of specific vehicle options like uberPOOL or uberX, but we're happy to help with any issues on specific trips that you may have had." And later in the note, echoing Uber's logic regarding why drivers can't reject less lucrative requests in favor of higher-paying, surge requests, the company added, "Accepting and completing all trips, both uberX and uberPOOL, is critical to ensuring a positive experience for riders who are relying on Uber to get to their destination. uberPOOL is one of our fastest growing and most popular products among riders, so accepting your uberX and uber-POOL trips should keep you busier every time you drive."

However, some drivers have persisted in their complaints and found success. A driver in Athens, Georgia, posted in a forum a response from Uber Support in the winter of 2017, which read: "I have gone ahead and removed the uberPOOL vehicle class option from your account." The uncertainty of Uber's dispatching policies and Uber's push to oblige drivers to accept jobs they want to reject are part of how Uber wields an information and power asymmetry against drivers. Limited by the rules enacted by Uber's algorithms, drivers are unable to pursue their highest economic or personal interests when accepting dispatches.

Uber drivers like Ron exemplify the driver autonomy dilemma. As Ron shuttles around New York City, he knows he will be sitting in traffic

UBERPOOL PICKUP WARNING

You picked up **less than 75% of uberPOOL requests again** over the past week.

Continuing to pick up fewer than 75% of uberPOOL trip requests may result in the **temporary deactivation of your Uber account**.

Top driver-partners **pick up at least 85% of uberPOOL requests** to provide a reliable experience for riders. uberPOOL fares are on average $16 higher than uberX fares when you make multiple pickups.

Figure 8. A screenshot of an email from Uber, which was posted in a forum in 2016, illustrates how the company disciplines drivers who refuse too many uberPOOL requests, chastising them with a sternly worded warning and bold print that points to selective policies. Another driver responded to the post to emphasize how this policy affected his employment status with the company. He wrote, "We really need to start fighting this because this is not independent contractor status.... Uber the new car sharing app[,] or can we just say crop sharing!!!!"

Figure 9. Uber CEO Travis Kalanick leaning in for a heated debate with his uberBlack driver. This is a screenshot of the video about the incident posted on YouTube in 2017.

for a good chunk of his trip to a New York City airport. Furthermore, the amount he will earn per minute is very low, despite Uber's insistence that its policy of blind passenger acceptance ensures that passengers receive reliable service. The company seems unconcerned that its practices severely limit drivers' ability to optimize their earnings. Algorithmic management is a system that works for the company—simple, efficient, and bureaucratic. But its drivers suffer as they are forced to accept the odds that Uber has designed in its own favor.

While drivers had long been aware of Uber's ham-fisted treatment of them, a video capturing Uber CEO Travis Kalanick in an encounter with an Uber driver showcased this dynamic to a wider public in February 2017 (see figure 9).[32]

The driver's dashcam recorded the interaction: The driver says he's bankrupt after investing ninety-seven thousand dollars in a high-end car to drive for uberBlack, because rates have fallen and the demand for uberBlack has dropped, given the availability of cheaper Uber services. He accuses Kalanick of constantly changing the conditions of his work and degrading his take-home pay. Kalanick contests the accusations and concludes the exchange by saying, "You know what? Some people don't like to take responsibility for their own shit. They blame everything in their life on somebody else. Good luck!" The driver replies, "Good luck to you, too. I know that you aren't going to go far." Later, this video of Kalanick chastising a driver for not taking personal responsibility for the damage wrought by Uber's rate cuts and business practices went viral. Media outlets like *Bloomberg* bludgeoned Kalanick for it.[33] He later issued an apology for the incident, but the damage was done: Kalanick and by extension, Uber, was perceived as indifferent to the plight of drivers.[34] The exchange between the indebted driver (defeated by Uber math) and an arrogant Kalanick (the winner in this economic relationship) has the caustic quality of a scene from the classic movie *Dirty Dancing*. Kalanick delivers a real-world version of the character Robbie, a *Fountainhead*-reading, Yale-attending antagonist who scoffs, "Some people count, and some people don't" as he declines to help a sympathetic but lower-class dancer whom he knocked up. Kalanick sends the same message in the dashcam video when he degrades the driver, but this specific articulation of it was not as important as it was newsworthy. Because of how Uber routinely treated them, drivers felt that the company saw them clearly as second-class citizens. Kalanick resigned as CEO in June 2017, several months after the incident, amid significant chaos at the company.[35]

Full-time, highly invested drivers are most affected by the conditions Uber sets for their work,[36] the very drivers whom Kalanick alludes to while chastising "some people" for not taking personal "responsibility." While the rhetoric of the gig economy implies that drivers have the information and power they need to make entrepreneurial choices, Uber's algorithmic manager effectively precludes them from making more "responsible" economic assessments of the work they take on. Even if, under Uber's model, drivers are not true entrepreneurs, their experiences of Uber's pros and cons do vary: these range from feeling excited to feeling trapped. The nature of their relationship to Uber depends in part upon their motivation, their competing options, the regional context of their work, and how long Uber has been established in their area. In interviews and conversations I had with drivers during my fieldwork, many willingly adopted the Uber slogan "Be your own boss" to describe their work. Despite their cooperative attitude, many often later admitted to conditions that they resent, and which narrow their autonomy at work, like rate cuts or the rating system. In some ways, there isn't that much difference between having a computer that delivers policies and communications, and having a boss who verbally tells you what to do. But it can *feel* different: having an app issue directives to workers creates a psychological distance from the idea that a boss is looking over your shoulder. Regardless, the result is a far cry from entrepreneurship.

CHAPTER FOUR

THE SHADY MIDDLEMAN

How Uber Manages Money

Silicon Valley is famous for "disrupting" business models and whole industries through innovative technology: this language—of technological disruption—is also a coded way of saying that a new middleman is in town. And it subtly suggests that new technology is inseparable from the business practices associated with it. This slippery rhetoric is part of how Silicon Valley companies create exceptions to the norms and rules of their industry competitors while subtly rewriting the rules. Fundamentally, Uber is a middleman. It collects and analyzes data from all of the drivers and passengers on the platform, and it displays some of this data to users, for example in the form of a surge-pricing map to a driver or a map of available drivers to a passengers. It also brokers ride requests from passengers, turning them into dispatches for drivers, and it handles payments for both sides. Individual drivers on the platform do not see the big picture. While it is normal that Uber earns a commission, lawsuits, journalistic exposés, and my own research suggest that Uber may be pocketing even more than agreed to, taking advantage of its position as an intermediary.[1] The result: passengers are charged higher fares, drivers are paid less than what the passengers pay, and Uber gets a bigger cut. At the beginning of this book, I discussed the myth of neutral technology and, in particular, the image of the algorithm as a neutral manager. But what about algorithms and money—specifically, how does Uber use its algorithms, channeled through its app and policies, to profit off of drivers and riders alike?

Dishonest dealings have existed since the days when herders bartered their sheep and cattle, but the advent of technology introduces entirely new dynamics. Technology companies claim that their platforms are neutral, driven by "impartial" algorithms. As a result, they can develop systems that produce self-interested and unjust results—and get away with it. Uber is engaged in all sorts of shady practices that contradict its status as an "intermediary," hands-off platform. How does this happen? First, Uber previously used pricing algorithms to estimate the price of a fare, based on variables like trip mileage, the duration of a trip, and price multipliers for Uber's estimate of supply and demand. Quietly, without announcing a policy change, it decoupled what drivers earn from what passengers pay. Then, in a departure from the calculation it previously used to estimate the cost of a fare, it introduced "route-based pricing." Using artificial intelligence, Uber identifies which users are part of an aggregate class of passengers willing to pay more for its services and charges them a higher fee. The company insists that this pricing practice is not personalized. To the public, Uber justifies route-based pricing in morally persuasive language. For example, it cites the possibility that passengers who travel between high-income areas might be charged more than passengers who travel between low-income areas.[2] And by citing "artificial intelligence" (AI) to describe the market logic of charging passengers what they are willing to pay, Uber harnesses technology to tell a more positive story about selecting which passengers get a surcharge. This price increase does not extend benefits to drivers, who are paid per minute and per mile at set rates. Uber didn't disclose its predictive pricing practices when it started experimenting with them. It was thus able to profit without notifying drivers or passengers that it was taking advantage of its position in the middle. A sense of mathematical objectivity—"It must be fair because the numbers, the algorithms, or the AI said so"—

legitimizes Uber's claim that it is merely an innocent and neutral technology platform.

Uber borrows its neutrality logic from consumer-facing companies like Google and Facebook (the putative empire-builders of Silicon Valley). Google's search results and Facebook's newsfeeds, both which rely on algorithms to sort information, may reflect a host of unexpected biases. It's difficult to distinguish between biases in society that are reflected back to us through search results, and algorithmic management practices that these companies use to manipulate users with information and inferences. But services like Google's search engine and Facebook's newsfeed are free, so consumers can't easily complain if the algorithms behind them are not neutral. As the rationale goes, unhappy users should just stop using these sites if they don't like them (although much evidence suggests that, in practice, it is difficult to opt out of using these platforms in everyday life).[3]

At Uber, however, the stakes are inherently higher, as algorithmic management affects the livelihoods of drivers. Despite the fact that its platform both faces consumers *and* organizes labor, Uber simply takes many of the same consumer-facing algorithmic management practices from Silicon Valley and applies them to an employment context. To understand how extractive practices have been woven into Uber's system requires leaving Uber for a moment in order to look at all the ways that other supposedly neutral systems can affect our lives in decidedly unneutral ways.

HOW PLATFORM COMPANIES PLAY YOU USING YOUR DATA

In our everyday digital lives, we interact with algorithms constantly, even if we don't realize it. Algorithms shape Facebook's newsfeed by selectively highlighting status updates, while YouTube and Twitter highlight popular trends such as the "most liked" or "highest rated" content in real time. The power of these algorithmic managers lies not just in their responsiveness or personalization but also in their capacity to obscure their work behind the scenes. As communications scholar Tarleton Gillespie observes of social media platforms, "They are curating a list whose legitimacy is built on the promise that it has not been curated, that it is the product of aggregate user activity itself."[4]

Consider Google: its search engine algorithm, called PageRank, is promoted as a neutral arbiter of information. PageRank measures the quality and number of links to a given web page to determine its order in search query results. In other words, it captures the wisdom of the crowd. Google has successfully cultivated a popular belief in the democratic and equitable nature of its search platform, despite critics who point out that algorithms often incorporate societal biases.[5] Similarly, Facebook touts its ability to increase voter turnout but denies that it has any impact on who people vote for: it dances on a tightrope that technology journalist Alexis C. Madrigal calls "the false dream of a neutral Facebook."[6] Uber's claim—that it is a platform connecting riders and drivers using neutral algorithms to set surge prices—rests on the same false premise of "platform purity."

The practice of using data-driven knowledge to influence consumer behavior is widespread in the tech industry. For example, *ProPublica* journalists Julia Angwin and Surya Mattu found that Amazon, which claims to put customers interests' first, steered customers to more costly products through rankings. By directing consumers to the sellers it charges for service, Amazon was able to improve its bottom line.[7] Effectively, the company put on a show of mathematical prowess: it analyzed dozens of pricing and shipping combinations, then used that information to ultimately disadvantage consumers with the results.

Price discrimination, or price gouging, is hardly new, but the rise of e-commerce businesses, like Amazon, that use Big Data to personalize product recommendations raises sharper considerations. Are customers being steered to higher-priced products without their knowledge? Are they charged higher prices for the same products sold to other, similarly situated customers? As several university researchers in computer science have shown, "personalization on e-commerce sites may also be used to the user's disadvantage by manipulating the products shown (price steering) or by customizing the prices of products (price discrimination). Unfortunately, today, we lack the tools and techniques necessary to be able to detect such behavior."[8]

On the Staples website, for example, consumers can be served different prices depending on their zip code. A consumer who is located farther from a Staples competitor, like Home Depot, is shown higher prices.[9] Airline and hotel brokers, like Orbitz, also use algorithmic pricing to serve higher- or lower-priced options or recommendations to passengers. They have learned that what passengers are typically willing to pay is related to the computer they have (Mac users get higher prices than non-Mac users), the type of web browser they use, and their physical location when they sign in.[10] (Incidentally, Orbitz is owned by Expedia, and the former CEO of Expedia became the new CEO of Uber in August 2017;[11] the former CEO of Orbitz, Barney Harford, was hired by Uber to be the chief operating officer a few months later.)[12] Although some argue that users should have a vested privacy interest in their phone's battery data or their geolocation, these variables are absorbed into pricing calculations by many software services. Data-driven sorting and customer segmentation are used across a variety of industries. For example, research by Evolv, a workplace data company, suggests that applicants who installed new web browsers onto their computers, like Google Chrome, rather than using the default, like Safari, were 15 percent more likely to stay at their jobs.[13] We can imagine that all sorts of personal data could be used to signal to platforms how we might perform as workers or what we're willing to pay as customers.

How information is represented to us is a source of great tension in technology culture beyond Uber. For example, we implicitly expect GPS navigation systems like Google Maps to have full and accurate maps, and we trust these services to produce accurate route recommendations for us. Artist and researcher Mimi Onuoha shows us that Google's maps have data voids—actual blank spots where whole communities live. She writes, "Google lacks mapping data on most favelas,

Brazil's infamous urban shantytowns (though not for lack of trying). In Rio de Janeiro, only 26 of the city's 1,000 favelas are mapped—this despite the fact that the favelas are home to over a million people and about a quarter of the city's population."[14] These inconsistencies raise real questions about who counts in how we map the world. But our societal belief that algorithmic technology supplies us with objective truths influences how we assess the fairness of the actions of companies like Uber.

THE MYTH OF THE NEUTRAL PLATFORM

These very real questions expose the fact that algorithmic systems aren't neutral. In other cases, however, algorithms can also surface latent biases held by society as a whole. Research by computer scientist Latanya Sweeney found that when African American names, like "Darnell," were plugged into Google's search engine, the site returned advertisements for criminal justice background checks, evoking the possibility of a connection between anyone with an African American–associated name and a criminal background.[15] When white-dominant names were used, like "Jill" or "Geoffrey," the advertisements served had no connection to criminal justice. What's pertinent is not just that Google made these associations but also that users of the Google search engine were then more likely to click on criminal justice advertisements when searching for black names, thereby training the algorithm to learn society's racist attitudes. In other words, seemingly impartial technology can showcase existing biases in society, supporting the idea that algorithms themselves merely reflect the conditions of society. In other instances of bias, research shows that when Google displays job advertisements in its search results, it displays lower-paying job offers to women than to men.[16] Meanwhile, Safiya U. Noble, a communications scholar, discovered that a Google search for the term *black girls* surfaced primarily pornographic associations in the first pages of search results and in the advertisements, such as "Local Ebony Sex."[17] Society does hypersexualize black girls, but Google distills and amplifies that social bias through explicit messaging, and it profits from it by generating ad revenue. Writer Hans Rollman summarizes Noble's findings this way: "Imagine if you walked into a library seeking information for your children, asked a librarian what information they had about young black girls, and had a stack of pornographic magazines tossed at you because librarians were paid kickbacks to get people to read porn."[18]

A supposedly neutral system can pick up the cultures it's embedded in: consequently, in Uber's case, its rating system may absorb the biases held by the consumers who rate drivers, which in turn affects their employability.[19] Anything associated with drivers—from their race or gender to the clothes they wear—could be used either for or against them in the ratings they receive from passengers. How we experience algorithmically curated information in digital life sets up our expectations for commercialized, digital transactions, as well. The myth of neutrality can relax our guard against manipulation. When Uber's surge-pricing algorithm surfaces higher prices for different but similarly situated users, it plays passengers, thereby profiting from the general belief that its algorithm is simply reflecting the supply and demand of the marketplace.

How society is reflected back to us through "neutral" technology platforms can amplify issues of bias and raise moral questions about the politics of algorithms. Platforms do more, however, than simply mirror society. It's difficult for a user to know whether the price they see for a given service or product is the result of "society" or a particular move implemented by the company. That distinction can make all the difference between a business or technology practice that is simply profit-driven and one that is manipulative or even abusive.

A broker's capability to take advantage of users goes beyond price considerations, too. For example, one of Facebook's most familiar products is the newsfeed, a personalized list of status updates and news from one's network of friends that is displayed to users when they log in to their profile. The newsfeed is curated algorithmically, and it is implicitly understood to be "neutral" even though Facebook regularly experiments with it (such as through A/B testing). Facebook sparked a public outcry after it quietly experimented with the psychological states of select users by displaying happier or sadder posts to them in their newsfeed.[20] The results of their study suggest that people are vulnerable to mass emotional contagion: users who saw happier posts generated more positive status updates and users who saw more negative posts generated more negative status updates.[21]

This power of algorithmic manipulation has recently been brought into sharp focus through alarming public mishaps. In particular, Facebook's role in distributing Russia-linked propaganda and the impact of media manipulation on the 2016 U.S. presidential elections has sparked intense debates across society about the role of technology tools in our daily lives.[22] Nonetheless, the consumer-facing platforms of Silicon Valley downplay the role of opaque algorithmic management when it applies to their "end users." Similarly, although Uber acts as a supposedly neutral middleman, it violates the spirit of neutrality when it adjusts the prices that passengers pay without compensating drivers accordingly. Corporate practices that may be considered deceptive in a consumer context, however, take on different implications when they are used to manage labor in an employment context.

WHEN THE ALGORITHMIC BOSS DECEIVES: WAGE THEFT, PRICE GOUGING, AND UNPAID LABOR

Silicon Valley spins algorithmic management as being neutral, yet we've now seen why this claim is not true. But there is a range of deceptive algorithmic practices in the workplace: in some cases, Uber uses its intermediary position as a shady middleman to algorithmically or technologically squeeze out extra dollars and cents, and this often looks like wage theft. In other cases, algorithmic managers may simply mislead drivers about their prospects for pay premiums through inaccurate reflections or predictions about surge pricing. The main techniques I have identified in Uber's employment practices include unpaid cancellation fees, so-called up-front pricing, the potential for missing tips, and manipulative surge pricing. In addition, Uber provides obtuse "customer service" for drivers as their main point of communication with the company, another example of how Uber treats drivers as low-status consumers rather than as workers.

How does Uber get away with all of this? Uber's unique brand allows it to constantly mask its manipulative activities. Its most frequent excuse is technology: to rationalize missing wages, it uses language like *server error, features, glitches, algorithms,* and *neutrality.* Typically, when Uber faces severe criticism and the threat of sanctions, it simply changes its identity (such as from a taxi company to a technology company), confusing which rules in fact apply to it. At other times, it lobbies lawmakers to change the rules. If Uber's drivers are consumers, do we describe missing payments in terms of unfairness and deception and apply to the Federal Trade Commission for redress? Or if Uber's drivers are workers, do we turn to labor law to redress wage inequities as such? The wrong may be the same in both cases, but how we explain the exploitation determines what path we take to remedy it. This, too, is strategic: Uber's multiple identities force us to contend with an escalating series of arguments depending on how we look at the company. Meanwhile, it takes advantage of this dance to pad its bottom line. How society grapples with the political power of platforms on a grand scale is a question for debate. On the granular scale of Uberland, technology is the language of power that Uber's business practices have over the livelihoods of its drivers.

HOW UBER POCKETS MORE FROM PASSENGER WAIT TIMES

In the relationship between Uber and its drivers, Uber is both the employer (one of the two parties in the workplace relationship) and the umpire (responsible for negotiating disputes between the two parties). This puts Uber in a powerful position. When Uber's policies and practices don't square with driver experiences, it is Uber who stands as judge. One of the benefits of app-mediated work is that work time and activities are monitored. This should, in theory, reduce inequities like prospective wage theft. But technology doesn't produce accountability automatically. In its system, Uber has the power to enforce or determine what is paid (e.g., cancellation fees are designed to be paid) and what isn't (e.g., lost items are not designated to be compensated), or what is tracked and what isn't. Drivers have very little recourse in negotiating inequities in the system.

Many who discuss the gig economy or the sharing economy assume that technology always works as promised or as outlined by company policies.[23] In reality, however, there are gaps in the implementation of tech that negatively affect drivers on the ground. Below is a series of issues that come from drivers' experiences. Some of these issues, like inconsistencies in how cancellation fees are paid, are potentially automated wage theft at scale; others center on questions of fairness. While these issues don't necessarily signify bad intentions by the company, they are interesting indicators of how age-old employment issues can emerge in different forms through software.

Uber drivers receive cancellation fees in two situations. The first occurs when a passenger cancels the trip after more than five minutes has elapsed since making the request (see figure 10). The second occurs when a driver arrives at the passenger's location but the passenger is unreachable or not ready to ride. In this instance, in order to get a cancellation fee the driver must wait five minutes before canceling the ride: the passenger is then charged a cancellation fee.

Some drivers describe, in forums and interviews, having waited the prescribed five minutes before claiming a cancellation fee, and later finding, when they check their paystubs, there's no cancellation fee despite their having requested it and despite their certainty that they waited six or seven minutes just to be sure. Tim, an Uber and Lyft driver in San Francisco, whom I introduced in chapter 1, has worked in customer service for twenty-five years. Our interview continued for hours as he explained to me, with examples from numerous incidents, both missing pay and incentives that didn't work out. With an edge of

Figure 2 (color). "Freedom Pays Weekly," a 2015 screenshot of an Uber driver recruitment ad on Facebook. The driver is depicted as a fashionable millennial dressed in a pink shirt and a pink-striped scarf. The image gentrifies a job typically associated with immigrant people of color in major metropolitan areas (where ridehailing companies have achieved significant market penetration). The ad also recruits drivers using American flag–themed stars in red, white, and blue, reinforcing the message that Uber delivers freedom and an American cultural ideal of independence.

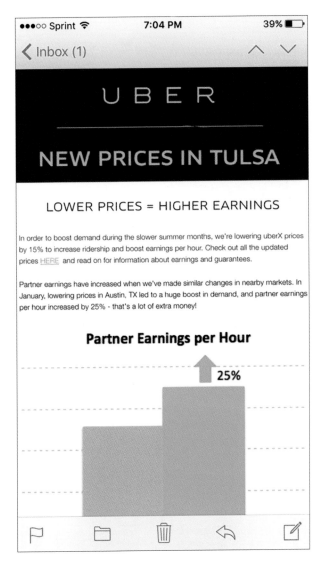

Figure 3 (color). A message Uber sent to a driver. The aesthetic design of the app communication, and the veneer of objectivity provided by the graph, emphasize Uber's authority to make claims based on the data it has. The design also leaves no space for negotiation over Uber's message—"lower prices = higher earnings." The simple bar graph uses bright blue to highlight the 25 percent increase in partner earnings, while the lower earnings preceding the rate increases are illustrated with a short gray column, conveying a duller prospect. This message was posted in a forum in 2015.

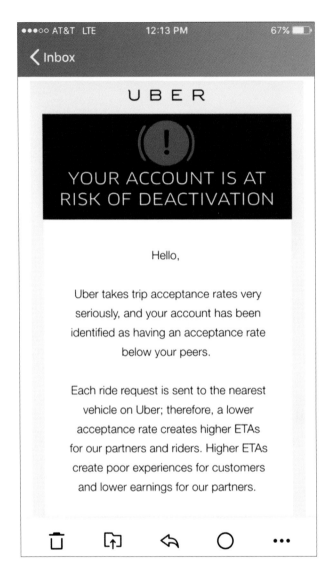

Figure 4 (color). How Uber breaks the news: a sample email the company sent to warn that a driver's account was at risk of deactivation because their trip or ride acceptance rate was too low. The warning is emphasized by an exclamation mark encased in a bright red circle at the top of the message, conveying the threat of imminent hazard. It was posted in a forum in 2016.

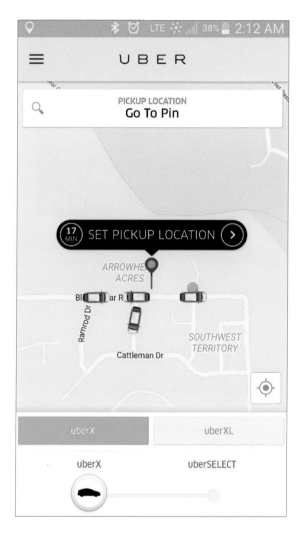

Figure 7 (color). This screenshot of phantom cars was sent to the author in 2015. The black sedans are typical representations of available Uber cars that passengers see displayed on their Uber passenger app. The blue dot indicates the location of the passenger who is requesting a ride. A green pin marks the pick-up location for the (same) passenger. The app indicates that the passenger will have a seventeen-minute wait before the nearest driver arrives. Visually, however, the cluster of sedans implies that four uberX drivers are available immediately next to the passenger's pick-up location. They are "phantom cars" because they don't physically exist at that time in that place.

Figure 18 (color). An example of a driver who relocated to a surge zone but waited for half an hour in an area of "high demand" without receiving a ping (ride request). The surge zone is demarcated with red, a color associated with urgency that alerts drivers to a time-sensitive pay premium within the surge-zone boundaries. The figure "2.1x" indicates that if drivers pick up rides within that area, they will earn double their usual rates. A red bar with a lightning bolt at the bottom of the app emphasizes "SURGE PRICING." In contrast, if drivers provide rides that start outside of the red boundaries, they earn the regular pay rates. This screenshot was posted in a forum in 2015.

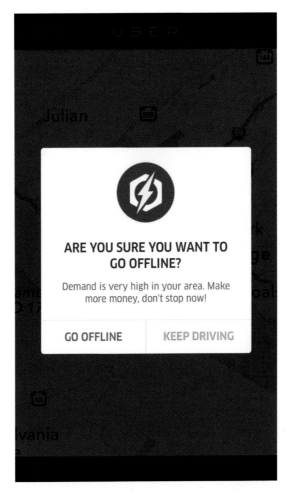

Figure 20 (color). An example of how Uber tries to dissuade drivers from logging out. The driver clicked the button to go offline, but instead of logging the driver out, Uber's app displayed a message that questioned the driver's decision and strongly suggested that the better alternative was to keep working. The urgency of the directive was conveyed by a surge pricing icon—a lightning bolt on a red background—that told the driver they could earn a pay premium above the base rates. The driver was given the option to continue logging out by selecting the offline button, displayed in black, or to accept Uber's prompt to keep driving, displayed in a more inviting blue font. A background map showcased the area where the driver could continue working. This screenshot was posted in a forum in 2015.

Figure 21 (color). An example of the kind of message Uber sends to convince its drivers to accept more rides. The driver clicked the button in the app to go offline, but instead of logging the driver out, Uber's app displayed a background map of the local area with a message superimposed reading "YOUR NEXT RIDER IS GOING TO BE AWESOME! Stay online to meet him." The driver was then offered the choice to go offline, presented in a black font, or to keep driving in the local area, presented in a more inviting blue font. This screenshot was posted in a forum in 2015.

PROBLEMS REPORTED

There were a few things riders in your city commonly reported. Here are some tips on how to improve:

 Service
Riders give the best ratings to drivers who:

• Never ask for a 5-star review, but focus instead on providing an excellent experience
• Stay calm, patient and polite with riders and other cars on the road
• Go above and beyond to make the experience special, such as opening doors for riders when possible

 City Knowledge
Riders want to be sure you're following the best route. It helps to:

• Ask if the rider has a preferred route
• Always use GPS until you know the city well (remember to press BEGIN TRIP after you enter the destination)

 Professionalism
Riders count on Uber for a comfortable, relaxing experience. They prefer for drivers not to promote other businesses during the trip

RIDER FEEDBACK

On the bright side, you received **23** five-star reviews out of 26 rated trips in the past two weeks.

Figure 23 (color). How to be a five-star driver. The theme of this message from Uber is introduced with the text "PROBLEMS REPORTED" in bold, black capital letters. The categories of problems that drivers should be aware of are listed in red and illustrated with icons that emphasize that these suggested behaviors conform to the workplace standards of professional men. For example, "Service" and "Professionalism" are represented by an icon showing a button-down shirt and tie. (There is no equivalent female professional dress.) This screenshot of an email that a driver received was posted in a forum in 2015.

HOW ARE CANCELLATION FEES CHARGED?

Riders may cancel without incurring a fee for up to five minutes
after their initial request. Cancellations made after five minutes
will incur a fee to compensate you for your time.

If you're running more than five minutes behind the provided
ETA and the rider cancels the request, they will not be charged a
cancellation fee.

Figure 10. Uber's stated policy on cancellation fees as of May 30, 2015. This
message was transcribed from a screenshot.

frustration in his voice, he told me, "I never worked for a company in
my life where I had to check my paycheck before."

Provision 2.2 of Uber's contract (December 2015) with its driver-
partners states, "In order to enhance User satisfaction with the Uber
mobile application and your Transportation Services, it is recommended that you wait at least 10 minutes for a User to show up at the
requested pickup location."[24] While five minutes is the standard waiting period, after which drivers are to collect their cancellation fee,
Uber "recommends" drivers wait at least twice as long for the passenger
to show up, essentially generating goodwill for the company through
the driver's unpaid waiting time. In 2016, I wrote a detailed blog post on
The Rideshare Guy website about long-standing driver reports of missing
wages, and about drivers who had mixed experiences with the policies
(see figure 11). Fees vary by city and tier of service (and select cities, like
Houston, have no cancellation fee policies). But generally, the passenger should be charged a $5 cancellation fee for uberX in either scenario,
and the driver receives $3.75 after Uber's 25 percent cut. If the driver
cancels before the five minute period is up, the passenger is not charged
a fee. To improve this inequitable dynamic, Uber has started testing
shorter wait times in some cities, where a passenger is charged the

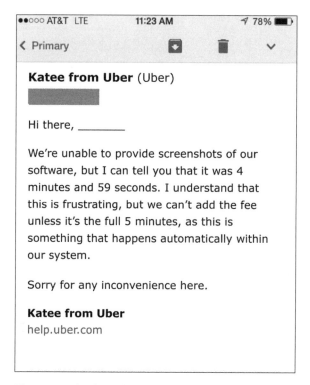

Figure 11. Uber's explanation of why it did not pay out
a cancellation fee to a driver who waited, posted in a
forum in the fall of 2015.

going rate per minute after a two-minute waiting period.[25] Uber's policy indicates that cancellation fees are automatically ("will incur")
charged to passengers and remitted to drivers, while in reality the company places the onus on drivers to claim fees formally after they request
their cancellation fees. When drivers cancel a ride because the passenger did not show up, they have the option to *not* levy the fee (which
newer drivers might do if they feel the passenger was not in the right
place, for example; see figure 12). But drivers' recurring complaint after
requesting the fee is that, even though they have done everything right,
the fee still doesn't come to them. While it could be that some of these
drivers have not truly waited the full five minutes, or they were not in

```
CANCEL TRIP
⊘ Do not charge rider
⊘ Rider no-show
```

Figure 12. Uber gives drivers the option not to levy the cancellation fee. Transcribed from a screenshot of the Uber app from 2016.

the place they said they were when canceling the ride, what is more concerning is when drivers don't get the fee when they know that they waited in the right spot for five minutes.

Under an earlier policy, Uber offered passengers the first cancellation free but passed that expense on to drivers, who were not paid for first-time passenger cancellations (see figure 13). Thus, some drivers might explain the missing fee as a first-timer thing, but how can drivers *know* when it's an absentee passenger's first cancellation? And why should the onus be on them to do uncompensated work to improve customer satisfaction? The terms of Uber's policy regarding cancellation fees assert that drivers will be paid a cancellation fee, not that it will be selectively enforced (although Uber reserves the right to change compensation structures in its contracts with drivers). Arguably, Uber may have violated its contract with drivers, but it also emphasized that drivers are expected to do "extra work" on Uber's behalf.

What could be happening here? There are at least three potential explanations. Perhaps Uber is automatically charging the passengers for the cancellation fee but not remitting it to drivers. (If this is so, drivers are at an informational disadvantage—they don't *know* if the passenger was charged.) Another possibility is that Uber is not automatically charging the fee after the driver cancels, even though the driver is owed a fee. Or, it could be possible that drivers did not actually wait five minutes for a no-show before departing.

Effectively, drivers are in an arrangement with Uber whereby they pay ahead with their time and effort and expect to be reimbursed later

Hi [driver's name censored],

We have an important update regarding our cancellation policy and we just couldn't wait to share it! Please see below for more information regarding the change to Uber's cancellation policy. We hope this information will help you continue to provide an awesome experience for riders.

New Cancellation Policy

We want you to know that we have heard your feedback and have made some changes! Starting today we have ELIMINATED the free cancellation for first time riders.

What does this mean?

Now any rider who cancels a trip more than 5 minutes after requesting will be charged and the fee will be reflected on partner pay statements. This change will go into effect immediately.

Figure 13. An Uber message to drivers received in the winter of 2015 regarding free cancellations. This message was transcribed from a screenshot.

on. After the fact, the company ultimately determines whether their expenses are reimbursable. Analogously, when an employee puts work items, such as business travel expenses, on her personal credit card and has to submit her receipts for reimbursement, she runs the risk that the employer will determine that some expenses are not reimbursable. For drivers, however, it's a pretty straightforward issue: did they wait five minutes, and is Uber obliged to reimburse them automatically after they request the fee, in accordance with the company policy?

For years, there was no timer in the app to count down the minutes until five had passed. Whether this was because adding a timer was not a priority for Uber or because its absence was intentional, the effect was the same: the lack of a timer encouraged drivers to wait beyond the five-minute period, just to be sure they'd receive their fee. This design was reinforced by Uber's contract with drivers, which "recommends" that they wait at least ten minutes. Seeing that the specific problem of unenforced cancellation fees was such an issue for drivers, an app developer created the Rideshare Timer app for them.[26] To their credit, in July 2016, Uber finally added a timer to uberPOOL pickups. But no timer was added to other core services, like uberX. Then, in June 2017, Ryan Calo and I presented a paper addressing many of these inequities in front of a federal trade commissioner (an Uber lawyer also attended this meeting). Right after this, Uber implemented a timer for regular trips, which improved the company's transparency and accountability to drivers who claimed cancellation fees. (Presumably, these changes were in the works. But given the high level of scrutiny an absent timer received at the largest gathering of law and technology scholars in the country, I speculate that changes like this might also be expedited.) Fundamentally, these examples demonstrate how deeply exploitation is embedded in the ways that we engage with technology.

HOW UBER POCKETS MORE FROM UP-FRONT PRICING

Starting in 2016, Uber quietly implemented a practice called "up-front pricing," which supposedly fostered greater transparency. Passengers could now see in advance what a fare would cost based on Uber's "best guess," or estimate of the trip tally, rather than waiting for the tally at the end. The problem: not everything about "up-front pricing" was so up-front. Months before Uber finally admitted that it was charging passengers a higher fare while paying drivers based on a lower fare, drivers were raising alarm at discrepancies they were noticing. Some drivers tried to crowdsource data about up-front pricing from other drivers online,[27] as well as through in-person meetings with labor organizers like the Independent Drivers Guild. The amounts they observed ranged from small discrepancies, like a few dollars, to differences that were much larger.

Meanwhile, Uber declared that all the discrepancies generally evened out, but it refused to reveal how often the house won.[28] So drivers, passengers, researchers, and reporters started investigating. As journalist Alison Griswold reported, "Up-front pricing certainly allows riders to make a decision about what the trip is worth to them, but it could put them in the position of paying more than what the service actually costs."[29] Before up-front pricing was institutionalized, a passenger who waited in his driver's car after his trip could compare notes to identify how much the passenger paid versus the fare the driver earned. Passengers would see their total amount paid, and drivers would see a trip summary (containing their fare breakdown, Uber's commission, and fees, such as tolls) instantly after a trip was complete. But around the time Uber officially implemented up-front pricing, drivers, like driver-blogger Harry Campbell, began to notice a delay (often about ten minutes) before their trip summaries would appear. Many drivers speculate that this time-elapse tool was intentionally implemented by Uber to prevent passengers and drivers from comparing notes.[30] Nevertheless, Uber argued that its practices were transparent. In a lawsuit drivers brought against the company, alleging that the practice violated Uber's agreement with drivers, Uber claimed that up-front pricing was "hardly a secret," because "drivers also knew that they were not paid until the end of the ride and could have simply asked a User [passenger] how much he or she paid for the trip to learn of any discrepancy."[31] Beyond the awkwardness of asking to see passengers' phones and receipts, the prospect of waiting for ten minutes after arriving at the passenger's destination is a real obstacle to transparency.

In practice, the effect of up-front pricing is that passengers may be unwittingly overcharged, or even price-gouged in more extreme cost discrepancies, while drivers may be unwittingly receiving far less than they signed up for. I interviewed Ron, whom I introduced in chapter 3, in 2015 and spoke with him again in the fall of 2017. He said, "I remember the first time a passenger and I started talking about it during the trip, and he offered to show me his invoice at the end of the trip. I had heard about it—but seeing it for real just outraged me so much! It was like somebody had cheated on me. He could see my disappointment [in

Uber] and kind of shrugged it off, until I told him, 'You know, they charged you forty dollars, but with the time and distance we drove, they should have only charged you twenty-eight dollars.' Then, suddenly he got it too!"

Uber contracts with drivers to take a certain percentage from the total fare as their commission (which varies by market, and among individual drivers and tiers of service), such as 20 percent, 25 percent, 28 percent, and so on. At the same time, it also charges a "booking fee" (formerly a "safe rides" fee) of at least one to two dollars that gets added to most fares. This means that on short trips, where drivers may earn only the minimum fare, Uber's 25 percent commission can effectively be 30 percent to 50 percent.[32] With up-front pricing, Uber was able to raise its take without notifying drivers or passengers that it was taking advantage of its position as the go-between. In New York City, I found a way to determine how much Uber's take had increased after being tipped off by the city's Taxi and Limousine Commission, which was seeking proof to substantiate a torrent of driver complaints. The sales tax that passengers pay on their fare is visibly deducted from the driver's pay, so several driver-bloggers and I were able to calculate the amount passengers were paying by working backward from the sales tax percentage, which is 8.875 percent in the city. When Uber takes advantage of unwitting passengers and drivers, it could be within its rights to do so, but this contradicts Uber's description of its business model: in legal forums and in its contracts with drivers, the company says it provides a platform that connects all its users, implying that its technology is neutral, like a credit card processor. In one court hearing, Uber's lawyers used rough metaphors to explain its logic in oral arguments, saying, "Uber, its technology which connects people together in real time can be used in other applications, as it is. People demand ice cream. We have vendors, vendors who produce ice cream that are able, through our software, demanded [sic]—on demand to people that want ice cream. We facilitate that transaction. We're not in the ice cream business, you know."[33]

When Quiang, a full-time driver in New York City, joined Uber three years earlier, he was paid a thousand-dollar sign-up bonus. For Quiang, the small discrepancies and small amounts were inconsequential: in the big picture, Uber was providing employment and bonuses to many drivers. Reflecting on up-front pricing discrepancies, he observes in slightly broken English,

> It's happened to a lot of people, and it's happened to me too. My personal thing is that it's not really a big deal. You know what, what really happens, it's a system issue, though. Sometimes when a passenger requests an Uber, it sends a flat fare to the passenger. For example, if the driver drives too fast, faster than the app supposed to be [*sic*], then the driver gets less than it used to be. Sometimes Uber gives you a guaranteed share. For example, the passenger pay five dollars, and pay the driver fifteen dollars. So we don't always get less, we sometimes get more. Sometimes this Uber credit us so money [*sic*], working opportunities, making so many people survive. Focus on the big part, not just like this passenger paid, you know, two dollars, I will sue this, that. No, no.

But even if some drivers didn't take issue with the company's pricing methodology, Uber's implementation of up-front pricing was largely seen as underhanded because drivers weren't alerted to it in its experimental phase. Because up-front pricing affected passengers too, the issue received significant media play as a form of passenger price-gouging, even though it was drivers who initially discussed it as a violation of their contracts with Uber. Interestingly, not all Uber drivers experienced this "unmasking" of Uber's practices evenly or universally. Months after up-front-pricing investigations revealed that what Uber billed as transparency was in fact another form of opacity, I spoke with drivers in Montreal who were just starting to identify unexplainable discrepancies between the price Uber charged passengers and the fares drivers earned. Back in the United States, Lyft quietly adopted a similar practice to mirror Uber's. Abraham, an Ethiopian Uber and Lyft driver I met in Washington, DC, in the fall of 2017, showed me the amount he earned on an airport run with Lyft—about eight dollars—

while the passenger was charged about sixteen dollars. "Oof," he exclaimed while he showed me photo comparisons. He added, "It's not the end of the world," though he was clearly still jaded by the fare.

RUMORS: DOES UBER POCKET MISSING TIPS?

Uber drivers were thrilled when Uber introduced in-app tipping in 2017, and many felt vindicated after years of complaints about the absence of a tip function. However, there are rumors flying around driver forums that Uber may sometimes convert the tips that passengers leave for drivers into a "service fee" that Uber pockets instead. In one example from the summer of 2017, a driver reported to a forum that he watched his passenger enter a tip into the passenger app, but on his waybill, he could see that the tip was classified as a "service fee." He posted screenshots and comments of the incident in a forum that read: "Keep an eye on your rides. I had a rider last night tip me $10 while sitting in my front seat via pax [passenger's] app. It never showed on my end. What did show was a large service charge for Uber and I got $6 for a $20 fare charged to the rider. Looking at the same route on the pax app it was a $10 ride. After going back and forth with Uber via support messages with redundant auto responses, they finally gave me my tip from their inflated service charge." (See figures 14–17.) In an effort to increase transparency, Uber has made changes to show drivers not only what they earn, but also what passengers pay. This eased some transparency concerns about up-front pricing: drivers now examine these amounts closely.

Drivers I interview and speak with often affirm that Uber pays on time, which is one of the positive features of the job. But there are discrepancies in the compensation system that give drivers pause, too. If Uber fudges the tip and pockets it as a service fee, it could be the result of a technical glitch. But this type of glitch (or business practice) is part of a pattern of missing payments to drivers, as I've written about on Harry Campbell's *The Rideshare Guy* blog.[34] Even if this type of

Driver: I watched my pax enter a $10 tip intro his phone while giving me a 5* rating for my excellent service. Why is it that the rider magically paid $10 more than it shows for that same ride on the pax app I would like my tip applied to this ride. This is a known issue having tips absorbed into the service fee.

Figure 14. A driver's message to Uber about his missing tip. This message was transcribed from a screenshot posted in a forum in 2017.

RIDER PAYS

Rider Payment	$21.26
Total	**$21.26**

Includes any booking fees, pass-through fees, contributions, and reimbursable costs such as tolls paid by the rider.

UBER RECEIVES

Service Fee	$12.45
Booking Fee	$2.20
Total	**$14.65**

Negative numbers represent an amount paid for by Uber and related entities. Does not include weekly promotions.

Figure 15. What the passenger paid. This message was transcribed from a screenshot posted in a forum in 2017.

YOU RECEIVE

Base Fee	$0.71
Distance (6.61 mi x $0.6825/mi)	$4.50
Time (10.95 min x $0.0975/min)	$1.07
Wait Time (3.38 min x $0.0975/min)	$0.33
Booking Fee	$2.20
Total	**$6.61**

Your earnings are always calculated the same way. On every trip
you take, you earn your base fare, plus time and/or distance rates
for the length of the trip, plus applicable tools, fees, surge/Boost,
and promotions. To see your rates anytime, see Fares in the menu.

Figure 16. What the driver received. This message was transcribed from a
screenshot posted in a forum in 2017.

Uber: Thanks for reaching out, [driver's name censored].

We've received this trip and can confirm that the tip of $10 was
correctly applied to this trip.

It will show in your next weekly statement, please check the Other
section to review.

Thank you.

Figure 17. After several messages, Uber finally confirmed to the driver that
his tip would soon appear. This message was transcribed from a screenshot
posted in a forum in 2017.

discrepancy is rarely happening with tipping, rumors fly because wage theft has been substantiated in the past.[35]

The larger question of whether "the machine" was eating drivers' tips has to do with visibility and the transparency of the app design. Because it's impolite to ask a passenger if she has tipped, drivers don't know whether they were meant to receive it. How, then, can drivers know if their algorithmic manager is cutting into their tips? This sort of moving money can be caught only when a driver knows for certain that his passenger intended to leave a tip. Otherwise, the opaque nature of these tech-driven platforms makes injustices much harder to spot. The only recourse that drivers have is to follow up with Uber's community support representatives, often through multiple email chains, to fight for their lost wages.

DON'T CHASE THE SURGE: HOW ALGORITHMIC MANAGERS MISLEAD

Not all algorithmic deceptions reach the threshold of wage theft, but they might nonetheless give us pause. Algorithmic systems can treat similarly situated users differently, even if the systems are supposedly operating neutrally. Take Uber's surge-pricing algorithm. Travis Kalanick, Uber's cofounder and former CEO, reiterated the neutrality of Uber's surge algorithm when he said, with reference to surges, "We are not setting the price. The market is setting the price."[36] However, Uber appears to be charging different prices for similarly situated customers—a practice known as dynamic price discrimination, which some customers and commentators find alarming. Research by computer scientists Le Chen, Alan Mislove, and Christo Wilson measured the prices that Uber's application programming interface set for rides for various passengers during customer surges in various areas, then examined those prices against the prices passengers actually received (the surge premium displayed in the passenger app).[37] They found a discrepancy, with users in the same surge zone at the same time receiving different prices. Uber explained this as a bug in the system.[38] A possible technical explanation for this discrepancy has to do with server infra-structure:[39] "Achieving consistency of prices across a distributed net-work of services is challenging."[40] Some suggest that Uber may in fact be allowing this system of discriminatory pricing to persist because it gives them access to a wealth of data about passengers and their will-ingness to pay within a range of price tiers. Regardless of the reason, it's clear that the new rhetoric of algorithmic neutrality has done nothing to change older practices of price discrimination.

The "neutrality" of algorithms has different implications in the con-text of employment and algorithmic management. Surge pricing is used as a tactic to provide drivers with the hope of extra wages, which they may never receive (see figure 18). Drivers are led to believe that surge pricing is a highly accurate reflection of the real-time conditions of the supply of drivers relative to the demand of passengers. They receive notices, including texts, emails, and pop-up notifications, telling them that a "surge" is taking place, or that "demand is high." The algorithm purportedly has "the data," or recognizes where demand is high, and it advises drivers on where they can expect a pay premium if they relo-cate to a specific place at a specific time. When drivers follow this advice and find that they have been dispatched to pick up a passenger for a nonpremium-priced ride, meaning that surge pricing has disap-peared, they feel tricked.

Drivers also receive notices of demand that imply that Uber can predict the conditions of supply and demand with the same accuracy with which it can measure it in real time, even though this is effectively a lower-confidence recommendation.[41] The language "demand is ex-tremely high" is similar to the language in a message another driver received from Uber in Lehigh Valley, Pennsylvania, in the winter of 2016, which predicted surge pricing for a certain Saturday night because "we saw huge demand last night." (See figure 19.) A second text message followed, in which Uber announced, "The weekend is here, and demand is on the rise in Lehigh Valley! Plan to go online tonight, and keep an eye out for SURGE around the area, where you can earn over 3X on fares!

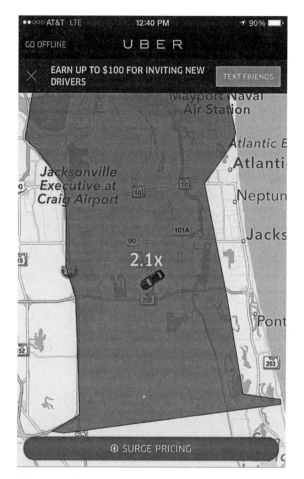

Figure 18. An example of a driver who relocated to a surge zone but waited for half an hour in an area of "high demand" without receiving a ping (ride request). Posted in a forum in 2015. (This figure also appears in the color section following page 116.)

Stay online through midnight to take advantage of the highest fares. Uber on!" The message Uber communicated was much more than an exhortation from a traditional manager to work late. Within the context of Uber's app, the text message on a screen from Uber's algorithmic manager resonated with the broader claim Uber was making—that it

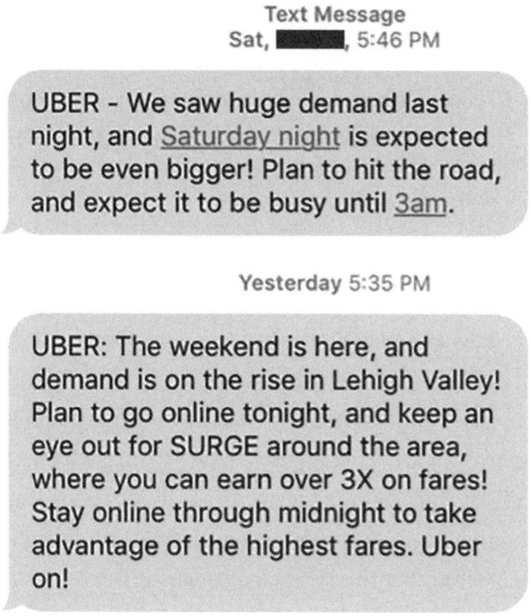

Text Message
Sat, ▮▮▮▮, 5:46 PM

UBER - We saw huge demand last night, and <u>Saturday night</u> is expected to be even bigger! Plan to hit the road, and expect it to be busy until <u>3am</u>.

Yesterday 5:35 PM

UBER: The weekend is here, and demand is on the rise in Lehigh Valley! Plan to go online tonight, and keep an eye out for SURGE around the area, where you can earn over 3X on fares! Stay online through midnight to take advantage of the highest fares. Uber on!

Figure 19. A screenshot of one example of Uber's predictive messages to drivers, posted in a forum in 2016.

had the technological capability to reflect forecasts of demand back to drivers.

Some drivers may feel they have been taken on a ride by the company if they follow lower-confidence recommendations that predict demand, only to find that business isn't as hot as they were led to believe it would be. As Luke Stark and I observed in advance of New Year's Eve 2016,[42] one driver posted a received message in a forum that read, "We also want to remind you that we predict New Year's Eve will be the busiest night of the year. With such high demand, it will be a great night to go out and drive!" This expected high demand did not materialize, however. A different driver asked, "Why send messages to me saying it is the biggest night of the year when everything is dead?" In a rare admission by Uber that predictive demand does not imply the same accuracy as real-time notices of high demand, the community support representative replied, "We try to predict how busy it is going to be based on the historical data from previous years. This is never going to be 100% accurate." The implication is that Uber may have successfully cajoled many drivers to come out on New Year's Eve to provide a demand for the high supply of passengers, so that a surge would not materialize and surge pricing would not go into effect. This directly undermined the interests of individual drivers but benefited the company and passengers. After using its data to nudge drivers about "high demand" and thereby leverage control over when and where drivers work, Uber deflected responsibility for its misleading nudges and communications, an example of behavior that has become a source of distrust in the Uber-to-driver relationships. To describe the trust dynamics, I try to think about this as analogous to a social arrangement. For example, imagine that two friends, Becky and Carl, make plans to meet the following evening. Becky advises Carl that there is a very high chance she will meet him downtown between seven and eight P.M. Obligingly, Carl travels downtown and waits for Becky. She never shows up or notifies him of a change in plans. When Carl confronts Becky over his spoiled evening, Becky explains that, technically, she didn't guarantee she would meet him, because she used the language of high probability. Essentially, Becky used a slippery technical disclaimer to evade social responsibility for misleading Carl. Technology services can similarly trade on our good-faith assumptions to mislead us, but we may remain unaware of how data-driven recommendations are used to manipulate us. Of course, users of algorithmic systems do not respond to algorithmic prompts in the same ways,[43] and drivers may not blindly follow the suggestions of their algorithmic managers. However, they learn to make sense of Uber's algorithmic practices over a period of time and, sometimes, with the advice of other veteran drivers. (One of the most common pieces of advice veteran drivers give to new drivers in forums is: "Don't chase the surge.")

Other commonplace services, like GPS navigation systems (such as Google Maps or Waze), make algorithmic recommendations to users on the routes they should take, seemingly according to the goals the users have selected, such as "shortest route" or "least traffic." But as Tim Hwang and I documented, users of mapping apps are generally unaware that they may unknowingly be sent on a nonoptimal route in order to generate data for the data-centric system on the road less traveled.[44] The majority of the time, users are routed to whatever is considered the "best" route according to the information the system has on all traffic conditions. At other times, in our hypothetical example, users are sent on the road less traveled as *explorers*. An unwitting consumer is thus used to gather data that will benefit the system as a whole; but a route that benefits the system may not be optimal for the individual user.

An algorithmic dispatcher has the power to quietly turn users into explorers. This creates the same kind of tension that Uber drivers experience when their algorithmic dispatcher sends them to a fake surge zone, or when it blends a high-confidence assessment of real-time demand with a lower-confidence recommendation of predictive high demand.[45] The friction that drivers experience under algorithmic management reveals the changing dynamics experienced by users of technology services more generally.[46] In particular, these experiences illustrate that while algorithmic management may produce a broad social benefit for the majority of platform users, it can deceive individual users along the way.[47]

The promise of a surge is the carrot dangling in front of drivers—a tactic that Uber uses to shape their behavior. In a sample message below, a driver tried to log out, and her app displayed the following message, with a surge-pricing, lightning-bolt icon: "Are you sure you want to go offline? Demand is very high in your area. Make more money, don't stop now!" (See figure 20.) Of course, there is no guarantee that drivers will actually earn extra money from "high demand" (a common euphemism for "surge pricing"), but the hope offered by surge pricing serves as a "herding tool."[48] In another instance, when a driver who wanted to go home for the evening attempted to log out, Uber

Figure 20. How Uber tries to dissuade drivers from
logging out. Screenshot posted in a forum in 2015.
(This figure also appears in the color section
following page 116.)

displayed the message "Your next rider is going to be awesome! Stay online to meet him." Only then was he given another option: "Go Offline" or "Keep Driving" (see figure 21). Some drivers report that such a message can be tempting, especially when Uber alerts them to imminent surge pricing. For some, this means that even when they really are too tired to keep working, they continue.

Some drivers mention that they wake up dreaming of a surge,[49] while others refer to it as a lottery. Not everyone follows the prompts Uber sends, in part because they presume that all the other drivers are following them and, therefore, negating the premium levied for "low supply" compared to "high demand." Doberman, an Uber and Lyft driver in Baton Rouge, Louisiana, whom I interviewed in the fall of 2017, said, with a thick Italian accent, "Unfortunately, I have two reasons why I can't follow these advertisements. First is because my schedule doesn't match with them. There is going to be a mistake. Second is because if all the drivers are going to be outside driving, trying to hunt surge pricing, ... then it will be hard to get a surge ride. So, no, I don't really feel that very enthusiastic when I see those offers."

Uber monitors driver behaviors in a calculated and systematic way, and nudges are just one tool that the company uses to incentivize, cajole, manage, and control their behavior. These nudges have changed during the time I've studied Uber, and they run the gamut from playful ("Your next rider is going to be awesome!") to helpful ("Demand Alert: 3–7pm and 10pm–12am") to pleading ("Don't stop now!" or "You're $1 away from earning $40") to informative ("Mets Game at Citi Field 4:05–8:45 pm"). The app is known to display information about local happenings like sporting events to drivers so they can anticipate demand.

While nudges are not necessarily manipulative and do inherently provide nudge-recipients with a sense of choice or agency,[50] they are nevertheless highly influential in setting expectations. The recommendations that individual drivers receive from Uber may be the product of mathematical data science, but it's not clear that Uber is an honest broker of that data. Moreover, when drivers use that data to their own

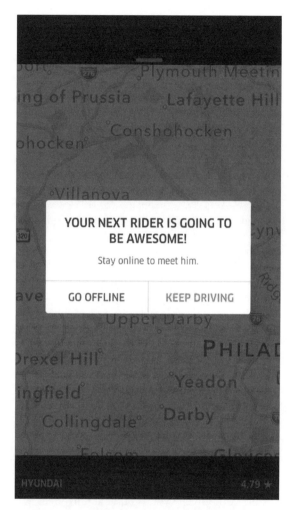

Figure 21. An example of the kinds of messages Uber sends to convince its Uber drivers to accept more rides. Screenshot posted in a forum in 2015. (This figure also appears in the color section following page 116.)

advantage, such as by rejecting a nonsurge dispatch when they are located in a surge-pricing zone, in order to wait for a surge-priced dispatch, they risk being fired. In other words, drivers are not merely consumers of free data-driven analysis, like users of GPS navigation services. What they can do with that data is constrained by the rules set by their manager, which directly affects their livelihoods.

This type of algorithmic management highlights the fact that "neutral" algorithms that appear to provide an objective data analysis of supply and demand can manipulate drivers. Although algorithmic management of Uber's drivers shows us how unneutral platforms can take advantage of workers, Uber's practices shed light on how the data-centric algorithms that emerge from Silicon Valley can impact us all.

CHAPTER FIVE

BEHIND THE CURTAIN

How Uber Manages Drivers with Algorithms

In Los Angeles, Jose and I are chatting in his car when I ask him if he ever avoids certain neighborhoods when he drives for Uber and Lyft. He admits he stays away from areas like Compton, but his voice wavers off before he completes his sentence. Destination-based discrimination is frowned upon in Uber's system, as well as in the taxi industry. It's also illegal in some cities. Refusing service to specific neighborhoods that are perceived as "dangerous" is often analogous to refusing service based on race, and the taxi industry already has a long-standing history of not stopping to pick up black (and particularly male) passengers.[1] There are many concerns that drivers for Uber and Lyft perpetuate this type of discrimination, too.[2] Going silent, Jose removes his smartphone from its mount and covers it with his left hand, pressing it into his leg, before resuming our conversation. Uncomfortable discussing a taboo, he switches topics, but eventually he explains that he hid his Uber phone because he's worried that the company is watching. He says that every time he opens his Uber application, Uber watches through cameras that film his interactions with passengers. "He feels that Uber does so for his own safety as well as the passengers, but "sometimes you just make comment they don't want you to heard [sic]," he stresses.

While Jose's claim is inaccurate (as far as I know, Uber is not listening through the mic or taking control of the camera), he's not exactly wrong. Uber *does* track driver behavior, such as through the rating system and, more recently, through telematics (how drivers brake, accelerate, and speed).[3] It's not a stretch for drivers to presume that the boss is listening and watching too. By trying to track driver movements in granular detail, from the shakiness of their phones to their passenger-sourced ratings for each trip, Uber employs a type of workplace surveillance that contradicts its claims that it has a "hands off" management style. For example, the app displays a safe-driving report with two categories, Smooth Breaks and Smooth Accelerations. One driver had smooth breaks 219/264 times, and the app displayed the message "Several harsh breaks detected." Meanwhile, the message "Great work!" followed their grade of 210/247 smooth accelerations. (Some drivers refer to this level of monitoring as "Big Brother" in forums.)

As noted earlier, Uber uses the data-driven algorithmic recommendations and behavioral interventions to control the flow of money. To collect that data in the first place, Uber monitors the behavior of both drivers and passengers as users of their respective Uber apps. Data surveillance does not produce accountability automatically for all users of the Uber platform, however. Leticia Alcala, who used to drive for Uber and Lyft in California, relocated to Dallas, where she continues to work for both companies. She administrates multiple driver forums online, too, and she is especially proactive about helping other female drivers. During a long interview over the phone, Leticia recounted to me one especially hazardous incident with two passengers:

> It was two men talking dirty to me. Fortunately, this was a short ride, but they really scared me. They seemed like the type that wouldn't take no for an answer. They started talking about boom-boom, and a threesome, and all this stuff, and just scared the crap out of me. Luckily, it was a short ride, but then I couldn't get one of those guys out of my car. He wouldn't leave until I gave him my telephone number. So finally, I gave him a fake telephone number, and he finally got out. I reported it to Uber, but that one really terrified me.

I mean, I went straight home after that. That was really, really scary. And I'm not one of those women who is easily scared; I'm a pretty tough cookie. But you could tell which type were dangerous, you know what I mean?

I had a pretty good idea, but I asked her to say a little more. "They were white males from Oklahoma, but country boys," Leticia added, her voice deepening. "They were low class, low-class types, the way they spoke to me. And the dirty terms that they used. See, the other ones were being dirty and everything, but I could tell they were educated businessmen; they were just being stupid. I wasn't scared, I was just bothered by all their sexual talk, stuff like that. These guys really, really scared me. So I got a dashcam, and since then, any incidents that *start*," she emphasized, "I just say, 'Smile, you're on camera,' and usually that shuts them up." Many drivers, like Leticia, discuss using dashcams to achieve the kind of accountability they don't get from Uber.[4]

Leticia's experience diverges from Jose's. Whereas he assumed that Uber was watching at every moment, Leticia was sure they weren't paying attention to the passenger behavior that most affected her. After several incidents of harassment from riders, she had come to understand what "data" Uber was and wasn't collecting. Her subsequent communications with Uber convinced her that keeping harassing passengers off the platform wasn't central among Uber's priorities. Uber prevented her from being matched with select passengers again, but, she lamented, the company still granted those passengers access to other drivers.

In this chapter, I show you some of the many ways that Uber takes advantage of the data it collects from users of its technology services. But first, I must explain that, to Uber, its drivers and passengers are equally "consumers" of its technology services. This is a significant and surprising claim. Uber has used technological, organizational, and rhetorical strategies to keep drivers from being considered "employees." Treating drivers as consumers opens them up to a broader logic, inherited from Silicon Valley, where Uber was founded. This broader logic is that user data—collected from both drivers and passengers—is a source of value for Uber. How Uber manipulates and exploits this data is identifiable not only as a business practice based on market logic but also as a facet of technology culture. In what follows, I discuss how Uber treats its consumers, both drivers and passengers, and how that raises questions about whether consumers are fairly treated by platforms.

WHO'S WATCHING YOU AT WORK?

Uber's management practices borrow heavily from how Silicon Valley platforms manage and manipulate their users. Many digital platforms track what users like or click on, gather up these preferences, and make "personalized" recommendations to users based on the preferences and clicks of other, like-minded users.[5] Netflix uses algorithms to produce data-driven recommendations on movies we may be interested in, Facebook recommends people we might know, Amazon suggests purchases we might desire, and Google produces search results for us to review—all using the data that these platforms have mined from user activities. These algorithmic recommendations can provide us with great benefits as users. People trust data and algorithms because they are presented as objectively and mathematically true and inclined toward benevolence.[6] Uber applies these same principles to the world of employment.

When Uber describes its technology as merely a way to connect two groups of end users—drivers and passengers—it underplays a more important feature of that technology: Big Data. Smartphones are basically ubiquitous sensors, and smartphone apps can collect data through these devices. The data-driven Uber platform gives the company a wide view into how drivers do their work in certain respects, though it lacks the ability to examine the more qualitative aspects of the job. Although Jose's ideas about Uber surveilling its drivers with cameras may be inaccurate, Uber has at times implemented programs that monitor whether drivers' phones are shaky, on the presumption that shakiness indicates a work habit that negatively affects how well drivers do their jobs (see figure 22). Lots of part-time or new drivers keep their phones on their laps or near the central console, although many eventually acquire phone mounts so they can

New Feature: Phone Movement Notification

Uber is continually developing new ways to improve safety for you and your riders. Using smartphone technology, we can now identify when your phone maybe unmounted during an Uber trip. Starting today, you may receive a SMS or in-app message informing you that we have detected possible phone movement during trip.

Phone movement while driving can be reduced by using a phone mount. Using a phone mount can help make the ride safe and ensure your rating stays high.

Figure 22. Uber announces a new feature, phone movement notifications. Transcribed from a screenshot posted in a forum in 2016. (Misspelling of "may be" in the original.)

consistently look at the app while they drive. Even if a phone mount actually has no bearing on how well a driver is doing her job, its stationary position allows Uber to more easily take in accurate data to feed its navigation services or collect sensor data. Quantitative tracking gives off the impression that driver behavior is being monitored within the driver's own car, even if a human manager isn't looking over the driver's shoulder.

For some drivers, company monitoring provides a sense of security in their interactions with passengers. With both the driver's and the passenger's personal information and geolocation on file, drivers and passengers alike may take comfort in knowing there is some presumed accountability if anything goes wrong. It's a type of trust verification for relationships mediated by platforms for clients and service providers.

In addition to providing a sense of security, Uber's access to phone data also gives the company a remarkable opportunity to proactively intervene in driver behavior. While drivers are free to log in or log out of work at will, they receive a continuous onslaught of nudges urging them to behave in particular ways, as discussed in chapter 4.[7]

HOW UBER TREATS DRIVERS LIKE CONSUMERS

We've seen how algorithmic management can produce biases and manipulate consumers of Facebook, Google, and the products of other Silicon Valley companies. Similarly, inequities among drivers can emerge when algorithmic bosses deceive them. We also know that Uber monitors drivers through the data they generate on the job to control their behavior in a workplace context. Yet in some ways, Uber explicitly adopts a model of *customer* service communications in managing drivers as workers. Beyond intense supervision, Uber controls drivers by creating an appeals process that limits their ability to find resolutions to their concerns. For example, drivers' primary (and often exclusive) point of communication with Uber is by email, although toward the end of 2017, drivers gained in-person driver hubs (physical locations where drivers can receive in-person support) and a telephone number to call in some cities. Drivers don't have a dedicated human manager who responds to their inquiries. Instead, they have community support representatives (CSRs), located at the email equivalent of a call center, often located abroad, such as in the Philippines,[8] and managed by third-party companies, like Zendesk.[9] Effectively, Uber offshores and automates its main communications with drivers. Drivers receive automated replies to most of their inquiries, which often appear to be based on keywords in the text of their emails. In other words, Uber is managing drivers without a human that understands and is responsive to nuances. While automated responses might be practical for basic factual inquiries, they can prove woefully insufficient when a passenger overdoses in the backseat or harasses a driver. One driver, echoing a sentiment commonly posted in an online forum, remarked, "Not to trash Uber but the support is nil at best. Most of the responses I get are less than adequate to the topic at hand. It seems that if it involves something other than a rider issue or a fare not starting on time, no one understands wtf you are talking about even though you are speaking the King's English."

While we are all familiar with bad customer service, this takes a greater toll in an employment context because drivers depend on these CSRs to resolve questions related to their livelihood. Ramon, who drives for both Uber and Lyft in Atlanta, told one story in our interview about a passenger who accused him of drunk driving in the "passenger feedback" comments. When I interviewed him in 2017, Ramon went to great lengths to explain to me that he works at night, when many passengers have been drinking, and that they can leave the smell of alcohol in the car. Ramon, who is a diabetic, told me he would be passed out in the hospital if he had been drinking. Things didn't go well when a passenger complained to Uber. Ramon was instantly deactivated once the passenger submitted the comment, and he had to stop in the middle of working to write several emails to try to get reinstated. As Linda, a Boston-area driver who works for Uber and Lyft, told me during our interview in the winter of 2018 in reference to the benefits of not having a human boss, "It's better, except when something goes wrong."

One Uber driver, Jay Cradeur, authored an article on *The Rideshare Guy* detailing how he was deactivated for no reason, jeopardizing his livelihood, and then spent weeks trying to resolve the problem, without any success. He concluded:

> At this point, Uber can do whatever it wants. I have thrown my arms up in the air. I have no say in the matter. I have wasted hours defending myself to no avail. Uber boasts about their 180 days of change [a six-month effort by Uber to improve employment relations through driver-friendly features, like a tip button],[10] but they don't seem to understand the importance of the little things, like common courtesy, telling a driver the truth, using some real customer service, showing empathy, or justifying their brutal actions with sound rationale. I feel like an insignificant cog in a very big machine and dysfunctional machine.[11]

Because CSRs are responsible for mediating disputes between Uber's drivers and Uber's passengers, low-quality responses multiply the unfairness that drivers experience at work. The consequences of unfairness in rating systems are offloaded directly onto drivers, even when passengers put drivers in uncomfortable, dangerous, or abusive situations. For instance, a driver in Philadelphia remarked in a forum in mid-2015 that he or she had "kicked out a passenger due to her being intoxicated to the point that she called me a white piece of shit. I kicked her out of my car and she gave me a 1 star. My rating went down from 4.97 to 4.8 guess you have to risk ur life for 5 stars. I emailed Uber and the robot said that unfortunately there is nothing they can do [to] make bad ratings go away since I was verbally assaulted. It should have chosen a better route. LIKE WTF uber doesn't have real people answering their emails."

Situations like these are not the only types of interactions where CSRs serve as a poor replacement for driver management. In forums, many drivers comment on unpaid or missing wages that they tried, and failed, to collect. In the case of cancellation fees, drivers only have forty-eight hours to contest nonpayment of these fees, presumably so Uber has time to bill the passenger for the fee. But Uber also has a constant flood of new drivers who may be unfamiliar with the system. Many drivers check their paystubs weekly or monthly, while others don't look at them carefully until tax season. Let's say that a small percentage of drivers are actually going over their paystubs each night and manually tracking their wait times. Only a percentage of those are going to write to Uber to complain. If a driver is willing to go back and forth with CSRs, she might get her cancellation fee. But given the time that the accounting and communications process would take, how many drivers decide it's not worth it for what amounts to a little less than four dollars? Drivers would probably make more money by spending the same amount of time on doing an additional trip instead. Some say they give up after three to six emails with unfeeling CSRs because it's simply not worth the pocket change they might recover. Meanwhile, others demand satisfaction from Uber and showcase proof of their hard-won wages in forum postings.

The customer-service process essentially provides disincentives to drivers to collect the wages they're owed, which echoes the wage-loss concerns detailed in chapter 4. This practice is analogous to cell phone companies cramming small, unauthorized fees into customer bills.[12]

Only a low percentage of customers actively track their bills, and only a low percentage of those are willing to spend an hour on the phone with a well-meaning but ineffective customer service agent to get a refund. Effectively, in app-mediated work it's possible to withhold small amounts from wages ("fees" in Uber parlance) on a massive scale. Contesting this kind of wage omission doesn't make sense on an individual level—it makes more sense to address it as a systemic issue on behalf of a large constituency of drivers. But the fact that drivers have to contest missing wages through CSRs tells us something about how Uber sees and treats its drivers.

For Li, the issue of unfairness was central to his frustration with Uber's CSRs. He had plenty to say about it when we spoke in the fall of 2016. He drives for Uber part time, often in the Palo Alto area, though he works full time as an engineer in San Diego. On one occasion, he noticed that he was missing the payment for one of his trips. He happened to remember which trip it was, because the passenger had a name similar to that of his coworker. It took five days for him to receive payment. He sent the company a dozen emails, he says, and each time, a new CSR with a different Indian name wrote him back in an email thread (a strategy that presumably prevents the driver from faulting a specific CSR in his or her ongoing issue) with a response that didn't address the root issue. Eventually, he said, "Can you just count how many trips I did (47) and how many I got paid (46)? It's not about the money, it's like $11 or something, but I'm an engineer and when I do my job I want to do it right. I hate when people say, 'Ah, that's *about* right.'" (He gives his extra Uber income to his daughter so she can buy things on Amazon.) Finally, a CSR replied affirmatively, indicating that the computer had a glitch. "I told you all along your computer had a glitch," Li exclaimed. "This money is like peanuts to me. As an engineer, you make a lot more money. It's the principle. I hate that kind of stuff." The CSR offered to pay him the missing amount, eleven dollars, as a type of promotional pay, adding insult to injury. Li reiterated that he wants a fair result when he does the job right. Even if the trip has a low value, that's fine because that's the game he signed up for, but he hates it when he's being cheated.

The issue of CSR effectiveness is important, because Uber's technologically mediated employment is still plagued by classic workplace problems: beyond managerial deception, other issues like the sexual harassment and unfair reviews of worker performance also plague Uber's reputation.[13] Leticia, for example, shares with me multiple experiences she had of sexual harassment by male passengers. She reported these men to Uber, and the company promised not to match her with them again. "They may not match you with them, but they'll match other women with them," she fumes with a tone of resigned indignation. She drives late at night, when the bars are closing, because it's more profitable with surge pricing, but there is an added risk of badly behaving passengers. Other women and some men opt not to drive at those hours at all. On one thirty-minute trip, she picked up a male passenger and his friend. "They both started talking about sex and directing a lot of things to me. So I thought, 'Go along with it, just don't react'—that's generally what I recommend to women drivers. They stopped at a hamburger joint and I got out to stretch. Well, they saw my body. One of them [the passengers] started saying, 'With a body like that, she should be fucking me.' It's a thirty-minute ride, hearing all this BS."

Some drivers, like Mehmet (whom we met in chapter 2) prefer not to alert the company to bad incidents, fearing recrimination from passengers or the loss of their jobs. Mehmet's smile touches his eyes when he speaks in his assuring tone. Inside his spacious seven-seat SUV, the buzz of traffic recedes to a dull hum; I lean forward in my seat to catch his answers during a ride in New York City. "I'm from Turkey!" he declares, though now he lives in Long Island. He needs four thousand dollars per month to meet all his expenses, and he commutes an hour and a half to drive for Uber and Lyft. I usually ask drivers if they ever have passengers who behave badly. I'm often told about drunk passengers, but sometimes it's a different sort of trouble. Mehmet was driving a male passenger one day who asked him to stop by the side of the road so he could pee. "He's coming back and he show me *[sic]* his private things [genitals]," Mehmet says lightly, in the same gentle voice that he uses to describe routine transactions, like paying tolls. "He asked me, 'Did you get something, feel something?' I said, 'No,' and he asked, 'Not even a little?'" Mehmet tried to shift the conversation with his passenger away from that topic at the time. He tells me, "I'd rather just keep quiet," rather than raise the incident with Uber. On another occasion, another male passenger learned Mehmet was from Turkey and started in on a familiar bit, "I heard something about guys from Turkey ... big stuff," until Mehmet said he didn't want to talk about it more. Mehmet speaks in lowered tones as if these incidents are a slight deviation from a script of how interactions are supposed to go. What really strikes me about Mehmet is the way he downplays his discomfort in these incidents. Although he minimizes his own story, he communicates it to me in earnest. Mehmet's experience isn't visible to Uber, which doesn't collect this sort of qualitative data the way it does his GPS coordinates. He fears that if he reports such an incident, the passenger may turn the accusation on him. He could lose access to the Uber platform and his livelihood. That risk highlights an important tension in driver empowerment. Drivers know that Uber controls their access to future rides, and therefore drivers may just fold sexual harassment and other complaints into the cost of doing business.

Other drivers have appeared much more rattled by the generic responses they get to extreme situations. Even when Uber does offer a particular solution to an individual driver, it may not address the root cause or unfairness in the *system,* which irks drivers. For example, one driver in Fort Lauderdale, Florida, disputed a previously adjusted fare (where Uber claws back some of the driver's earnings following a passenger complaint), writing in an email to a CSR: "I had to end the trip early because the passenger got in the car, started to curse me out, [and] called me a dumb stupid nigga because I told him we was on an Uber pool. He said, 'You dumb stupid niggas can't ever get shit right.'" The CSR replied with generic Uber policy details and robotic emotional drivel ("We're sorry to hear about this. We appreciate you taking the time to contact us and share details") and emphasized, in bold print, that the passenger in question would not be matched with her as a driver again. Disgusted, the driver wrote back, "So that's means the next person that picks him up will do the same, while the driver gets deactivated. Welcome to America."

Drivers may grow resentful of the robotic managers that communicate with them, which can foment their distrust in Uber's system more broadly. But the fact that low-grade customer service handles their inquiries speaks to the combination of consumer logic and employment logic that we see in Uber's model. The role of CSRs substantiates the idea that Uber's drivers are consumers rather than workers. Similarly, millions of users on social media platforms are managed by the rules encoded in and automated by algorithms.

CONTROLLED THROUGH THE RATING SYSTEM

Weak customer service is one facet of Uber's management communications, but in other respects, Uber's management draws on a longer history of worker surveillance.[14] The rating system at Uber effectively makes management omnipresent, because it subtly shifts how drivers behave on the job. After each trip, passengers are prompted by the Uber passenger app to rate drivers on a scale of one to five stars on their mobile app. A driver's rating is the average of ratings from his or her last five hundred trips. Consumer-sourced rating and ranking systems are familiar to us from the digitization of other business evaluations, such as Yelp reviews of restaurants or Glassdoor reviews of jobs. While the rating system is described as a simple way to compare Driver X to Driver Y across Uberland and to scale trust between drivers and passengers, in practice its implementation has troubling implications.[15] In our case study of Uber's drivers, Luke Stark and I found that passengers effectively perform one of the roles of middle managers, because they are responsible for evaluating worker performance.[16] When workers are monitored through an opaque system like Uber's, it's much harder to see the extent to which control and power dynamics are at play.[17]

In addition to sending in-the-moment nudges to drivers, Uber also exerts longer-term performance management through weekly performance metrics. The company tracks a combination of personalized stats, including ratings, ride acceptance rates, cancellation rates, hours online, number of trips, and comparisons to other drivers (such as the driver's personal rating compared to the ratings of top drivers). Historically, drivers risked being deactivated if their ratings fell below a certain threshold, such as 4.6/5 stars; if their ride-acceptance rate fell below 80–90 percent; or if their cancellation rate climbed above 5 percent. Uber changed this in the summer of 2016: drivers now get temporarily suspended from the app if their acceptance rate is too low (although it's not clear what the cutoff is between temporary and permanent suspension).[18] These weekly summaries are sent after rides are complete. Despite the claim that Uber drivers are independent contractors and entrepreneurs, they must deliver a standardized experience to passengers or risk suspension, deactivation, or loss of pay.[19] The rating system functions as both carrot and stick, a mediating force to ensure that drivers fulfill the expectations that Uber scaffolds for the passengers who evaluate them.

Standards for driver behavior are periodically sent out as suggestions and advice by email and by text, but the all-powerful rating system stands in the background ready to enforce Uber's standards. Knowing that a direct approach, like a policy guide or employee handbook, could produce accusations that Uber is directly supervising drivers (signifying an employment relationship), the company instead words its expectations indirectly. Consider figure 23, an example of one of Uber's notices received by a driver. It reads, "Riders give the best ratings to drivers who" followed by a meaty list of expectations.

Drivers with low ratings are penalized, such as through temporary suspensions or termination.[20] When César, who drives in Chicago, tried to log in to work one evening, the Uber app advised him to log in with a

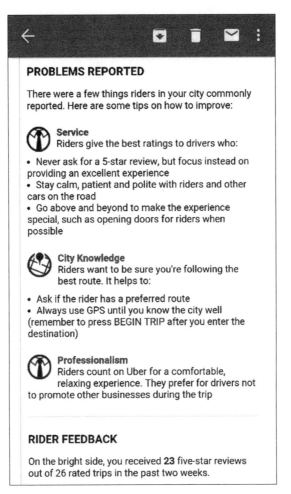

Figure 23. How to be a five-star driver. This
screenshot was posted in a forum in 2015. (This figure
also appears in the color section following page 116.)

different vehicle. Beneath the log-in screen, a banner message notified
him that "your driver account has not been activated." He posted this in
an online forum in the spring of 2015. César would later realize that his
inability to log in was not because he entered the wrong vehicle
information. He had been fired, and that's how he found out. It was the

equivalent of an employee badge that simply ceases to work when an employee tries to swipe it and enter the building for work that day. The threat of deactivation shapes how drivers interact with prompts and suggestions from their algorithmic manager. When they feel their job eligibility is on the line, the power of a nudge can be significant.

As many drivers have told me and commented in forums, ratings are everything. Drivers have limited interaction with their invisible manager, so this little number between one and five fosters a highly personal sense of responsibility and performance.[21] Drivers occasionally brag on forums about their positive ratings, too. One driver from Maryland posted his rider feedback and his rating of 4.77 stars in a driver forum in 2015, along with an excited caption that included the comment "I see so many money-bragging posts, and I always say to myself, 'that ain't what you're focused on. Continue to do you, and your rewards will come.'" Others strategize about how to interact with passengers in just the right way to sustain a high driver rating. A driver from New York posted the following advice in a forum in 2015: "The less you say to a passenger, the higher rating you get. A simple hello and Thank You have a nice day is more than enough. Passengers don't really want to be bothered when they have their cell phones to entertain them." She also perceived that drivers risked their ratings if they made comments outside of basic politeness, because passengers could be fickle or punitive: "Passengers use anything and everything against you if they dislike what you say, causing you to get a lower rating from them." Drivers who have tried to have unfair ratings removed from their average have said that Uber declines to adjust them.

Because passengers do not rate Uber separately from their driver, drivers are forced to assume responsibility for the entire Uber experience.[22] Drivers who work for multiple ridehail companies occasionally describe Uber passengers as "more picky"; fearing low ratings and deactivation, these drivers try to be extra nice to dissatisfied passengers when working for Uber.[23] Drivers thus take on the "care work" involved in managing Uber's relationship with passengers,[24] and they provide emotional labor, like making passengers feel good, as part of their service-economy job.[25] These little gestures, at least in the earlier stages of Uber's operations in a given market, might include providing care items like bottles of water or candy to passengers—gestures traditionally reminiscent of female service work (think of airline attendants, hostesses, and waitresses who smile at you).[26] After drivers have made an extra effort, the fact that some passengers don't bother to rate their trips also strikes some drivers as unfair. Although since 2017 Uber has often required passengers to rate drivers before they can order their next trip, that isn't universally true, because the rules of engagement for passengers and drivers are not consistent across the Uber app for all users in all places at all times. Doberman, for example, has been driving in Baton Rouge, Louisiana, since the winter of 2016. When I interview him two seasons later, he sounds irked when he comments, "I have two hundred unrated trips. I don't understand why Uber doesn't remind the passengers in a close period of time that they need to rate us. And if they don't do anything in this period of time, that trip should be counted as five stars for us. It's hurting when the passenger doesn't give a rating—they just get out of the car and slam the door, and they don't say thank you. It's hurting. You just realize how the people are."

How passengers behave can leave drivers feeling underappreciated and affect how they perceive their own sense of independence at work. Doberman continues: "They [passengers] expect water, and you gave them water and candies, and they [are] going to spill the water on your floor. They'll drop the candy wraps on the floor, you know?" Many drivers come to resent both the care work they must do and the cost of these extra frills after Uber drops the rates at which they earn their income. When I ask Doberman if he feels like his own boss, he replies tellingly, "No, I'm not, because mine is a service category of working for people. It's very hard. They make you feel like they own you, like you're supposed to do whatever they want most of the time." He's not alone. Aasim, who immigrated from Bangladesh and now drives in New York City, used to work for a black-car service in Long Island, before he switched to Uber, Lyft, and Juno. After a year, he left the ridehail world to become a Yellow Cab driver, a job he'd held for about six months when I interview him in the fall of 2017. I asked him if he felt like his own boss, and he paused reflectively for a moment before explaining, "I think the yellow taxi is your own boss; but with Uber you cannot be your own boss. Because with Uber, the passenger is rating you. You don't have any personality. Somebody has to rate you? Come on." Some drivers feel pressed to make a demonstrative effort to fulfill the needs of their passengers, whereas others, with different personalities and goals, feel comfortably in charge of their own environment.[27]

Deedra, a former nursing assistant who drives for Lyft in New Orleans, likes the feedback she gets from the platform through summaries of her passenger reviews and performance, like ratings and comments. She credits her high rating to her friendliness and the social connection she manages with passengers. She says, "My summaries are always the best, because I like talking to people.... I break the ice and ask them where they from. If I sense that— you know, you can tell I'm a friendly person, so once I see that they['re] really not into being bothered, I just cut it off. But if they say something back again, then I still talk with them."

The difference in how drivers experience the emotional demands of their job may derive partly from whether or not they have previously worked in customer service jobs. Patrice, a Montreal Uber driver I interviewed, summed up this difference nicely when he said, "I used to work at a call center, and I hated it. I got fired because my sales weren't up. I started doing Uber, and, um, I guess I'm very customer-related. All my life I've been doing customer-related jobs, customer service. And I find that this is one of the best, best jobs that I've ever had. It's been like five months, and I still have a five-star rating. It's rare. And I've gotten texts from Uber saying I've got one of the greatest ratings in Montreal." He takes pride in his individual achievement, which is illustrated by his high rating and company approval.

Many drivers, however, are vexed by the unfairness of the rating system. One driver posted a remark in a forum in the summer of 2015 about a passenger he had picked up who cursed and bashed Uber for doubling the cost of her ride through surge pricing, which was 2.1 times more than the base price. He wrote, "At the time I drop[ped] her off, she told me that since I can't go to the Uber office and complain for this, I'll give you a 1* [to] show [my] middle finger to them." Drivers are helpless against unfair ratings, a demonstration of the limits of their power in an employment relationship governed by inflexible algorithmic managers.[28]

The rating system also perversely shields Uber from potential suits over protected-class discrimination in the workplace.[29] A generation ago, a slew of court cases rejected the idea that companies could engage in discriminatory hiring practices in order to cater to customer preferences.[30] The argument was essentially that companies weren't biased when, hypothetically, they hired only white female clerks, and that their hiring choices reflected the preferences of their consumers, who preferred to shop at stores without black female clerks. Now, through rating systems, consumers can directly input their biases into worker evaluation systems in ways that companies cannot do on their behalf.[31] And, worse than the discriminatory hiring practices of the 1980s, the silent prejudices of passengers expressed through rating systems are much harder to detect, prove, or prevent. Uber is not alone in using consumer-sourced rating systems. Across the digital world, consumer-facing platforms like Yelp and Expedia also offer rating mechanisms for evaluating businesses and their workers. For each of these companies, it is impossible to say that the evaluations posted are entirely objective: consumer biases inevitably swing ratings higher or lower. In Uber's case, this means that drivers are managed according to the biases and whims of consumers, which, in turn, means that blatant passenger discrimination could negatively affect them. Yet because Uber drivers are classified as independent contractors, not as employees, they do not benefit from most workplace discrimination protections.[32] In this way, the rating system provides one of the clearest signals that Uber has taken on the role of managing drivers as *workers*. The combination of worker and consumer practices in Uber's model creates a blurred distinction between these two categories that we think of as separate. The company's ambiguity on this question challenges regulatory bodies in the countries where Uber operates to manage not only Uber's claims that it is a technology company, rather than a taxi company, but also its relationship to its drivers.

Around the world, the same tools that Uber uses to manage drivers have led to different opinions on drivers' employment classification. In Australia, the Fair Work Commission ruled that an Uber driver who alleged he was unfairly dismissed from his job was not protected from being fired unfairly because he is, according to their assessment, an independent contractor.[33] In Toronto, Canada, a class-action lawsuit filed in January 2017 contends that drivers are misclassified as independent contractors, rather than employees.[34] Misclassification lawsuits abound when it comes to Uber, but the various challenges to drivers' employment classification have had mixed results. In the United Kingdom, there are three worker classifications: employees, workers or dependent contractors (who are formally self-employed, but who are economically reliant on a single employer for their income), and independent contractors. On appeal, a UK employment tribunal confirmed an earlier ruling that asserts Uber drivers are not independent contractors. They are workers and, as such, are protected from unlawful discrimination and entitled to a minimum wage and holiday pay, among other benefits.[35] Conversely, in Florida, an appeals court ruled that drivers *are* independent contractors,[36] and later, the state legislated their status as independent contractors. The implication is that drivers are not entitled to unemployment benefits or most labor law protections. Meanwhile, the California Labor Commissioner's Office ruled that drivers are employees, not independent contractors, as early as 2015.[37] These rulings affect the working conditions of thousands of drivers, but it's clear that there is not a universal consensus on whether drivers should be defined as employees or independent contractors. Whether drivers should be considered workers at all, rather than consumers, is another question.

TREATING LABOR AS CONSUMPTION: HOW UBER JUSTIFIES ITS MANAGEMENT PRACTICES

The vocabulary of technology that Uber deploys to describe its drivers and its own practices has implications for labor: it treats drivers as end users of its software, rather than as workers at all. *End users* is a perfect example of the language of disinformation that distances drivers from employment. The term appears in court documents in lawsuits over Uber's allegedly illegal employment practices and in company communications with the public. The rhetorical impact of that language is clever: as a society, we might be persuaded to care about workers, but who cares about end users? By fudging the terms of employment within its control, such as by potentially misclassifying drivers as independent contractors, and by pivoting to frame drivers as customers or end users, Uber provides us with a template for questioning what we know about employment relationships. And although technology practices and rhetoric have ushered in another way of doing business, older problems, such as harassment, persist under the veneer of technological neutrality.

Using a thin argument about technological exceptionalism, Uber tried to maneuver around legal walls in the case of Douglas O'Connor, Thomas Colopy, Matthew Manahan, and Elie Gurfinkel vs. Uber Technologies. However, Judge Edward M. Chen seemed to find the company's reasoning highly improbable. When presented with the idea that drivers are customers, he said, "The fact that you screen drivers, select them, the fact that you, Uber, sets *[sic]* the fare, not the drivers, the fact that the company could not operate and exist as a company and make money without drivers, you think that does not establish, among other things, that these drivers serve Uber?"[38] Uber's shifts between the language of labor and the language of consumers evoke its earlier tactics of regulatory arbitrage. There's no "sharing" in the sharing economy it has come to represent. In practice, drivers are hardly "entrepreneurs" or true partners with Uber, even though the company calls them "Uber Driver-Partners";

drivers are not suspended or fired, they are "deactivated." This conflation of workers with customers is clearly cause for disbelief. And yet, the miscategorization has deep roots within Uber's claims about the employment relationship it has with its drivers. Regulators may support that blurring by using language consistent with Uber's own: in 2016, the Federal Trade Commission brought legal action against Uber on the basis that it had misled drivers about their earnings, but the FTC also referred to Uber drivers as "entrepreneurial consumers."[39]

On a cool evening in San Francisco in 2016, I find myself sitting across from a senior Uber employee. Employees had invited me to their offices in the past, but since I've declined to sign a nondisclosure agreement before holding meetings with Uber employees, I'm not able to meet with them inside. Instead, the senior employee and I are meeting at a "non-NDA" café near Uber headquarters. I ask if the company tries to build trust with its drivers, and the answer—that Uber cares about building trust with all of its end users—floors me. The fact that even in an informal interview this person is deploying the language used in the lawsuits gives me pause, and I will return to this moment over and over again in my mind in the months that follow. As our table becomes littered with cappuccino cups, the senior employee persists in asking me how Uber can improve its relationship with drivers. I can't help but think this is roughly akin to asking how to improve your relationship with your girlfriend after she discovers that she is, in fact, the mistress.

The implications are stark: if the problems that Uber drivers experience at work can be reframed as customer satisfaction problems, these drivers lose access to remedies like employment law, which is available to workers in other businesses to redress any harms they suffer as part of their employment. It isn't just Uber using this language—it's echoed by other companies, including Lyft and, across the ocean, a British food-delivery service called Deliveroo. The kind of employment relationship that Uber has with its drivers is not unique: rather, it signals a greater social force that is turning workers into customers through the power of technological tools and narrative. Deliveroo, for example, classifies its food-delivery people as independent contractors in a dozen or so of the countries where it operates, and classifies some, in other countries, as employees, such as in the United Arab Emirates. According to several Deliveroo employees I spoke with in 2017, this boils down largely to the laws that define employment relationships in those respective places. However, the company contorts itself in order to avoid giving the impression that its workers are considered employees. As one media outlet, among many, reported in June 2017, about a leaked doc: "It says bicycle couriers who work for Deliveroo are never to be referred to as workers, employees, or staff, and that the Deliveroo jackets they have to wear on the job are not uniforms but 'branded clothing'. These workers don't have 'contracts', says the document, but 'supplier agreements'. They don't 'schedule shifts', but 'indicate their availability'. And they can never get sacked—instead, they're 'terminated'."[40]

On a different occasion, I meet another senior Uber employee, who makes a comment that reflects the same "drivers-are-customers" sentiment. He arrives a few minutes late to our meeting, overtly casual in a white T-shirt with a matching white towel to wipe away the sweat of an early morning jog from his forehead. His casually authoritative energy on a variety of subjects reminds me of the way women strive to appear effortlessly slim as a practiced way of projecting status. When we hit on the topic of improving customer service for drivers, he explains that, if you count all of the people working in tech in every single function, and then you count all the people working in customer support, the latter is significantly larger. He indicates that there are twice as many customer support agents as employees. Taking it all in, I squint on the inside, and smile on the outside, before observing with a briny smile, "That's because you don't count your drivers as employees." Dipping his head, he concedes that drivers are a much larger group than either of those—about ten times bigger. The central conflict between how to categorize a driver, and how to consider work in the sharing economy more broadly, animates a lot of the conflict between labor advocates and Uber.

By treating labor as consumption, Uber can have its cake and eat it too. When Uber describes its technology as a way to merely (and neutrally) connect two groups of end users—drivers and passengers—it underplays a more pressing reality: Uber's algorithms give the company vast leverage over how drivers do their work. When drivers are misled by algorithmic bosses, it is merely an example of how Silicon Valley companies with power can play us all. Uber's employment conflicts reveal *why* drivers are unfairly treated in a legal framework, but the context of employment merely illustrates how technology platforms can take advantage of all consumers. The context of the workplace provides us with a lens for examining inequities that emerge and multiply in a tech-driven world. The question for us to consider is whether algorithmic management creates a qualitative distinction between work and consumption. Uber's arguments actually articulate dynamic changes in how employment and consumption are negotiated in digital spaces through algorithmic power and transparency.

WHEN THE PLATFORM HAS YOUR DATA

How Uber treats its worker-consumers raises questions about how Uber and other platforms treat customer-consumers. We generate data that companies collect every time we use our digital devices. Datacentric surveillance has prompted long-standing debates over how we protect the privacy of individual users, such as by de-identifying data that is collected from them. However, the idea that anonymizing data will protect us from predatory uses of aggregate data collection is misguided. The question that emerges as we explore Uber's practices is, how are individuals treated when they are identified as part of a class of users?

As a broker between passengers and drivers, Uber controls not only prices, wages, and work standards but also a host of confidential data in the process. Uber's data collection practices are leveraged in ways that can play consumers, such as by charging certain groups of passengers what they're willing to pay rather than a set price.[41] Simultaneously,

Uber is highly visible among consumers because of its vast popularity. Sometimes, the ways Uber uses its data is a signal that Uber's role as a broker can be abusive rather than just profit-driven. Up-front pricing hovers over that thin line, not because it is specifically bad to charge passengers more than the driver is paid, but because it violates how drivers understand their partnership and legal contract with the company.

The ways Uber uses data brings into question its role as a "neutral" middleman, but its more scandalous practices raise serious questions about the culture of consumer data protection more broadly. For instance, Uber obtained the medical records of a passenger who accused her Uber driver of rape—and they did so without her permission.[42] In another instance, Uber made threats against journalist Sarah Lacy as well as her family, suggesting that they would entertain the idea of a smear campaign against her because of her justifiably scathing critiques.[43] And during the legal proceedings of a suit launched by Waymo (Alphabet's self-driving car unit) against Uber for allegedly stealing proprietary trade secrets about self-driving cars, a former Uber employee accused Uber of massive corporate espionage.[44]

Uber has a history of breaking trust with its stakeholders. In 2011, for example, the company held a Chicago launch party for its black-car service. It allegedly displayed to guests a stalker-y data visualization of the movements and whereabouts of thirty New York City Uber users, along with a list of their names via "God View," Uber's global view of the geolocation details of its app users.[45] These incidents demonstrate a culture of data curation at Uber that can turn predatory. In 2015, *New York Times* reporters Natasha Singer and Mike Isaac highlighted allegations by the Electronic Privacy Information Center that upcoming changes to Uber's privacy policy would "allow the ridehailing app to collect more detailed data about customers' whereabouts and use their contact lists to send their friends promotional pitches."[46] The advocates urged the Federal Trade Commission to intervene.

Even when Uber's practices are not specifically abusive, they may nonetheless demonstrate that small tweaks to the design of an app can have significant effects on consumer privacy. To take a small example, in 2016, Uber updated its app settings so that passengers had to agree to share their location with Uber through their smartphone either "Never" or "Always." Most apps provide a third option: users can choose to share their geolocation data with an app only when that app is in use. Scrolling through one's phone to alter the privacy settings from "Never" to "Always" selectively each time a passenger wants to hail a ride is a pain. As privacy and legal scholar Woodrow Hartzog observes publicly on Twitter, "By not including a common option like "only while app is in use," they [Uber] manipulate users into sharing by making privacy costly."[47] (Uber later revised the settings when Apple made it mandatory as a condition of hosting Uber and others in its app store, though Android users were still affected before Uber changed course.) Most consumers, who are generally further removed from Uber drama, accept data practices that are not in their best interests simply because they want a cheap taxi ride and a convenient service. It is clear that consumers can be taken advantage of through data exploits.

And it's not just individual consumers who are vulnerable—large companies can also get duped by sly data practices. Apple's app store has specific privacy rules that all apps must follow, including the Uber app. But in direct violation of these rules, Uber continued to track iPhone data even after users had deleted the ridehail app from their phones, as Mike Isaac reported for the *New York Times*.[48] Normally, app developers who flout Apple's app-store guidelines risk being cut from the app store, which in Uber's case would have resulted in their losing access to millions of Apple customers. Given the stakes, Uber went to elaborate lengths to hide its noncompliance: the ridehail company purposefully set out to evade Apple's fraud detection protocols by manipulating what Apple's app-review team would see when approving the Uber app. Under orders from then-CEO Travis Kalanick, Uber's engineers duped Apple for a time by building a "geofence" around Apple's corporate headquarters in Cupertino, California. Anyone within that geofence (e.g., Apple's app-review team) would see a different version of

Uber's app. (It's a bit like if a company were to send a tech reporter a new smartwatch to test and review—under the pretense that it is their normal product—but the device sent to the reporter secretly includes a faster processor not available to everyone else, so that the tech reporter will give it a better grade.) In a meeting that took place years before the event became public knowledge, Apple CEO Tim Cook summoned a nervous Travis Kalanick to his office to discuss Uber's willful disregard for Apple's rules. Kalanick agreed to comply properly.

Between 2016 and 2017, Uber's many violations of the public trust were publicized broadly in the media. Because Uber's practices are representative of more common dynamics of how we use technology today, the company's actions have pulled the veil off of the way practices that bring us so many valuable services can also take advantage of us. There are rich privacy debates in academia on whether companies should be able to resell the data they collect about us, a practice that can take advantage of users.[49] Some thinkers, like computer scientist and philosophy writer Jaron Lanier, envision a future where people are paid for the data they generate online.[50] As digital labor scholar and computer scientist Mary L. Gray observes publicly on Twitter, however, "We have no evidence that people want to commodify their online lives. Does cash back make it OK for companies to resell my family pics or shopping history, as they choose? Maybe ask: Should we stop giving companies wholesale permission to sell our data to 3rd parties?"[51] She draws a distinction between repurposed social data and paid, digital knowledge work because, as she elaborates in conversation with me, immaterial labor isn't the same thing for everyone. Over time, privacy debates have become a symbol representing broader conversations about problematic technology practices in society. Uber may become a proxy battleground over consumer data privacy because it's an easier target for political entrepreneurs who want to move the needle on data-collection and privacy debates.

Kofi, whom I discussed in the introduction, is an Uber and Lyft driver I interviewed in Washington, DC. He was appalled when he learned first from the media in December 2017—rather than directly from his employer—that hackers had gained access to his personal data and that of 57 million Uber drivers and passengers from around the world in 2016, such as their names, email addresses, and mobile phone numbers.[52] In the United States alone, six hundred thousand drivers were affected by the hack, which compromised their driver's license information. Uber, which had paid the hacker a "bounty" to delete the data and keep quiet about the breach, later notified drivers by snail mail and email on November 22, 2017, a day after *Bloomberg* first reported it.[53] Before moving to the United States, Kofi had practiced law as an assistant attorney for a government agency in Ethiopia. "I expected Uber to do better when it comes to protecting private information, be it for customers or drivers," he told me. Uber later settled a complaint with the Federal Trade Commission over its deceptive privacy and data-security practices by entering a twenty-year consent agreement, which requires Uber to build a comprehensive privacy program with internal audits.[54]

Data practices at Uber raise questions about our trust in platform companies regarding how they use what they collect from us. Uber's activities reflect the larger practices of data collection and user manipulation common at Google, Facebook, and other Silicon Valley companies. Uber used its data to gain insight into who among their users had one-night stands ("Rides of Glory" as Uber termed the category in a blog post), highlighting just how much personal data companies collect on users as a seemingly benign part of facilitating transactions.[55] Uber isn't alone. The popular online dating site OkCupid asks its users a series of questions in order to create recommended matches between users based on how much they have in common. In 2011, OkCupid's cofounder Christian Rudder authored a blog post on the company's site that examined the data it collected from its users. As an example of what they could do, the company cross-matched the questions "Do you like to exercise?" and "Is it difficult for you to have an orgasm?" to determine that a woman will have greater difficulty achieving orgasm if she doesn't enjoy exercise.[56] Privacy violations in technology culture abound. Around Christmastime in 2017, Netflix joked publicly on Twitter, "To the 53 people who've watched A Christmas Prince every day for the past 18 days: Who hurt you?" The seemingly innocuous joke raised the uncomfortable specter of Big Brother–style surveillance: you watch Netflix, but Netflix watches you too.[57] The message is that your data can be used against you by the services that collect it, though that threat is usually more implicit. The ways that we interact with datacentric systems imply a contractual trust with platforms to protect our data privacy. And indeed, Netflix was roundly criticized for its privacy violations.[58] The particular examples that Uber provides us with might have simply joined a long list of "oops" moments in which technology hit a nerve. But Uber is different. It is the legacy of a technology culture that cautioned "Don't Be Evil," the slogan that came from Google's code of conduct around 2000. Similarly, Facebook, founded in 2004, announced that its mission was "to give people the power to share and make the world more open and connected" and, in 2017, adjusted it to: "Give people the power to build community and bring the world closer together."[59] Technology companies get the benefit of the doubt in American society, enjoying a high level of status and respect as powerful, entrepreneurial innovators that deliver a better future. But Uber gives us plenty of reasons to withhold that benefit of the doubt.

Unlike Facebook or Google, Uber provides physical services, and its service depends on the labor of thousands of people who see what they do as work. Uber drivers can be seen and ticketed by law enforcement for their activities, and the company can be literally kicked out of cities. Google and Facebook aren't getting the boot by municipalities; with Uber, however, regulators could sever the foot of the beast because the company is present in a tangible way. And while consumers would find it very difficult to functionally opt out of Google, they can opt out of Uber (though the company obviously delivers a service that people value beyond the merit of any particular scandal). For the moment, Uber has succeeded in bringing the world of algorithms to the context of employment, which has a host of implications for how drivers are treated and protected. Regulators and legislators are still working to catch up. Meanwhile, Silicon Valley companies like Uber are using data-driven algorithms to reshape the norms of employment and rewrite the rules of work.

CHAPTER SIX

IN THE BIG LEAGUES

How Uber Plays Ball

In August 2017, white supremacists rallied in Charlottesville, Virginia, and an Uber driver (who happened to be a woman of color) booted several Nazi ringleaders from her car after they made racist remarks.[1] Shortly afterward, Uber, along with leading tech companies like Apple, Google, Facebook, GoDaddy, and others, took a remarkable stance against hate speech. CloudFare, a popular website-hosting service, kicked the Daily Stormer, a Nazi website, off the Internet.[2] Uber proceeded to email drivers and passengers, citing the neo-Nazi demonstration and emphasizing that bigotry and racism are not permitted on its platform. The fact that the company had to take a stance against Nazis is a sign of how large Uber looms in society. Yet it is drivers who are on the battle lines Uber draws. If flagging Nazis is suddenly part of the job, drivers are the ones who shoulder the occupational risk of confrontation and retaliation, even as they remain "independent contractors."

Leveraging drivers in a show of anti-Nazism is one way of forming alliances, both with drivers who can feel confident that they won't be fired if they reject Nazi passengers, and with anti-Nazi civil-society groups and consumers. Yet ultimately, these politics are mercenary. They form one weapon in a whole arsenal of strategic partnerships that Uber builds as it grows. On a larger scale, these politics demonstrate how quick technology companies can be to intervene in social problems, but these interventions can fail to address downstream consequences. So much of what allows Uber to play us all is the fact that it has such a wide variety of stakeholders—drivers, civil rights groups, regulators, and even nonprofits supporting girls who code—who have uneven investments in its methods and its success. As I've examined Uber's politics in countless cities and several countries, I've found a consistent pattern. Uber seeks to cultivate allies quickly, leverages their support, and then moves on to the next series of crises—which range from misclassification lawsuits and Kalanick's publicized dispute with a driver, to accusations from Waymo that Uber stole its proprietary self-driving-car technology. The only constant logic is expansion and control.

We can see this in three major trends. First, as Uber enters a new space, it takes a direct-to-consumer approach, bypassing potential barriers, like regulations or political opposition, by winning over consumers with its effective app. It cautions opponents that might try to constrain some of its practices by conveying the message, "Be grateful for the disruptive innovation we bring, because what we offer is superior to the regulations that would hold us back" (what I refer to as "gratitude logic"). Because of its size and influence, it simply shrugs off regulation that it doesn't like. Then, Uber shifts and reshifts its identity, trying to find exploitable cracks and inconsistencies between various systems of rules and laws. Finally, Uber plays stakeholders against each other, using temporary alliances to gain a foothold wherever it goes. In many cases, drivers, passengers, cities, and others benefit from Uber's operations, but there are always others who are left behind.

The politics of Uber are simultaneously vast and local. Uber plays each of its stakeholders individually, but each of these individual battles simultaneously affects all of the rest. How drivers experience Uber's expansion varies in its different stages: at the beginning, drivers are often optimistic, and many grow jaded later, though some cite the flexibility of this job as the main reason they continue to appreciate it. After the first stage of Uber's arrival, it seeks to reach geographic density by recruiting drivers and passengers to its platform. Subsequently, the wait for a pickup grows shorter for passengers, drivers incur less downtime, and demand rises while Uber tries to lower prices in order to expand network utilization. The expansion of Uber initially benefits drivers, then hurts them: in the next stage, Uber typically cuts rates and floods the market. In Juneau, Alaska, Ignacio shows me how he uses a local ridehailing app, TaxiCaller, that alerts him and others nearby to dispatch requests. The app displays how long each driver has been waiting. There are a few ridehailing apps in this city of thirty-two thousand people, like Juneau Taxi and Tours. The spread of Uber and Lyft prompted local taxi businesses to build their own apps in many local cities across the United States and Canada, such as Plattsburgh, NY (Plattsburgh Taxi), and Montreal (Téo Taxi). Ignacio is optimistic about Uber's imminent arrival in the state. "I think it's good for consumers, more choices," he offers. As Ignacio articulates his thoughts on the arrival of Uber, Ralph Waldo Emerson's poetic line comes to mind: "America is another name for opportunity." On a recent vacation to country-music capital Nashville, Tennessee, Ignacio used Uber himself, and it worked well. But when he tried to go with his family to the airport, surge pricing was in effect. Rather than paying fifty dollars for a fourteen-dollar-trip, he hailed a local taxi.

Ignacio's optimism reminds me of the pessimism of Faiq, a driver in New York (whom I introduced in chapter 3). "When Uber came to the city, taxi business went down," Faiq had told me with a grimace, speaking in clipped tones. Analyzing the ridehail climate, he had said,

> I wouldn't recommend the driving industry to anyone anymore. It used to be very good. Now you kill yourself. You have to work thirteen, fourteen hours. Usually if you have family you cannot work that long. It used to be very good hours. You work nine to ten hours, five or six days. Now you have to work six or seven days, twelve to fourteen hours. . . . Uber, Lyft, the others, they take too much. In the city, we have our expenses. The TLC plate, the extra fee for that, extra money for the insurance, and the expense also. Some guys pay seven thousand dollars in insurance, some guys pay three thousand dollars. Plus the car payment and everything. Housing, too.

When I asked what his family thought of his job with Uber, he replied swiftly, "They don't like that I drive. They'd like me to find another job. They say nowadays I put in too many hours. I miss them too." Faiq's commitment to his family is a common theme of how drivers explain their long hours at work, in a grim triumph of their independence.[3]

For others, their working conditions with Uber *do* let them feel more free and independent than in their prior work as taxi drivers or at more heavily monitored workplaces like call centers.[4] Gurjinder, a taxi driver turned Uber driver in Montreal, whom I met in 2017, used to pay $600 per week to a garage to rent his taxi (which he kept for twenty-four hours a day, though many taxi drivers split their shifts). Per week, he also paid $200–250 for gas and other costs and took home $600 for himself. The dignity of keeping what he earns is an important part of the psychology of his transition into Uber driving. "When you make $600 and you give it to some someone else, it pains," he says, taking his eyes off the road ahead to look me directly in the eyes. Even though he could technically choose his hours, the stress of always needing to pay the rent made him anxious if he was late in the morning. If he sat at home for too long, his wife would harass him, asking, "How you will pay the rent? How you will pay the rent?" he says, adding, "That was a constant worry."

Gurjinder appreciates that, with Uber, he can use his own car, even though he's responsible for all the gas and maintenance, which he estimates at $2.50 for every $10 he takes home, plus another $1.50 in income taxes. "I am my own boss," he declares emphatically. "You can start whenever you want, you can stop whenever you want. I have a choice." He felt like his own boss driving a taxi, too, but now he feels more in control of his time. Earlier that day, when business was slow with Uber, he went home to eat his lunch and run some errands at the bank. Later, he mentions, "I was making more money before it [Uber] was legal. There were not a lot of drivers.... Where there was one driver, now there are five. [In October 2016, the Quebec transport commission and Uber started a pilot project that permitted Uber to operate legally under certain regulations.][5] Still, the money you make in Uber is the same, or maybe a little bit higher, than money you make from being in a factory or another something like that." Unless you are a white-collar worker in an office, driving for Uber is a good option compared to his alternatives, he explains. As I noted in chapter 2, drivers assess this job in comparison to their available alternatives. Evaluating Uber's impact on society, however, is always complicated by the mixed benefits it delivers to drivers, passengers, and other stakeholders, and by the divisions it sows in the process.

GRATITUDE LOGIC: MOVE FAST, BREAK THINGS, CITE TECHNOLOGY CONTRIBUTIONS LATER

In its initial rise, from 2009 to 2014 or so, Uber came to represent the sharing economy and was widely celebrated in forums on the future of work, in the media, and across academic and policy circles. Sharing-economy companies argued that they should not be put in the same categories as their industry competitors. In many ways, they successfully evaded pre-existing bodies of law regulating taxi services, accommodations, and employment, although some perished by this logic too (e.g., HomeJoy, a housecleaning company, went out of business after employment misclassification suits hampered its fund-raising efforts).[6] Uber banked on the political legacy of Silicon Valley to steamroll local governments that tried to regulate it, too: the technology industry has operated with low regulatory oversight because it successfully persuaded regulators, and society, that low regulation is essential to innovation. This social pact is morally persuasive because of a mainstream belief that the fruits of innovation—specifically, technology services and devices—benefit society. That relationship is characterized by sharing or reciprocity, which implicitly obscures the political power technology companies have over society.

This logic is especially salient because some corners of American technology culture de-emphasize the importance of a social welfare net and are receptive instead to the interventions of private wealth to salve public deficits. One of Uber's Silicon Valley neighbors, Facebook, received serious criticism when it took that attitude abroad. In a program called "Free Basics," Facebook aimed to bring the Internet to underserved populations in India on the premise that this program would bridge the digital divide between those who are connected and those who are not. "Free Basics" wasn't the Internet, though; it was a Facebook portal with some access to Facebook-curated content and limited access to other digital functions. In effect, Facebook positioned itself as the Internet. In a backlash that continues through 2018, Facebook's efforts have been widely decried as "digital colonialism."[7]

There is a certain receptiveness to tech companies who come in to replace public infrastructure, because they promise certain benefits, like free laptops or, in Uber's case, less road congestion.[8] *New York Times* journalist Natasha Singer identified these dynamics in a multipronged investigation of education-technology adoption in public schools.[9] Her investigation revealed that tech oligarchs were equipping schools with ed-tech programs and devices, and in the process they were changing the nature of the curriculum without any public reckoning of these changes. Microsoft, Facebook, Google, and Salesforce all backed Code.org, the main actor of this story, as the prototype for reform. Its founder, Hadi Partovi, likened Code.org's role to the sharing economy: "Airbnb is disrupting the travel space, but they don't own the hotels," he said, adding, "We are in a similar model, disrupting education. But we are not running the school and we don't hire the teachers."[10] In effect, he said that he is not responsible for the institution of education, stakeholder consultation, or the relationship that schools have with their employees. His digital intervention is capable of disrupting or seriously changing the school model without the responsibilities of ownership.

The *gratitude logic* of "accept our contribution, but don't expect us to submit to governance in this space" was similarly visible in an advertising campaign by Airbnb in San Francisco. A sample ad plastered to a bus stop shelter read, "Dear Public Library System, We hope you use some of the $12 million in hotel taxes to keep the library open later." The condescending ads, which hinted broadly at the city's ingratitude for the taxes that Airbnb's business generates, followed an $8 million lobbying campaign by the company against San Francisco's 2015 ballot measure Proposition F. Voters ultimately rejected the proposition, which would have restricted short-term rentals and thus undermined Airbnb's short-term-rental business model.[11] Gratitude logic is part of how Uber drums up popular support for its regulatory evasions. Even in cities like New York, Chicago, or Toronto, with strict quotas on how many cabs can be in operation, Uber prevails when it insists that it's not a taxi company but rather a technology company; the old rules don't apply to the digital world. For consumers, Uber disrupted a calcified taxi industry that was chiefly known for its inadequate service, while Airbnb undid the monopoly that expensive hotels had on tourism by creating a platform for hosts to rent out their spare bedrooms or homes.[12] The unrepentant politics of disruption became the social standard for assessing the value of technological innovation in society, against the value of entrenched industries.

Despite its reputation, Uber claims to have a cooperative attitude toward governments and regulators. The company wrote to me, "We are actually trying to get governments to update their regulations to use resources and infrastructure more efficiently."[13] Uber is, of course, willing to play nice with regulators as long as they cave in and accommodate the company's perspective. One senior Uber employee shared his theory about Uber's culture clash when we met, and it stuck with me for a while. He mused that Uber's conflicts were about the new world, represented by leaders like Uber cofounder Travis Kalanick, coming into *direct contact* with the old world of compliance, law, hierarchy, and order. The clash is big, public, and polarizing.

In California, where Uber started, the state government took real steps to align itself with advances in technology and society, attempting to be a dance partner in step with ridehail companies. Yet when the Department of Motor Vehicles developed a license for the budding self-driving cars developed by companies like Uber, Google, Lyft, and others, Uber refused to cooperate, contradicting its stated rhetoric. Instead, it debuted its self-driving cars without licenses in the streets of San Francisco. When the DMV and State Attorney General Kamala

Harris threatened legal action, Uber initially refused to back down. It offered a flimsy premise, that its particular technology was simply not subject to the rules the DMV had developed.[14]

The most important part of Uber's encounter with the California DMV was the company's rejection of the government's authority on principle. Citing Tesla's autopilot technology as an example of self-driving-car technology that doesn't require a permit, Uber argued that the testing permits the DMV devised for self-driving cars didn't apply to Uber's self-driving cars because they were, in fact, not yet capable of autonomous driving without a human overseer. Anthony Lewandowski, Uber's lead engineer on self-driving cars (who was accused of stealing Google's self-driving Internet protocol when he left and came to Uber), announced, "We cannot in good conscience sign up to regulation for something we're not doing."[15] Uber directly contravened the law with no remorse, and with no real impact. The attorney general's office wrote to Uber in response: "We are asking Uber to adhere to California law and immediately remove its 'self-driving' vehicles from the state's roadways until Uber complies with all applicable statutes and regulations[,] ... until it obtains the appropriate permit, as 20 other companies have done."[16] Rather than change its approach, Uber packed up its self-driving cars and delivered them to Arizona, with the expectation that regulatory requirements there would be minimal.[17] (In March 2018, Arizona suspended Uber's self-driving car tests after one of them struck and killed a woman as she walked her bicycle across the street in Tempe, Arizona.)[18] Uber's seemingly disingenuous protest against regulations highlights the power of technology companies to ignore the clear intentions of legal authorities.

At the same time, it's disconcerting to watch Uber raise the banner of illegality-as-innovation. Couched in the context of Silicon Valley disruption, however, this illegality-as-innovation can seem like daring entrepreneurial work. But this is a kind of privilege afforded billion-dollar corporations and their (often white) technologist founders that is denied to other segments of the population. Uber was flouting California's rules in 2016, whereas, two years earlier, Eric Garner was choked to death by police—allegedly for selling loose cigarettes.[19] On such a small scale, performed without technology and by a lower-income black man, illegality is not merely punished but punished swiftly and completely out of measure. When law enforcement goes easy on tech entrepreneurs breaking the law but cracks down on racial minorities peacefully living quiet lives, the cultural-privilege dynamics that Uber benefits from become plainly obvious.

What happens to Uber tells us a lot about who may break the law under the guise of innovative disruption with less severe consequences. For some critics, the disruption ethos of technology—often summarized as "move fast, break things" and "don't ask permission; ask forgiveness later"—eerily echoes rape culture, where entitlement and privilege supersede consent.[20]

Many advocates for labor and civil society have begun to push back against Uber and companies like it. Beneath the heady haze of debates over whether governments should be innovative and run society like tech start-ups, worker advocates and class-action lawyers have mounted cases accusing Uber—as well as other sharing economy companies, like Handy,[21] HomeJoy,[22] Lyft,[23] and others—of violating labor law meant to protect their workers. Regulators have struggled to "adapt multiple regimes of evaluation"[24] to the cases of Uber and other sharing-economy companies, which have flourished with a lot of law-flouting. For example, after researchers demonstrated that racism is evident on Airbnb's platform[25] and may violate fair-housing laws, the California Department of Fair Employment and Housing resolved a complaint lodged against the company by obtaining permission from Airbnb to audit certain hosts with "fair housing tests."[26] These processes highlight how challenging it is for regulators to enforce the law without having access to the data that companies hold.

When cities try to reign Uber in, municipal regulations can backfire. Consider what happened when Austin, Texas, passed municipal legislation to require Uber and Lyft to comply with fingerprint-based background checks. Both companies pulled out of the city in May 2016[27] and continued to lobby the state to pass legislation friendly to its business model.[28] Uber and Lyft succeeded a year later, when House Bill 100[29] passed the Texas State Senate[30] and was signed into law by Governor Greg Abbott shortly afterward. The bill, which overrides local ordinances, classified drivers as independent contractors and clarified that drivers would not be required to undergo fingerprint-based background checks.[31] A tension, like that between Uber's desirability and its irascibility, pervades its many partnerships. Uber's advances can sometimes seem like technological determinism; their advances rely on the idea that Uber and all its practices are inevitable. The National Employment Law Project, together with the Partnership for Working Families, provides another analysis, suggesting that Uber and Lyft deploy a two-stage "shock doctrine" to get their way. In the first stage, they manufacture a crisis with a municipal regulator, such as Austin, and in the second stage they appeal to the state legislature for relief. The goal of this approach is to rewrite employment laws by ensuring that state laws classify drivers as independent contractors. The rationale they use to justify their efforts, however, is that if regulations were left to municipal governances, the company would have to accommodate a messy patchwork of requirements. In forty-one states, Uber and Lyft have successfully lobbied politicians to pass laws that erase or mitigate how localities regulate these companies.[32] While this approach is rational (it's technically legitimate to change laws), it's also eyebrow-raising (because it confirms a certain contempt Uber has demonstrated toward existing laws). It's no wonder that any number of Uber stakeholders might feel uneasy in their alliances with the company.

After Uber and Lyft left Austin in 2016, I flew there to find out how drivers felt about being left behind. As I reported for *Motherboard* while conducting some of my fieldwork in spring 2016,[33] Karl, a former Uber and Lyft driver, said, "They claim that it was because the background checks … would take too long and so on, but there is a time frame from now to February 2017 for that, so they had a lot of time to do all the background checks." He signed up to work for GetMe, a local ridehail start-up, so he could keep working. "They [Uber and Lyft] didn't need to shut down and leave the city like they did." Thomas, a former driver for Uber and Lyft, said he believed both companies took a stand against fingerprints because of high driver-turnover rates. "I have no problem with doing it. I think most drivers would have been happy to do it. The problem is that Uber treats their drivers so bad that there's such a turnover that they have to constantly churn them. And the fingerprinting is just another hurdle for them to sign up."

Another incident occurred when Uber partnered with Carnegie Mellon University and the city of Pittsburgh to advance its self-driving car project, only to hire away nearly the entire robotics department of the school.[34] As Cecilia Kang reported for the *New York Times,* then-mayor Bill Peduto (a Democrat) announced Pittsburgh's excitement at the development, proclaiming, "It's not our role to throw up regulations or limit companies like Uber. You can either put up red tape or roll out the red carpet. If you want to be a 21st-century laboratory for technology, you put out the carpet."[35] The municipal government of Pittsburgh later complained that Uber failed to keep its word to the city as part of their agreement, not following through on offering driverless-car rides for free or creating jobs as promised in a high-unemployment neighborhood.[36]

UBER'S DOUBLESPEAK: JOB CREATION WITHOUT WORKER RIGHTS

Uber is a chameleon: it utilizes the art of doublespeak, which allows it to simultaneously maintain seemingly contradictory political stances. The company's reputation as a darling of the technology world lost some of its shine by 2015, when the aggressiveness of its tactics was beginning to give many people pause. And yet, the most notable attitudes of regulators at that time were censure or hesitation. Regulators seemed fearful of being accused of anti-innovation sentiments. The Federal Trade Commission, for example, endorsed the benefits of the sharing economy, styling Uber's drivers as "entrepreneurial consumers."[37] Politicians in cities where Uber wasn't legal yet, like Vancouver, started adding "Sharing Economy" to their own Twitter bios as proof of their pro-technology, progressive, business-friendly credentials.

178 / *In the Big Leagues*

More than 8,000 New Jobs

Uber empowers thousands of local drivers to benefit from the platform, and in turn helps boost local economies in Canada.

Thousands of Torontonians—working moms, young professionals, retirees, recent graduates, and more—are choosing to drive with Uber. We hear everyday from driver partners that the flexibility of earning on the Uber platform is one of the things they love the most because it means that they can supplement their income and achieve their goals whenever works best for them.

By creating the equivalent of over 8,000 new full-time jobs in 2015, the potential for growth is so strong that Uber is on track to generate more opportunities in Toronto than any other new business in the city. (note: full-time job equivalents based on a 40-hour week)

Figure 24. Copy from Uber's website, Toronto, 2015. Source: Ian Black, "Strengthening Toronto's Economy with Thousands of New Jobs," *Uber Local Blogs* (on file with the author), April 21, 2015.

As one example of doublespeak, the company claims that it's not an employer in the sharing economy, even while it touts job creation as its main benefit to cities and other stakeholders.[38] Uber marketed its growth in Toronto by announcing on its website, "By creating the equivalent of over 8,000 new full-time jobs in 2015, the potential for growth is so strong that Uber is on track to generate more opportunities in Toronto than any other new business in the city. (note: full-time job equivalents based on a 40-hour week)" (See figure 24.) Although Uber draws on the characteristics of employment measures like "a 40-hour week" to underscore its claim, it also rejects the notion that it is an employer that leverages significant control over its drivers through management. Uber brands itself as a job creator, but it generally decouples employment from employment rights.

Another example of Uber's doublespeak presents itself in the question of how drivers are treated. Although drivers are typecast by Uber as free and willing participants in "turnkey entrepreneurship," the company shifts gears when drivers start to organize for better working conditions. In an effort to combat labor organizing and unionization efforts among drivers in Seattle, Uber sent drivers in-app messages with cautionary alerts like: "The City recently granted the Teamsters' [a union for drivers] approval to begin pressuring drivers for support despite the Teamsters' long history of fighting for taxi and against independent rideshare drivers. Check out our latest podcast for info on how you can protect your freedom" (emphasis in original).[39] (Incidentally, the company could potentially then gauge driver interest in unionization and intervene accordingly based on who clicked on podcast links and other prompts and how long they listened to them.)[40] Uber's refrain emphasizes that drivers are free, but a closer look shows that the company is actually arguing that drivers should have freedom *from* collective organizing.

HOW UBER PLAYS STAKEHOLDERS OFF EACH OTHER

When Uber is playing one hand, it's also playing three other hands simultaneously. In concrete terms, it looks like this: let's say Uber and others are working to get approval from municipalities to test autonomous cars. Behind these particular negotiations is a larger, cultural conversation in the United States which says that advances in automation will result in mass joblessness. Against this cultural backdrop, Uber simultaneously approaches state regulators to pass laws that legislate the independent-contractor status of drivers,[41] even stripping them of worker rights. But the logic of automation debates frames this effort as a small concession: ceding workers' rights seems relatively innocuous if their jobs give way to a future with autonomous cars, a future that renders driving redundant. "Robots are taking your jobs" is an

all-too-common refrain in debates about the future of work. This man-
tra can shed light on the importance of protecting workers and finding
new ways to create jobs in the New Economy. It can also be used, however, as a subtle propaganda tool to justify poor working conditions:
improving employment becomes less important if robots are coming
for these jobs anyway. While drivers may have a viable legal claim to
employee status under labor law, the culture of technology is pushing
us past those considerations in more diffuse ways.

Interrelated issues draw in different sets of actors, and Uber can break
promises to one without necessarily hindering its relationship with
another, because Uber represents more than a single actor. For instance,
Uber may never create jobs in a high-unemployment neighborhood near
its driverless car track in Pittsburgh, even though it promised to do so
when it began operations there. Other regions, like New York State, may
continue to welcome the company's expansion as a sign of certain pro-
gression in the digital economy. Despite Uber's mixed track record as a
sometimes friend, sometimes foe, Governor Andrew Cuomo signed a
bill to legalize ridehailing in the state on June 5, 2017. Uber was beaten
over the head with a bat in the press for months before the bill's passage,
for its scandalous behavior at corporate headquarters, in cities, and in
various countries, and for its treatment of drivers and sometimes passengers. The notable economic and labor historian Louis Hyman voiced his
support for Cuomo's seal of approval, observing, "We should not think
of this development as the coming of Uber and Lyft but rather as the
expansion of the on-demand digital economy. These particular companies are only two of a vast world of new kinds of work that Upstate New
Yorkers will be encountering over the next few years. They will disrupt
assumptions about what work is, and where it will take place, but at the
same time, will create new opportunities."[42] In other words, Uber's
expansion is synonymous with the expansion of digital economies.

Governor Cuomo's signature on the bill to legalize Uber and Lyft
symbolizes the pathways these companies blazed for the future of work,
yet these platforms have their local detractors. Initially, Westchester

County, adjacent to New York City, considered opting out. In a response that is typical of the Uber political playbook, Safraz Maredia, an Uber general manager from the tristate area, penned an op-ed titled "Westchester Would Send Anti-business Message by Opting Out from Ride-Hailing."[43] Politicizing consumers with messages that support innovation, business, or employment opportunities is a classic Uber move.

As we saw earlier, anything that is an obstacle to Uber (such as regulations designed to govern it like a taxi business) is positioned by sharing-economy and Uber proponents as an obstacle to innovation, opportunity, and the future of work. It is indisputable that companies like Uber provide valuable services to consumers, and as a result regulators in particular may hesitate to block "innovation" when it comes to such a popular service. One way to see this clash between the old establishment and new-technology commerce is to look closely at the competing logic of Uber's stakeholders. Uber is embroiled in a long game of circumventing unfavorable regulation at the municipal and state levels.

Two years earlier, in New York City, then-mayor Bill de Blasio had tried to limit the number of cars on the street in the summer of 2015. The city has long had a limited number of medallions available for taxi drivers. When users opened up the Uber app, they were met with a "de Blasio" version of the app, one with no cars available (see figure 25).

Uber users were flooded with emails from the company encouraging them to protest the government's efforts, a strategy that Uber had employed as part of its political organizing elsewhere.[44] (Uber was sued for doing this via text and phone in Austin.) As author Nikil Saval observes with reference to David Plouffe, former senior vice president of policy and strategy for Uber, "What Plouffe and the ridesharing companies understand is that, under capitalism, when markets are pitted against the state, the figure of the consumer can be invoked against the figure of the citizen. Consumption has in fact come to replace our original ideas of citizenship."[45] Uber's ominous threat to rally consumers (who love the convenience of its service) against regulators (who reign in the company) is a gambit predicated on the idea that consumer

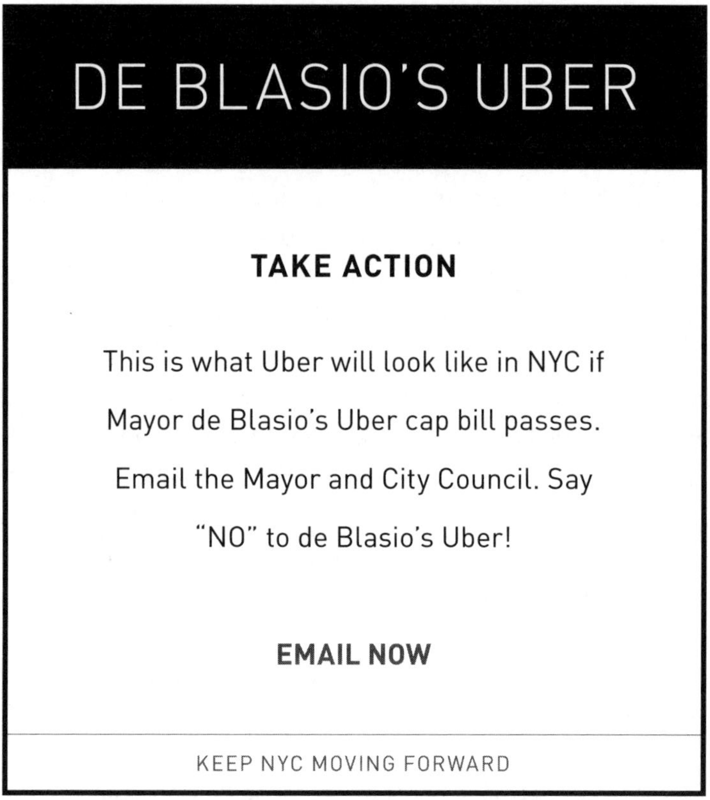

DE BLASIO'S UBER

TAKE ACTION

This is what Uber will look like in NYC if

Mayor de Blasio's Uber cap bill passes.

Email the Mayor and City Council. Say

"NO" to de Blasio's Uber!

EMAIL NOW

KEEP NYC MOVING FORWARD

Figure 25. This message from the Uber passenger app in 2015 accompanied what Uber called "the de Blasio map": the map displayed no available Uber cars and signaled a long wait of twenty minutes or more.

trends are bellwethers of political sentiment.[46] It also speaks to a larger strategy. Uber has been repeatedly hauled before courts for allegedly violating laws and threatened with legal action by a variety of actors, but it has largely escaped criminalization. Instead, it does encourage customers to operate as voting citizens to back it up when it comes under threat of sanction.

Uber's messaging is adaptive to regional, cultural, and political contexts: it is a local, global phenomenon. In western Europe, which is grappling with the effects of immigration from the Middle East and

Africa (including Syria, Iraq, and Libya), anxiety about newcomers runs high. Uber's pitch is that it can help hordes of young men assimilate on the job by giving them gainful employment, connecting them with locals and improving their language skills. In Slovakia, which has a legacy of communist rule, Uber's pitch to Slovakian policymakers in 2015 reportedly stated that, "although Uber is often accused of being a linchpin of predatory capitalism destroying job security and reducing welfare, Uber is in reality a socialist project of sharing aimed at providing ordinary people with more economic opportunities and improving their lives." (The excerpt circulated on Twitter, though the original policy document did not. Although I could not confirm its veracity, it strikes me as entirely plausible based on the logic of Uberland.) Rhetoric reveals how Uber consolidates decentralized nodes of its network into an adaptable global force. It reminds me of Genghis Khan, who let people keep their gods as long as they swore allegiance to the marauding troops of his empire.[47] This sense of American global intrusion is a source of tension in Uber's reception abroad, where the company is implicated with the outsized role that American technology companies play in the civic life of other nations. Many stakeholders want to get a grip on the fruits of disruption, but this competition can produce internal strife in the most parochial battles for Uber's partners.

Uber's politics can produce odd bedfellows in a phenomenon that author Tom Slee terms a "marriage between commerce and cause."[48] Uber drew support from the New Jersey National Association for the Advancement of Colored People (NAACP) for its efforts to recruit three thousand new drivers from low-income, minority neighborhoods to drive for Uber.[49] The company received a Sponsor Award from the civil rights group in 2016.[50] In 2016, Uber also announced a hiring policy intended to support criminal justice reform in society: applicants with a history of certain nonviolent crimes would not be disqualified from driving for Uber.[51] The U.S. criminal justice system disproportionately arrests and incarcerates people of color, which creates cumulative racial disparities in access to employment, among other things.[52] While reducing barriers to employment is a noble civil rights goal, this effort also services another of Uber's business practices: when Uber first arrives in a city, rates are higher and drivers are often happier. Then, it floods the market with new drivers, sometimes by widening eligibility criteria (such as by extending the range of cars drivers can use), and often lowers the rates at which drivers earn their income. By creating a job for everyone, Uber can undermine the interests of dedicated full-timers. In effect, one civil rights cause—equality of access—is pitted against another cause: job security. The sheen of civil-society partnerships gives Uber cover for practices that negatively affect drivers in other arenas.

There are many examples, even in very recent history, where a coalition of civil rights activists finds common ground. In March 2017, for example, faith and civil rights communities joined labor advocates to show support for workers at a Nissan plant in Canton, Mississippi, the majority of whom were African American.[53] They carried signs with slogans like "Labor rights are civil rights" to demonstrate for safer working conditions, to protest intimidation tactics used against union organizers, and to push for a reduction in the use of permatemps (who qualify for inferior benefits compared to regular employees). The multiplying numbers who hold a stake in Uber's future can create paradoxical clashes between civil rights and labor rights efforts when they might otherwise be aligned, because organization in favor of or in resistance to Uber is not uniform.

The specter of managing labor's economic relations along racial lines evokes other social struggles in American history. For example, historian Nancy MacLean reminds us that at the turn of the nineteenth century, a battle brewed in Tennessee between free miners and employers who (in collusion with the state) were keeping wages low by renting cheap convict labor. "The widely reviled system, so redolent of slavery, created a perverse incentive to lock men up for petty offenses so the state could rent them out to coal companies as dirt-cheap labor to take the jobs of free miners, who had organized the United Mine Workers of America to demand living wages and decent treatment."[54] In today's climate, Uber's stance against a heavy-handed criminal justice system—which disproportionately affects people of color—is laudable, but it smacks of civil rights theater for well-managed race relations.

This strategy works: a loose "partnership" is a feature of the company's expansion of its brand across 630 cities globally by July 2017. Partners are useful allies in this effort, but their common bond is predicated on their fairly mercenary agendas that converge on higher-order articles of ideology, politics, or causes. Uber partners with drivers, groups, campaigns, universities, cities, politicians, and governments in an effort to build a socially desirable enterprise, a technique it may have learned from Google's example. When Uber initiated a self-driving-car research unit in Toronto in 2017, it promoted "Toronto" as its partner, even though no representative of the city had actively "partnered" with Uber in any official capacity.[55] That is a bit like booking your vacation in Israel with the declaration that you've found a potential partner for peace in the Middle East. The only connection Uber appeared to have to Toronto was that Raquel Urtasun, a University of Toronto computer science professor, had joined Uber's research efforts. Uber is relentlessly social like that, but it has created legitimate partnerships with cities in other capacities. The cities of Innisfil, Ontario, and Altamonte Springs, Florida, both agreed to subsidize Uber's services as a substitute for expanding public transit options.[56] When cities advocate reduced public services in favor of private options, the results are not always spectacular. Consider the relationship between cities and the National Football League: cities invest huge sums in building sports stadiums for teams and give the league's operations huge tax breaks, but sometimes the NFL pulls out later on, leaving behind empty stadiums and cities holding empty promises about the business revenues that football traffic would generate for them.[57] For cities, these alliances can be a poor return on their investment of tax dollars.[58] At times, Uber's enterprising efforts at forming alliances feel like emotional ransom, a delicate form of insincerity that becomes part of its hustle.

Because digital culture is a web of overlapping interests, Uber's interactions with one ally can produce a domino effect, with consequences for all of its other stakeholders. Furthermore, the company's self-conscious branding with a multitude of partners and causes, from the sharing economy to the NAACP, is part of what opens it up to so much criticism regarding the authenticity of its self-promotion.[59] Shortly before New Year's in 2014, a holiday infamous for alcohol consumption, Uber announced, "We're partnering with Mothers Against Drunk Driving (MADD) and asking everyone to pledge not to drive drunk."[60] And this news isn't just a public talking point. In the Uber passenger app, a passenger might find a plug for MADD Canada beneath his destination details, with features like: "During a cold night in Toronto, Shelly shares her story with her riders about the consequences of impaired driving and how her life was changed forever."[61]

Uber and Lyft both joined the cause against drunk driving, marketing their services as a hedge against death. And yet, New Year's Eve is also a huge moneymaking event. Drivers are swarmed with notices alerting them to high demand, though some cry foul when "the biggest demand of the year" doesn't result in the predicted pay premiums. As noted earlier, on some such occasions driver supply seems to have been sufficient to meet passenger demand and didn't result in surge-pricing premiums. Additionally, many municipalities already offer or support designated-driver services, some of which are free, to ward off drunk driving on key holidays.[62] The lure of false promises of wage incentives leaves some drivers feeling jaded, but the cognitive framing of Uber as a substitute for drunk driving is powerful. During my interview with Karen, who drives for Uber in New Orleans, she recalled a time when she was pulled over:

> I had four young boys in my car at a D.U.I. checkpoint. I have an Uber sign that I usually have on top of the car, but the cop didn't see it. He pulled me over and was, like, "Please step out of the car," so I started getting out. As I was getting out, he looked in and saw my passengers, and he said, "Where's your sticker?" I pointed it out, and he says, "Okay, go ahead, get out of here." He didn't check to see if I was drunk or nothing. I was sober, of course, but Uber got me out of being stopped at the checkpoint.

Karen is a white woman with grown adult children. The contrast between her and her passengers might have helped prove that she was, in fact, working. "I just thought it was funny that the cops recognized by my passengers that I was an Uber driver. It was four Asian boys that were, like, college students," she explains, before joking, "You know, that's my boyfriend, ha. That was funny." But, she adds, she's heard stories of Uber drivers driving drunk, and she doesn't think the police should place trust in a brand alone. (One driver I met in Los Angeles suggested that some people who intend to drive drunk purposefully add an Uber or Lyft sign to their vehicle so that they don't get stopped, though I don't know of specific instances where this has occurred.)[63]

The effects of such messy partnerships have consequences for drivers. Because Uber is always in the press, its drivers command a great deal more attention for their working conditions than their taxi industry competitors do. Moreover, drivers learn how to make sense of their jobs partly through Uber's media narrative. One Uber driver, commenting on a near-accident she was in, posted in a forum, "The crazy drunk that almost killed me was an Uber driver. WTF?!!! We are supposed to keep people safe, not contribute to the problem." Drivers in forums are avid consumers of media messages about the company and the ridehail business that affect drivers across regions. Derek, a driver in Colorado Springs, posted a story from San Diego, California, titled "Combative Uber Driver Accused of DUI Crash." Derek introduced the posting by saying, "Another driver making us look bad." Uber optimizes its presence through regular displays of prominent partnerships, but it also risks losing control of the narrative it shapes.

NOT EVERYONE DANCES TO UBER'S TUNE

As a company, Uber has put forth many of the same arguments that Internet giants make about their own services. In December 2017, the European Union Court of Justice dealt a serious blow to the power of that rhetoric when it ruled that Uber is a cab company, not a technology company.[64] For perspective, there is no equivalent ruling in the United States that undermines Uber's "we're a technology company" spin.

Not all groups that Uber works to conscript are equally cooperative. The United Nations women's group cut off their partnership with Uber shortly after banding together in order to create 1 million jobs for women by 2020, after the UN realized that Uber is associated with undermining labor protections and hurting marginalized workers.[65] Additionally, in 2017, a former Uber engineer, Susan Fowler, penned a firsthand account of the sexual harassment she experienced while she worked at Uber's corporate office, which sparked a much larger cultural discussion of the sexual harassment in Silicon Valley. She writes,

> On my first official day rotating on the team, my new manager sent me a string of messages over company chat. He was in an open relationship, he said, and his girlfriend was having an easy time finding new partners but he wasn't. He was trying to stay out of trouble at work, he said, but he couldn't help getting in trouble, because he was looking for women to have sex with. It was clear that he was trying to get me to have sex with him, and it was so clearly out of line that I immediately took screenshots of these chat messages and reported him to HR.[66]

She goes on to report that after she reported him to HR, the company protected her harasser because he was a "high performer," and that HR did the same to other women who brought allegations. She outlines the corporate culture that contributed to harassment, including the *Game of Thrones*–style politics among upper management: "It seemed like every manager was fighting their peers and attempting to undermine their direct supervisor so that they could have their direct supervisor's job." Furthermore, she observes, "we all lived under fear that our teams would be dissolved, there would be another re-org, and we'd have to start on yet another new project with an impossible deadline. It was an organization in complete, unrelenting chaos."[67] Ultimately, the fallout from this controversy culminated in the departure of Uber's CEO, Travis Kalanick, in June 2017.[68]

In the wake of these events, Uber endeavored to ally with the cause of "women who code" by pledging a $1.2 million donation to the nonprofit organization Girls Who Code,[69] but not all of its potential allies were receptive to its overtures. Girls Develop It, a nonprofit organization that offers education in software development to adult women, announced in August 2017 that it had turned down much-needed funding that Uber had offered. Corinne Warnshuis, executive director of Girls Develop It, explained it in a tweetstorm:

> FWIW [for what it's worth]: re Uber's GWC [Girls Who Code] donation. We've turned down $$ (that we could really use) because we didn't want to clean up a bad tech co's brand. We don't want to have our name & brand associated w/ your clean-up campaign. We're here for women, not the tech industry. On one hand, it's like "Wow, a lot of good will come from a million dollars!" OTOH [on the other hand], it's just a drop in the bucket, a marketing line item.

Warnshuis continued tweeting about the connection she saw between the stakeholders that her organization represents (women who code) and what it means to ally with Uber, adding, "I'm not going to promote working w/ or at a place like Uber (!?!) What's the point of offering women avenues to learn web/software skills ... if we're going to then lead them astray by recommending they work at a company that actively harms them? That's the worst outcome." At that point, Kimberly Bryant, founder of Black Girls Code, chimed in with the information that they similarly turned down Uber's offered donation (though it was a fraction of what GWC was offered).[70] The causes tied to Uber will continue to fight for space whether or not the company is faithful to its alliances.

Uber inspires a mix of disgust and appreciation for its "take no prisoners" attitude. People admire Uber the same way that they venerate fighters who exhibit their toughness through violent exploits.[71] Unroll.Me, a service that unsubscribes people from emails, became the center of a storm when it was revealed that Uber purchased data from the service, on Lyft, its competitor, to gauge how Lyft's business was faring. This incident articulates how Uber evokes both disgust and admiration for the sheer boldness and cleverness of its daring feats. Responding to the controversy, Perri Chase, a founder of Unroll.Me, said:

> Travis Kalanick is out of control and no one can stop him. No one except a board who refuses to hold him accountable for his disgusting behavior. Yeah. As a woman I think he is disgusting. As a founder, the truth is I'm like DAMN. That guy is willing to do whatever it takes and I have a mild amount of envy that I'm not a shittier human willing to go to those lengths to be successful. *(Oh and since this has been misinterpreted so many times in comments— let me lay this out for you.* I AM NOT WILLING TO BE A SHITTY HUMAN TO BE SUCCESSFUL. *That is what that means.)*[72]

Uber's adverse exposure in the media displays a small triumph of information over the power of a $68–70 billion behemoth with a reputation for lawlessness. This exposure is magnified by Uber's efforts to participate in politics at a national level. Kalanick became an early member of President Donald Trump's technological advisory council, a move widely derided by anti-Trump liberals. Trump used the vital, embryonic stage of his presidency to impose a travel ban on Muslims and refugees. In reaction, two hundred thousand Uber users deleted their accounts in a #DeleteUber protest against the company's alliance with a man who contradicted their values.[73] Uber banked on irate consumer-citizens to fight its battles with Mayor de Blasio of New York City and with cities across America, but consumers can also turn against the company when Uber undermines their politics on another front.

The #DeleteUber protest was a momentous response to a specific instance of Uber's behavior, but it tapped into a greater agitation in the air. The 2016 U.S. presidential election made it clearer than ever that Americans live in a divided country. On January 28, 2017, the powerful New York City Taxi Alliance—the majority of whose members are immigrants, many of them from South Asian countries—had called a strike at the John F. Kennedy International Airport to protest President Trump's travel ban. Uber's city manager decided to turn off surge pricing during the strike, though not necessarily in response to the strike.

Quartz reporter Alison Griswold suggests that Uber's actions were responsive to announcements by the Port Authority about airport safety concerns as protestors swarmed.[74] Uber's suspension of surge pricing, however, was widely panned as a form of strikebreaking against taxi drivers. Uber carried such a reputational debt that it was an easy mark for an outraged consumer base with an appetite for political action and a willingness to believe bad things about Uber. Deleting an app is a low-barrier action. Only a sliver of the same pointed protest was directed at Lyft, Uber's main competitor, even though its primary investor, Peter Thiel, was the number one technology-industry booster for then-presidential candidate Donald Trump. Kalanick, under pressure created by consumer upheaval, left the advisory council. In a climate of political discontent, Uber is often treated as a scapegoat for larger frustrations on the political scene. A senior employee at Uber opined to me that all the liberal indignation directed against Uber has to do with the close association between its founder and President Trump as a result of Kalanick joining that council. Uber's cultural impact on society stems partly from its outsized visibility in the press. The high-conflict relationship between Uber and its stakeholders, however, also shows us just how far we've come from the sharing-economy promise of cooperation between trusted strangers.

After the ruckus, Uber subsequently offered immigration support for drivers stranded abroad by the presidential travel ban who were no longer able to earn a living. It was clear to many drivers that this was a political gesture aimed at garnering support from Uber's consumer base. The responses from drivers that I saw were more muted: they grumbled that Uber would make large gestures for, say, five hypothetical Yemeni drivers, but they couldn't even add a tip button for drivers in the United States.

Playing numerous stakeholders, Uber trivializes driver concerns until it is prudent to address them as part of a larger instrumental threat to the corporate social order. At certain key moments, though, it has felt as if drivers are at Standing Rock, a major site of protest against a pipeline project in North Dakota that, as author Sherman Alexie described, brought a rare contingent of multiple native tribes, veterans, environmentalists, and others together.[75] #DeleteUber had a similar energy signature, suddenly the center of a fashionable cause. When it is cool to condemn Uber, drivers find themselves unexpectedly flush with allies, including consumers, labor advocates, and business school professors. Sociologists nodded somberly at their precarity, while slacktivists (or clicktivists) online lobbed a steady stream of criticisms at Uber for practices that some perceive as exploitative. For a brief time, the fate of drivers was of unusually deep concern to Uber's users and stakeholders.

The backlash to Uber's practices has been immense yet hollow. I speculate that many must have furtively re-downloaded Uber as the company promised change, though #DeleteUber reputedly spurred growth for Lyft, as users downloaded an alternative. Despite the ongoing unrest, Uber hit a milestone of 5 billion rides by late June 2017, a mere five to six months after the travel ban episode. When a renewed travel ban was produced that would effectively discriminate against Muslims, the protests did not recur. Amid all the ups and downs, it's easy to forget that Uber is basically a high-profile taxi company with Napoleonic ambitions and the reputation of expired mackerel. Meanwhile, drivers repeatedly meet with the pain of realizing that their frustrations don't merit much more than auto-replies from Uber Support, while the company amasses a global following. Far removed from the company's central operations, and left with little support, it's easy for drivers to feel they have been left behind by Uber. Still, Uber breeds possibility, as well as uncertainty, a sentiment that becomes quickly apparent among taxi drivers who jump the fence to drive for Uber instead.

WHEN UBER'S HOUSE OF CARDS BEGAN TO COLLAPSE

By 2016, Uber had been massively exposed by a torrent of bad press. Later that year, the company was accused of stealing Google's intellectual property regarding its self-driving car. In early 2017, it hired a former attorney general of the United States, Eric Holder, to lead an independent investigation into its corporate culture following allegations by a former employee that its toxic culture permitted sexual harassment to flourish at work. Uber has become a permanent media beat: it's rare for more than a few days to go by without news of its latest developments. The sheer number of self-revelatory scandals overwhelms Uber coverage, each reduced to a line or a paragraph in a roundup piece instead of a full story. The cultural and business practices at Uber are crucified in the court of public opinion, but the persistent poking and prodding at one living voodoo doll in the press is a striking phenomenon. It speaks to a cultural desire to purge *something* unsettling and powerful from our midst.

In the wake of Uber's many scandals, crestfallen tech and business optimists have moved from rapturous approval of Uber's rise, to ponderous self-reflection on the wildfires of scandal tearing through its executive core. Some have proposed that Uber's business model is broken. Benjamin G. Edelman, a law professor at Harvard, penned an op-ed for the *Harvard Business Review*, commenting on Uber's toxic leadership: "Uber Can't Be Fixed—It's Time for Regulators to Shut It Down." In it he opines, "Uber's business model is predicated on lawbreaking. And having grown through intentional illegality, Uber can't easily pivot toward following the rules."[76]

While Uber fights with Google over the patents to self-driving-car technology that are up in the air, drivers are in the trenches eking out wins, such as bathrooms at John F. Kennedy International Airport in the cell phone parking lots where they wait for ride requests.[77] They had been fighting for port-a-potties for months, revealing the starker inequalities at work, while tech pugilists with high-powered lawyers sought domination over the future of driving. Both of these items made it to the front page of the *New York Times* around the same time, because Uber is a symbol for all the ways that technology shapes power.

By the summer of 2017, Uber was blighted by a rush of scandals that built on the previous three years of conflict it had borne, and which revealed a darker side to its technological promise to society. Wave after wave of stories hit the front pages of the *New York Times*. Uber was accused of owing drivers potentially hundreds of millions as a result of wage theft,[78] and it reportedly facilitated subprime, predatory lease terms for drivers it recruited.[79] Moreover, Uber drivers in the United States didn't always earn enough to ward off homelessness,[80] and some Uber drivers were setting up camp in parking lots because they migrated in for their shifts and were unable to go home before getting some sleep.[81] Female drivers were subject to sexual harassment and assault, and Uber was said to have offered them no meaningful recourse.[82] And reportedly, in Singapore, Uber knowingly leased cars with faulty parts to Uber drivers through third parties—the cars were liable to burst into flames.[83]

As critiques mounted, the sharing economy crystallized long-standing concerns over the eroding political and economic power of labor while invigorating enduring debates over the future of work. By the end of 2017, driver pay had fallen precipitously. In internal company documents, Uber quietly cited Lyft and McDonald's as its primary competition for recruiting drivers.[84] The fight over Uber became a proxy for larger ideological battles between pro- and antiregulatory lobbies, and between sharing and taking and social inequality.

Two trips to Salt Lake City, Utah, remind me that Uber isn't a centrifugal political force for everyone in Uberland. Ted is an Uber and Lyft driver whose license plate on his car doesn't match the identification I have for his car in the passenger app. I double-check his driver app to ensure I'm the correct passenger before we depart. "Why are you visiting? Are you Mormon?" he asks, before launching into a tirade of conspiracy theories about black supremacy, Black Lives Matter riots, and illegal aliens, whom he asserts comprise 90 percent of the employees in factories. With a practiced mental calm, I gently meet his provocations with light, curious inquiries and answer questions he has about socialized medicine in Canada. Ted generously concedes it must work better in its Canadian form, though he's aggressively derisive of Obamacare. He also adds that he's almost Jewish, though he hasn't brought himself to fully convert yet, before turning the subject to government efforts to put gluten in bananas (even though they are naturally gluten-free). Driving is a full-time job for Ted while he goes to school to study computer science, though he's struggling to meet his rising health-care costs, between the cost of school and his driver earnings. Notably, Uber is not a proxy for any of his varied concerns.

A year later, I visit Salt Lake City again and hail a ride while I wait at the front entrance to a building that is closed for seasonal activities. Despite the empty lot, the driver hesitates to pull up to the entrance because a sign advises drivers that the entrance throughway is for specific vehicles only. Her respect for the rules sticks out in my mind when she starts to speak vociferously about her support for the National Rifle Association, and how she would fight the government if they ever came for her guns. Her views echo a popular position in the gun culture debates that are central to American politics in the United States. While cultural polarization characterizes the United States more broadly at this time, Uber can be simultaneously in the foreground of those conflicts in some cities, like New York, while it remains in the backdrop elsewhere.

Meanwhile, in Silicon Valley, an exodus of C-level executives left a power vacuum at Uber, and former Uber employees were asked in interviews by future employers to explain why they should not be regarded as assholes.[85] Uber was widely reputed to be a blemish on their records, according to HR insiders in Silicon Valley.

Uber continues to control the narrative of what technology will do for society in the future, in part because of the company's strategic public relations efforts. Uber usually distracts the media and society with shiny future technology after a cluster of scandals. In the 2017 spring roundup of Uber's failings, including the sexual harassment scandals[86] that culminated in the departure of Travis Kalanick,[87] the company selected Dallas and Dubai as the cities where it planned to launch flying cars in 2020.[88] Just a few months after Susan Fowler's sexual harassment allegations, lawmakers from the Congressional Black

Caucus stepped forward to make the case for African American leadership in Uber's future.[89] The earnest hopes of select black lawmakers for technological inclusion in what was quickly becoming a vortex of scandal made sense to me only after I took a moment to think about what Uber represents for the future. A wide spectrum of stakeholders are invested in Uber because it spins in so many different directions and is a force to be reckoned with. Perhaps Uber's creative destruction will unlock some breakthrough in social inclusion in the future of technology. That glint of possibility is how Uber continues to attract new allies. At a watershed moment between technology and society, civic society leaders who scaled the ladders of opportunity in the Old World still want a piece of the pie. There are some who won't be thwarted by scandals.

CONCLUSION

The New Age of Uber—How Technology
Consumption Rewrote the Rules of Work

Cole is a part-time Uber driver in Atlanta. On his first week on the job, he finds himself driving a man who has clearly had too many drinks.[1] The passenger, a new arrival to the city, wants to know what to do and where to go, so Cole informs him of several tourist destinations. "Out of nowhere," Cole recounts, "he yells at the top of his lungs and slams his hands on my dashboard. 'Dude, shut the F up. Seriously, just shut the F up or I'm going to have to hurt you.'" Stunned at the sudden outburst, Cole finds his bearings and quietly adjusts his hands on the wheel, careful to keep them loose in case he needs to ward off his aggressive passenger. They ride on in silence. A little while later, Cole's passenger asks if he can smoke in the car. Hoping to appease him, Cole pulls over, so the stench doesn't ruin his car interior—and possibly land him in trouble with a future ride. Each of them smokes a cigarette standing at opposite ends of the car. When they arrive at their destination, Cole's passenger invites him inside to smoke marijuana, and after he declines, suggests another cigarette instead. Feeling agitated and eager to keep the peace, Cole doesn't feel he can easily get out of this one.

"I didn't know the Uber guidelines then," says Cole. Company rules advise that riders who behave disrespectfully can lose access to the Uber platform. But even knowing the guidelines isn't enough to negotiate all the exigencies of a ridehailing job. "If I knew then what I know now, the second he got out of the car I would have driven off. But I didn't know that. I didn't know the kinds of repercussions at the time, having been on it only for a week." His passenger asked for a hug before Cole left, and it lasted too long. Drawing on the customer service skills he had honed at his primary job, Cole brought his hand in front of his chest and gently broke the embrace.

Nearly a year after that first harrowing incident, Cole still drives for Uber, part time. But he also wears another hat: he's a forum administrator, one of many across the globe who put in countless hours managing unofficial online communities where drivers who work for Uber, Lyft, and other ridehail services share advice and warnings, answer questions, and provide a rare sense of camaraderie. Another driver, Doberman, who is also an administrator of a forum group for Uber and Lyft drivers, in Louisiana, says about his own group, "I didn't create the group to learn something from somebody, but to get together with some people." When I interviewed him, he emphasized that he's trying to foster an environment where drivers can coach each other. "I want caring and more sharing when someone has a problem, not just to look over it." Ridehail drivers at Uber and elsewhere have no way to speak with one another through the app. Instead, the forums—along with journalism, social media, and in-person conversations—are providing a vital source of information for workers trying to navigate a new set of labor practices.

Drivers enjoy the formal freedom to log in or log out of work when they want, but that freedom is constrained in practice. As drivers do their work, they must continually deal with Uber's shifting pay rates, experimental policies, and incentives. An employment relationship like this, which evolves with iterative features, produces instability for drivers as workers, not just as users. Technology companies create products that shape the user's experience of their services; but when the user is a *worker*, these experiments change the nature of work, with mixed effects. Nonetheless, Uber's drivers continue to reap benefits, from the scheduling flexibility to the social connections they make with passengers.

As legal scholar V. B. Duval said to me about the growth of insecure work (particularly with regard to the deregulation of the taxi industry), "The good things about this work don't necessarily go away even if you no longer have benefits or security. The affective benefits, like the community you build with other drivers during down periods, continue."[2]

Nevertheless, some of the drawbacks of algorithmic management center on information scarcity, rather than on discussions of employment benefits. Drivers don't have an employee handbook when they start out: instead, they learn what the rules are over time through hundreds of text messages, emails, and in-app notifications. To manage the cognitive load of rapidly shifting terms and conditions in their employment, some drivers turn to information-sharing forums online. On these driver-led forums—on Facebook, on message boards, and on chat apps like WhatsApp, Zello, and WeChat—drivers are forging their own informal information networks, outside the algorithmically proscriptive realm of the ridehail apps. Drivers are always playing catch-up to Uber's iterations. Uber may be changing the rules of work, but thanks to digital communications, drivers, too, are creating a workplace culture. These centers of community create an institutional memory that persists even when Uber's practices change. What remains to be seen is how these drivers and their new workplace practices will influence broader culture—including other jobs and other technology companies—because Uber, as the cultural icon of the New Economy, has already left an indelible mark on far more than ridehailing.

HOW DRIVERS ROLL IN A NEW WORLD OF WORK

Ridehail drivers are among those in the New Economy adapting to working for a faceless boss. In our early research, my colleague Luke Stark and I found that an algorithmic manager directs how Uber drivers behave and when and where they work, using responsive incentives and penalties that affect their pay. This finding held true even years later as I continued my research. As Ricardo, a New York City driver who works for

Uber and other ridehail companies, puts it, "You don't have a boss over your head—you have a phone over your head."[3] While automated feedback may be effective for standardizing how hundreds of thousands of drivers behave, it can't address all the possible variables that drivers like Cole and Doberman face—everything from pay inequities to safety threats. For many drivers, learning the basics of driving for Uber is only a fraction of the knowledge work they do on online driver forums. When Uber was quietly testing out its new policy of up-front pricing in 2017,[4] drivers learned of the scheme in part by comparing screenshots of their passengers' in-app receipts with their own wages, and then wrote about the difference in forums and in public blogs like *The Rideshare Guy*.[5] With app screenshots of their work proliferating across forums, driver-to-driver comparisons spread across a disaggregated workforce located in diverse cities, fueling a pervasive sense of unfairness: the group dynamics of online forums derive from a common sense of the inequities that affect all drivers. At an individual level, some of the Uber and Lyft drivers I interviewed shrugged off pay discrepancies, while others were disturbed by them. (The combination of tipping and up-front pricing can also produce surprising benefits to drivers. For example, when Uber ran A/B experiments with the tipping function, they allowed some passengers to tip based on a percentage, while others could add only a limited dollar amount. In the resulting discussions in forums, some drivers posted screenshots of their pay stubs to illustrate that although they earned a lower fare than the amount that the passenger was charged through up-front pricing, they still did all right. Because a tip based on a percentage of what the passenger paid would be higher than if passengers tipped on the fare that the driver earned, drivers speculated that there was a hidden benefit to up-front pricing in the tips department.) Comparisons between drivers can emerge closer to home, too.[6] Cole's fiancée, for example, occasionally drives for Uber when she's not at school or at home with their newborn son. Cole told me that she receives better wage promotions than he does because her driving schedule is more sporadic. Although he is more reliable, he said the company seems to work harder to retain her, which strikes him as unfair.

Meeting in digital common spaces allows Uber drivers to trade notes in a job that is otherwise highly isolating. It's not clear how many drivers participate in driver-led web forums and chat rooms, but the forums I follow boast hundreds of thousands of members and serve local, national, and international regions (though there's no guarantee that all members are, in fact, humans or drivers). Many of the forums have developed membership requirements and gatekeeping processes over time, meaning they technically aren't open to the public. Often, drivers work for both Uber and Lyft, and even when drivers start Uber-focused forums, these quickly expand to include members who work for multiple employers. Drivers I spoke with in person in 2017 were often familiar with the online forums. And forums can shape the workplaces even of drivers who have never used them: online driver discussions influence how the media report on their work, and this offers more visibility and transparency to drivers. For instance, in July 2017, the *New York Times* found evidence that Uber had deducted hundreds of millions of dollars inappropriately from drivers' paychecks through faulty tax calculations.[7] Meanwhile, the New York–based Independent Drivers Guild reported that Lyft was engaging in a similar practice.[8] As these reports circulated among drivers both inside and outside of forums, they validated a much longer institutional memory of pay frustration.

Although they often surface drivers' concerns about ridehail work for a wider public, forums are primarily sites of communication for routine workplace matters. For example, one common piece of advice I have found in driver forums is that drivers should refrain from reporting to Uber or Lyft when they have a fender bender or any light vehicle incident, like a scratch: drivers risk deactivation if they do. And not all forum discussions center on challenges; many of them are positive, regarding appreciation for high ratings, complimentary passenger feedback, profitable trips, and the occasional on-the-job humor. Still, rate cuts, commission hikes, and pay inequities often blend together on forums, creating a sustained current of resentment. When a driver sees that what happens to him is happening to other people too, he gains a wider perspective on his workplace environment. For some, these independent networks can help fill the information gap that characterizes disaggregated work on platforms.

Drivers also band together on forums and chat apps to protect themselves, not from ridehail platforms, but from local authorities. For example, in Montreal, where Uber drivers operated illegally before ridehail work became legal, drivers showed me the Zello chats they used to update each other on the whereabouts of the transportation police, or on hostile cab drivers in the legitimate workforce who had tried to intimidate or had even attacked them. Drivers are on the lookout for information to help them adjust to the changing conditions of their work. By filling in gaps neglected by the platform economy, these informal driver networks help reduce that instability. As drivers like those in Quebec band together to manage some of the risks associated with their employment, they are also, in effect, helping their employers maintain the practices that produce the risks in the first place.

HOW UBER CHANGED US ALL

Driver forums provide one illustration of how Uber pulls together two of the most significant social trends of our day: the growth of contingent labor and the primacy of digital communications networks in society. Employers are distancing themselves from workers, such as through subcontracting arrangements, and Uber is no exception, classifying its drivers as independent contractors, treating them like low-value consumers, and managing them through algorithms. As the company builds off of labor trends by scaling opportunities for work among a disaggregated workforce, algorithms enact the rules that Uber sets. Algorithms manage users on consumer-facing technology platforms like Facebook and Google. Distanced from their employers, drivers turn to digital culture to crowdsource information that they don't get directly from their algorithmic bosses. When employers disavow responsibility for workers, they open up a gap in workplace culture.

Meanwhile, the Internet and digital culture have opened up a second wave of opportunities for workers, and others, to network their resistance. This doesn't prevent exploitation, and it isn't foolproof. In a job where the conditions of work are subject to frequent changes, partial information—about a discrete experiment, an emergent pricing policy, or a test feature—can spread quickly. If misinformation is spread by the same channels, the credibility of driver discourse might be jeopardized. These dynamics, from algorithmic management to networked resistance, illustrate that Uber makes more than a splash in society. The company creates an infinite series of ripple effects in every place it lands.

Beyond Uber's practices or its discrete impacts, a theme that emerges over and over again throughout Uberland is how Uber uses the language of technology to disrupt the role of identity. Uber self-identifies as a technology company, not a transportation company, and it uses that distinction to justify why it does not have to comply with the Americans with Disabilities Act and provide wheelchair-accessible transit. Hundreds of thousands of workers find jobs on Uber's platform, but Uber distances itself from the role of employer. Uber bills drivers as free and independent entrepreneurs but, through automated, algorithmic managers, obscures the control it leverages over how drivers behave at work. Because technology is "connective," Uber identifies the work and services it provides as a type of sharing in the sharing economy, a message that effectively devalues and feminizes paid work. Issues like missing wages are attributed to technical language, such as "glitches." The market logic of price discrimination is reframed as an innovation of artificial intelligence. Over and over again, we see how the language of technology is used rhetorically to advance the argument that what we think is one thing is, in fact, another. Uberland is driven not just by the mechanics of technology but also by the substantive sway of technological persuasion in American culture.

The number of Uber drivers in the American workforce is small overall, but these drivers have come to represent the role of technology in popularizing and expanding a longer-term trend in the growth of contingent work. Two leading economists, Lawrence F. Katz and Alan B. Krueger, found that "workers who provide services through online intermediaries, such as Uber or TaskRabbit, accounted for 0.5 percent of all workers in 2015."[9] But Uber's impact on the culture of technology, business, and work is vastly larger than its workforce numbers suggest. Technology ideology is a powerful cultural instrument of Uber's success, no less than the mechanics of its operations. The popular culture of Silicon Valley technology in American society prepares us to accommodate Uber's technology model of employment. Uber's disproportionate impact on culture emerges through its ubiquitous presence as a service and as a fixture of media attention because it is a magnet for conflict. And the terms that Uber has set for its drivers shapes the terms on which we negotiate technology's role in the future of work.

Travis Kalanick, Uber's most prominent cofounder, has come to represent Silicon Valley warrior-kings. Despite Uber's status as a "decacorn" and its valuation of approximately $70 billion dollars, Kalanick finally resigned in June 2017 because endless scandals were jeopardizing the company's future. Sarah Lacy, longtime Silicon Valley journalist, observed in a keynote speech at Startup Fest in Montreal on July 14, 2017:

> Silicon Valley is a homegrown culture: whoever the highest-value company is, disproportionately impacts the entire culture of that era. Starting with Uber, the highest-valued company in Silicon Valley history from a pre-IPO standpoint, $70 billion—never seen anything to this level before. Total founder control. Founder finally gets ousted because of three years of scandal. Because the disruption and lawbreaking that got them so many billions of dollars, all of those valuations and magazine covers—it turned out they didn't know the difference between breaking taxi laws, breaking labor laws, stealing trade secrets. It was just a lawless organization.

Uber's aggressive disregard for proper adherence to normative restrictions on their behavior is part of the macho attitude of disruption that the sharing economy popularizes in American society.

Yet Uber's reputational roller coaster doesn't necessarily affect its larger legacy: the idea of Uber is important to how we imagine the desirability of technology in society. In its ascent to global heights, Uber has become a shibboleth for technology optimists. For many cities, having Uber is the mark of being on the cutting edge, or at least being part of the global technology-business marketplace. When Uber and Lyft turned swiftly on their heels and left Austin, Texas, in May 2016, in a show of protest against regulatory efforts to impose requirements on them (like data-sharing and fingerprint-based background checks for drivers), the moment was captioned in the press by disdainful headlines such as "By Losing Uber, Austin Is No Longer a Tech Capital."[10] In Vancouver, which has been the least-eager major city in Canada to accept sharing-economy companies,[11] worried University of British Columbia alum and community experts at the university participated in panels such as, in late November 2016, "Why Has Vancouver Been So Slow to Join the Sharing Economy?"[12]

The absence of Uber in metropolitan places is a wrinkle on those cities' reputations, a symbol that they lag behind their more forward peers. The use of Uber has become infrastructural in some cities, a default method of private transit for many. In May 2017, a Painesville, Ohio, municipal judge ordered convicted DUI offenders to download Uber and Lyft onto their phones as part of the conditions of their probation.[13] To consumers, the experience of traveling to an Uber-free zone can feel like culture shock, as disconcerting as when Americans and Canadians go to Europe and learn that they have to pay to use the toilet.

Uber is more than an app you download onto your phone: it changes the way we move around cities, like WhatsApp does in Brazil or Waze does in Israel. Turning off WhatsApp in Brazil would destabilize communications nationwide; likewise, when Waze erroneously advised drivers in Israel to avoid a major roadway, mad traffic jams ensued.[14] The idea of Uber and the logic of its business model have already surpassed Uber itself.

Both as workers and consumers, we have integrated the algorithms of Silicon Valley into our daily lives. The case of Uber shows us that technology has changed work in ways that are unexpected and potentially irreversible. The sharing economy popularized wider changes to work culture by conflating work with altruistic contributions, bringing into question the identity of workers and devaluing work itself. Meanwhile, Uber advanced its own vision of the legal status of its workers, emphasizing that they were closer to technology consumers than workers. This seemingly legalistic nuance is in reality a cultural sea change in how we categorize work.

Uber's employment model, driven by algorithmic practices, represents how technology is permanently altering not only how we define work but also how it is organized. I doubt that Uber set out to undo how work is defined. Rather, as it navigates the challenges to its business, Uber seems to sense the broader cultural undercurrents and know how to effectively mobilize them to defend its practices. The conflicts it raises along the way illustrate how we chafe against those practices, but ultimately, the success of Uber as an idea condones the practices that made it a billion-dollar, global reality. And regardless of what happens to Uber now, the changes are already here.

The conflicted relationship between Uber and its drivers is an example of how labor relations are being shaped in our new, digital age. The rise of algorithmic management of consumers is prominent across Silicon Valley's data-driven technologies. You can't go far in daily life without encountering these systems: GPS navigation apps, like Google Maps, generate route recommendations and crowdsource traffic routes, while Facebook relies on an engine of algorithms to curate the information we digest. We don't imagine Facebook or Google as part of the sharing economy, but Uberland brings to light the power that technology platforms have to disadvantage users even as platforms are shielded by the rhetoric of neutrality.

On the surface, the company's self-serving argument that its drivers are consumers of its technology, like passengers, appears to be just another play to escape regulation. After all, Uber has developed a reputation for changing course whenever the rules catch up with it. But upon closer examination, Uber does treat drivers both like consumers and like workers. By blurring these lines, Uber creates a legacy for how we all identify as workers or consumers. Uber benefits from this strategic ambiguity because it's hard to decide *which* rules apply to its model. If drivers are unpaid for work they perform, should they allege wage theft under labor law, or seek redress for unfair and deceptive practices under consumer protection law? Uber broke norms, not just laws, exposing the fragility of both. It remains an open question whether the new norms Uber ushers in are better or worse for labor and for consumers.

The impact of Uber is profound. Despite the scandals it weathers, and perhaps because of its sustained coverage in the media, Uber is objectified as the future of work in the popular imagination. At the same time, the story of Uber is just one example of how we are all being played by the technologies that have become commonplace, because, simply put, we want to use them.[15] With an unorthodox approach, Uber has changed the playing field in significant ways for a host of stakeholders—from drivers to passengers, from workers to consumers, from the technology industry to the taxi business, and from governments and regulators to civil rights groups. Yet perhaps more importantly, by working the rules of the system to its advantage, Uber used Silicon Valley algorithms to rewrite the rules of work.

METHODOLOGY

How I Studied Uber

My research methods stem from the fact that I'm a hybrid of a few different types of scholars—I'm a social scientific researcher, an academic author, and a journalistic writer and blogger. These identities and their different methods of uncovering and synthesizing knowledge shaped the way I pursued this research over the past four years, and the way I wrote the book. For this reason, my research methods relied on a number of different conventions and professional communities that I endeavor to explain here. While much of this book draws on the scholarship I have done in my capacity as a researcher and a multidisciplinary scholar, not all of it falls strictly under an academic mandate. The research I have done stems from two formal research projects,[1] one of which expanded into a research project that drew comparisons between ridehail drivers and care and cleaning workers. Each of these research projects began with its own set of starting assumptions and protocols, though the findings are blended together in this book. Some of the text of this book draws on the public-facing writing I have published over the years in the media, rather than in academic publications. Occasionally, I blog snippets of field notes, and sometimes I gather and report what I find in the course of my research from a journalistic perspective. I have also cross-published my findings in academic journals; as journalistic accounts; and in blogs, including Harry Campbell's *The Rideshare Guy* blog and my own *Uber Screeds* blog. These outlets also shaped what I explained to drivers about what I do. I would typically provide the context that my job is to study how technology affects work, and would also share that I primarily research Uber and ridesharing (a term more familiar to drivers than "ridehailing") from the drivers' perspectives, and that I publish my findings both in academic journals and in public-facing outlets, including media. After I started the process of writing a manuscript, I began adding, when I spoke to drivers, that I was also writing a book.

Within academia, I have used my ethnography as the basis of broader intellectual projects, such as collaborations with legal scholars and social scientists to explore questions related to subjects ranging from bias and discrimination to consumer protection. I mention their application as part of my methods because the collaborative, interdisciplinary conversations I had at different stages helped me process and analyze what I continued to observe in my qualitative research, as well as suggested what to look for as my research project evolved and continued. For example, I intermittently consulted with computer scientists, both regarding what was technically possible and about information security practices for conducting my research. In particular, the Labor Tech group run by Winifred Poster and the Privacy Law Scholars Conference are generative spaces for receiving invaluable feedback from engaged scholars. Throughout the course of this research, I've also benefited from conversations with leaders across many different communities: academic, policy, regulatory, and business. These conversations informed my analysis but should not be considered a part of my formal interviews. (They served as an important background as I refined and developed my ideas.)

Throughout my years in Uberland, I collected different types of data in different ways. At first, I learned primarily through driver forums online— where I still spend hours nearly every day: I actively read posts, and the minute-by-minute updates of forum culture are always in the background during the time I spend on the Internet. Against what I read in forums, I compared much of what I'd gathered in interviews with drivers across the United States and Canada, as well as in scattered interviews with other stakeholders, like chauffeur industry executives.

My research method is qualitative ethnography. As part of my formal (and cumulative) research studies, I made participant-observations with over four hundred drivers by riding as a passenger. One hundred twenty-five of the interviews I did with drivers animate this book; although the styles of these interviews varied, they were designed to be semistructured. As a researcher, I compensate subjects for their time with a nominal amount for their participation, and I reassured all drivers that I give everyone five stars. I conducted seventy-five formal interviews with drivers, interviewing them in their cars, by phone, and rarely, by instant messaging. When drivers agreed, these interviews were often recorded. Sometimes drivers agreed to be interviewed but declined to be recorded. In other cases, I conducted formal interviews without a recorder and relied on my notes and memory to paraphrase their accounts in this book. Many times, I'd hail a ride as a passenger and, early in the ride, ask the driver to do an interview with me; sometimes I'd conduct the interview from the front or backseat of the car, and other times I'd follow up at a later date. Some drivers declined to do interviews, at which point we may have ended the trip after reaching a prescribed destination, or we may have continued to chat. As in the case of my conversations with Uber executives, I don't consider these conversations interviews, and they served as background information that informed my understanding.

In addition to the formal interviews, I conducted fifty informal interviews and chats. In these instances, I rode as a passenger but announced that I was a researcher and often asked questions similar to those I asked in formal interviews. Throughout this book, I have quoted drivers from the full range of interviews, including what I jotted down in notes. These informal interviews tended to be much more conversational—rather than conducted in a more interrogative style—and involved a greater exchange of information between myself and the driver. For example, in some cases we compared notes on raising families. During other trips as a participant-observer, I asked lighter, less-structured questions, often involving jokes or driver-led prompts during the conversation. I also focused on observing how drivers worked and on their car environment, such as how they managed ride requests from multiple apps, like Uber and Lyft, often from multiple phones. I'd observe the ways drivers personalized their cars (or not), or the placement and number of charger cords, whether they provided snacks or beverages for passengers or even brown-bagged their own meals (which was rare), and whether there were photos, emblems (such as religious symbols), and so on, to help make up these unique workspaces. I'd watch for changes in body language during the interview, the attention paid to other drivers on the road, and how drivers oriented themselves to me as a passenger in the car during our chats. As a passenger across hundreds of trips, I found that my conversations with drivers could evolve into formal or informal interviews, but they could also be sites primarily of participant-observation. These rides might involve little to no conversation, or low to high engagement on a range of topics, such as on religion, family, real estate, guns, politics, health care, travel, or immigration. They do not necessarily focus on the Uber driver app, technology, or labor, but they usually involve a few questions that I might ask a driver I interview more formally, such as their motivations for driving or their views on Uber and Lyft generally. I still gather information on the driver experience through my observations and engagement as a passenger. The book draws on these trips as background, as well as on small anecdotes that drivers relayed during these trips. I did my best to preserve the integrity of what people told me, retaining their tone, speech patterns, accents, and grammar. In some cases, I've mentioned a driver's speaking style up front and avoided drawing attention to their irregularities of English, using the "[*sic*]" stylistic notation sparingly to preserve flow. Where a driver's mistakes might be misunderstood as typographical errors, I preserve their wording with a more liberal use of "[*sic*]." In all cases, my goal was to retain the accuracy of drivers' statements while making the book as readable as possible.

Throughout the course of my ethnography, undertaken within cities and on the Internet, I crossed more than twenty-five cities during my years on the road with drivers (primarily ridehail drivers but also some taxi drivers, particularly in pre-Uber cities). Because drivers often work in extended urban centers, for analytical purposes I treated regionally connected cities that drivers routinely traverse as "one city"—for example, the Dallas and Fort Worth area, New York City and the portion of New Jersey close to the city, the Boca Raton and Miami area, and Cambridge and adjoining Boston. These groupings reflect the way that I traveled through them: for example, Boston is a more dominant city, but Cambridge was more often my main base. Similarly, San Francisco and Palo Alto are interrelated, but I made a larger number of distinct observations on my trips within Palo Alto and within San Francisco than on my trips between the two cities, or between other nearby cities, such as San Jose and San Francisco. New York City was my main base for New York and New Jersey trips, but these states had different implications for drivers: drivers who were free to deliver passengers to New York from New Jersey were unable to pick up passengers for the return trip if they were not licensed to work in New York. However, New York drivers could deliver passengers to, say, Connecticut or New Jersey and pick up passengers on the return trip. But the rates for the return trip tended to be lower than the rates for trips that began in New York City. The field sites that are the subjects of deeper ethnographic and investigative analysis include Austin, Texas; Dallas and the Fort Worth area in Texas; Orlando, Florida; Cambridge and adjoining Boston, Massachusetts; San Francisco and Palo Alto, and Los Angeles, California; New York City and the New Jersey area close to the city; Salt Lake City, Utah; Atlanta, Georgia; New Orleans, Louisiana; Washington, DC; and Montreal in Canada.

Within that range, there were select cities I visited repeatedly, or for longer cumulative durations, from 2014 to 2018, including Montreal and New York, and my observations collected from those reflect a deep analysis. And while I did visit and observe drivers on trips in Los Angeles, the city is an exception among my fieldwork sites because my interviews with drivers and my understanding of their experiences came more from phone-based interviews while I was remotely located than from trips within the city. In the spirit of ethnography, I also had a handful, a few, or one-off rides in cities that I was traveling to or through, where I conducted additional interviews or made observations with drivers (this method is referred to as "flash ethnography"). These include Ann Arbor and the Detroit area in Michigan; Denver, Colorado; San Jose, California; Boca Raton and the Miami area in Florida; Juneau and Anchorage, Alaska; Seattle, Washington; Charleston, South Carolina; Bozeman, Montana; Winnipeg, Manitoba; Vancouver, British Columbia; and Toronto and Ottawa, Ontario. In addition, I conducted phone interviews with people both in cities where I have done physical fieldwork and in cities I have not visited, which include Savannah, Georgia; Baton Rouge, Louisiana; Houston, Texas; and Raleigh, North Carolina.

All driver names are anonymized throughout this book, other than those of drivers who gave me explicit, written consent to use their real names; and some details of driver experiences are altered to maintain drivers' anonymity. As detailed in the introduction of this book, I used a variety of accounts with different ridehail services. I used my name for some accounts and several aliases for other accounts, both with ridehail services and in online forums. Throughout the book, I have scrambled details of screenshots and driver experiences, such as dates and names, to protect driver anonymity, though I have made every effort to preserve the accuracy of their accounts. Three drivers whom I interviewed preferred to have their real names used: Leticia Alcala, Nicholas Stewart, and David Aguirre; I included their surnames in the book, in contrast to those of other drivers whom I interviewed. The surnames of more public figures, like bloggers, are also included in the text. In places where screenshots or images have been transcribed from publicly available forums, I have omitted links to their locations, such as on driver websites and public Facebook groups. Although these may be public postings, my prerogative as a researcher is to err on the side of protecting those who posted them from publicity.

The second major way I conducted research was through online driver forums, which are virtual field sites. Some of these are open to the public, some aren't. In the case of closed forums, which have gatekeeping functions, I sought permission to observe as a researcher. By the end of 2017, I was actively following forum groups, blogs, digital chats, and websites, which have a combined total of about three hundred thousand members. I observed some much more closely than others, though all of them inform how I understand driver networks online. Websites that host these forums include sites like Facebook. Facebook's algorithmic curation of news can amplify or obscure different parts of driver conversations, as well as highlight specific forums over others. For example, we might imagine that Facebook's newsfeed highlights more engaging posts, such as those that are more controversial, or it may highlight forum groups that I click through more often. Facebook's own algorithms have thus affected my observations of driver groups in ways that are not transparent to me.

The organization of these forums often evolves over time, and a public forum might later become closed, or private, usually with the intention of creating an environment for drivers only. In my applications to join new groups on sites like Facebook, in digital chats, and at Uber-dedicated websites or blogs where I located forum administrators, I announced who I was. This included my research intentions and often a link to my professional profile or to my website. I explained my goal in joining these forums, which was to observe driver activities and to occasionally seek out select drivers to interview. For this, I generally used profiles with code names and not my real name, so that another person or representatives of ridehail companies would not necessarily be able to identify me from the forum membership rolls. Earlier in my observations in forums, select administrators were curious to see artifacts of my research processes, such as consent forms, which I readily shared. I presume this vetting was partly to ensure I was not an Uber corporate spy, a concern that some drivers raised individually to me over the years. (I learned early on that my depth of knowledge of and profound interest in their work could raise red flags for drivers in person and online; it was much easier for me to show proof of my intentions after I had published work in media that I could share with them, or that explained some of my findings thus far.) Outside of hailing a ride, I also recruited drivers to my studies in online forums. In reaching out to select drivers, I announced who I was, my role as a researcher, and later in my studies, showed drivers articles I had authored.

It was extremely rare for me to participate actively in forums, such as through comments or posts; but in some cases, nominal participation was required in order to be able to message other member participants. There were also drivers whom I recruited for my studies after they got in touch with me on their own or through referrals. I also conducted formal interviews with two businessmen in the chauffeur industry so that I might learn about their perspectives on the advent of Uber and Lyft as part of my formal research. While much of my recruitment relied on my personal outreach to drivers, in some instances I received referrals from other drivers.

In my role as a researcher at the Data & Society Research Institute, I have received funding and generous support from Microsoft Research, Open Society Foundations, the John D. and Catherine T. MacArthur Foundation, and the Robert Wood Johnson Foundation.

Some of the text of this book comes from work previously published under my own name, such as blog posts and media articles, as well as from collaborative, interdisciplinary work with other scholars, including Dr. Luke Stark, Tim Hwang, Ryan Calo, Dr. Julia Ticona, and Alexandra Mateescu. The latter publications are reproduced in part and cited throughout the text of this book, with the permission of my coauthors.

RIDEHAILING BEYOND UBER

Meet Lyft, the Younger Twin

Uber may be the dominant player on the ridehail stage, but many Uber drivers work simultaneously for Lyft and other competitors. Lyft was founded in 2012 in the United States: by 2017, it had become available in forty states.[1] Lyft achieved an $11 billion valuation by the fall of 2017.[2] *Recode* reported that Second Measure, a research firm that tracks credit card purchases, determined that Lyft had 23.4 percent of the ridehail market share in the United States and Uber had 74.3 percent.[3] The corporate practices of Uber and Lyft in managing drivers aren't identical, but their similarities vastly outnumber their differences. They both track drivers' ride-acceptance and cancellation rates. Both dispatch fares through an automated system (Uber claims the nearest driver is dispatched, while Lyft claims the nearest driver is dispatched and determines how long a driver has been waiting for a dispatch). Both companies use a passenger-sourced rating system to evaluate drivers. And both companies permit drivers to rate passengers. After a Lyft driver or passenger rates the other with three or fewer stars, the two are not paired again; Uber does not have the same policy. Both use the threat of deactivation to penalize drivers for ignoring rules and norms of the system. Both rely on outsourced customer support to communicate with drivers, although Lyft also has a mentorship program in various cities. In this program mentors, who are usually drivers as well, provide help to new drivers. Both companies use premiums and pay incentives to encourage and attract drivers to their platforms, and both unilaterally set and change the rates at which drivers earn their income.

Finally, for users, both apps function in much the same way. In major markets, Uber and Lyft are both viable options: in San Francisco, for example, the two ridehail companies each make 170,000 trips per day, according to a report in June 2017—about twelve times the number of taxi trips made within that city.[4] In November 2016, Uber confirmed in a response to me that it had 600,000 "active" drivers, defined as drivers who had completed four or more trips in the previous month. Lyft claimed at the same time that it had 300,000 "active" drivers, but it refused to say how it defined *active*. Both companies continue to grow. In 2014, Uber had 160,000 drivers, and 400,000 by 2015. By November 2017,[5] it had 750,000 active drivers in the United States and about 50,000 active drivers in Canada. Still not defining *active*, Lyft says its active drivers increased to 700,000 by November 2017. Yet Uber and Lyft are so similar in the ways their drivers are dispatched, evaluated, and managed that drivers often treat them interchangeably, to the point where some get confused in describing their Uber or Lyft experiences. A driver might be frustrated at Uber for not respecting a rule set by Lyft, for example, but for the most part this ambiguity centers on issues of pay, safety, and policies. For example, both services use an algorithm to raise prices in times of high demand, but Uber calls this a "surge" while Lyft calls it "prime time." Even in an Uber-dominated ecosystem, Lyft is part of the equation; I even heard about it from drivers in Canada, where Lyft launched its first operations in Toronto at the end of 2017.

Among most drivers I meet in person, and the countless number I've observed in online forums, there is a near-universal consensus that Lyft treats its drivers better than Uber, such as through friendlier communications. But drivers get more business through Uber. Drivers cited Lyft's driver-friendly tip button as a stark contrast to Uber's policy of actively discouraging passengers from tipping. (Uber finally added a tip button in June 2017, after years of protests and feedback from drivers.) Some of the differences drivers describe are similarly reflected in corporate messaging. The first section of Lyft's homepage in February 2018 promotes three main points, including "HAPPY DRIVERS. HAPPY RIDERS."[6] This emphasizes the idea that happy drivers are an important part of the service Lyft delivers. The first section of Uber's homepage in February 2018 focuses more on passengers, with three slogans: "Easiest way around," "Anywhere, Anytime," and "Low-cost to luxury." Both companies include a link on the top right-hand side of the page allowing readers to sign up to be drivers.[7]

Drivers' primary point of contact at Uber is a group of email-based community support representatives; drivers describe Lyft's emails and messaging as more driver-friendly than Uber's. My focus has been on how drivers evaluate Uber's CSR's, though I see frustration across both companies with automated replies.

Ramon, whom I introduced earlier in this book, drives with both Uber and Lyft in Atlanta, Georgia. He told me about one of his most memorable incidents: while he was taking several passengers to their destination, another driver slipped over the lane divider and Ramon had to quickly switch lanes. His passengers, who were busy joking in the backseat, didn't notice what happened, except for the sudden lane shift. Ramon prided himself on being a proactive driver with a 360-degree view of what was happening in the street, but these particular passengers alleged that his driving was impaired. Uber took the passengers' word over his in the lane-changing incident, but when a passenger on Lyft accused him of impaired driving in a separate incident, Lyft accepted his explanation: he is a diabetic, and drinking would have landed him in the hospital. For competitors looking to improve on Uber's model, the key may be simply to treat drivers with greater consideration and respect for their side of the story.

Frank, an Uber and Lyft driver whom I interviewed in Dallas in 2016, assessed the differences between the two companies according to their passenger bases. He observed, "Uber passengers are a little more knowledgeable, a little more up-class, in my experience. Most of the people that call me on Lyft got kicked off of Uber, or their credit card got screwed up or something." While Frank's explanation of Lyft passengers is on the margins of what other drivers have said, it's not uncommon for drivers to describe Uber passengers as higher class, but also as stuck up, and to say they prefer Lyft because the passengers are more friendly or engaging. This distinction may originate with the different branding of the companies. Uber advertises itself as a chauffeur service with slogans like "Your private driver"; drivers say that Uber passengers sit in the backseat and stare at their phones. In contrast, Lyft advertises itself as "your friend with a car" and encourages drivers to fist-bump their passengers, who are welcome to sit in the front seat and chat with the driver. Lyft drivers reported higher rates of job satisfaction in a 2018 survey conducted by blogger Harry Campbell.[8] In interviews and observations, many drivers indicated that Lyft is superior because it has an in-app tipping function (which Uber took a long time to introduce), which made it a bit more expensive for passengers but more satisfying to drivers. Some suggested that Lyft is just more respectful and nuanced in its appreciation of drivers' concerns. Still, drivers indicate that they drive more for Uber than Lyft because they get more business through Uber.

"Uber is like Walmart, and Lyft is like Target" is how one driver in Salt Lake City succinctly summarized it. "You'd rather go to Target for a bit better quality, but Walmart is cheaper so you usually go there." Despite the different cultures of Uber and Lyft, most drivers describe the actual business practices of the two as interchangeable. However, the fact that Lyft gets *so* much less flak than Uber does from the popular press, consumers, and other stakeholders, despite the fact that both companies have similar employment practices (a signal of Uber's brackish reputation), suggests to me that the popular divide over these two companies emerges not from their employment practices but from Uber's highly visible conflicts. Uber is important not only as a company but also as a political scapegoat for unwashed feelings people have about technology and society.

In my travels, some regional differences have emerged over time in how drivers assess Uber and Lyft. In Salt Lake City, Lyft seems to offer enough work that drivers don't need to seek work from more than one company. When drivers choose to work for Lyft, it's not necessarily out of an antipathy they developed toward Uber. And in Atlanta, Nicholas Stewart told me he prefers to drive for Uber over Lyft because "they've been more loyal to me, so to speak." He went on to say, "I know a lot of the management team. And, when I need an issue solved, it's easier to get in touch with Uber than it is to get in touch with Lyft. They have more on-the-ground support than Lyft. That's been frustrating not only for me but a lot of other drivers as well."

NOTES

INTRODUCTION

1. An investigation by *Bloomberg* reporter Eric Newcomer found drivers setting up to sleep in parking lots all over the country. See Eric Newcomer and Olivia Zaleski, "When Their Shifts End, Uber Drivers Set Up Camp in Parking Lots across the U.S.," *Bloomberg Technology*, January 23, 2017, www .bloomberg.com/news/articles/2017-01-23/when-their-shifts-end-uber-drivers-set-up-camp-in-parking-lots-across-the-u-s.

2. Andrew Ross, *Nice Work If You Can Get It: Life and Labor in Precarious Times* (New York: New York University Press, 2009); Arne L. Kalleberg, "Precarious Work, Insecure Workers: Employment Relations in Transition," *American Sociological Review* 74, no. 1 (February 2009): 1–22.

3. This figure is specific to New York City, but it was circulated in the media to describe the benefits of this job more widely, beyond a city-specific focus.

4. Uber builds on long-standing trends in contingent work that affect both the taxi industry and other sectors more broadly, but it goes a step further. It reproduces these same patterns, with a technology-driven narrative.

5. V.B. Dubal, "The Drive to Precarity: A Political History of Work, Regulation, and Labor Advocacy in San Francisco's Taxi and Uber Economies," *Berkeley Journal of Employment and Labor Law* 38, no. 1 (February 21, 2017), https:// ssrn.com/abstract=2921486.

6. Researchers at Carnegie Mellon described this as algorithmic or data-driven management. See, e.g., Min Kyung Lee, Daniel Kusbit, Evan Metsky,

and Laura Dabbish, "Working with Machines: The Impact of Algorithmic and Data-Driven Management on Human Workers," in *Proceedings of the 33rd Annual ACM SIGCHI Conference, Seoul, South Korea, April 2015* (New York: ACM, 2015), 1603–1612, https://dl.acm.org/citation.cfm?id=2702548.

7. Uber Help, "Insurance," February 14, 2018, https://help.uber.com/h /a4afb2ed-75af-4db6–8fdb-dccecfcc3fd7?state=x31lXMTG_n8G9rQNXx_ 5L3qgzdIE8–7bHzhAoksAf1g%3D&_csid=KofAFMlupm3NY9go3SoD_A#_.

8. Alex Rosenblat and Luke Stark, "Algorithmic Labor and Information Asymmetries: A Case Study of Uber's Drivers," *International Journal of Communication* 10, no. 27 (2016), http://ijoc.org/index.php/ijoc/article/view/4892.

9. Douglas O'Connor, Thomas Colopy, Matthew Manahan, and Elie Gurfinkel v. Uber Technologies, Inc., August 16, 2013, http://uberlawsuit.com /Complaint.pdf.

10. The quote, by Robert Jon Hendricks, comes from Douglas O'Connor, Thomas Colopy, Matthew Manahan, and Elie Gurfinkel vs. Uber Technologies, Inc., no. C 13–3826 EMC, "Transcript of Proceedings," p. 17, U.S. District Court, Northern California: January 30, 2015, http://uberlawsuit.com/Uber%20-%20Transcript%20of%20hearing%20on%20summary%20judgment%20-%201–30–15.pdf.

11. Philip M. Napoli and Robyn Caplan, "Why Media Companies Insist They're Not Media Companies, Why They're Wrong, and Why It Matters," *First Monday* 22, no. 5 (May 2017), http://firstmonday.org/ojs/index.php/fm /article/view/7051/6124.

12. The quote, by Judge Edward M. Chen, comes from Douglas O'Connor et al., Plaintiffs v. Uber Technologies, Inc., et al., Defendants. No. C-13–3826 EMC, "Order Denying Defendant Uber Technologies, Inc.'s Motion for Summary Judgment," p. 10, U.S. District Court, Northern California, March 11, 2015, https://onlabor.org/wp-content/uploads/2015/05/uber-order.pdf.

13. Helen Christoph, "Judge Advances Men's ADA Complaint against Uber," *Courthouse News Service,* March 1, 2018, www.courthousenews.com /judge-advances-mens-ada-complaint-against-uber/.

14. Napster changed the trajectory of the music industry by allowing users to share files without paying for them. Facebook's social media platform spread news more quickly, but journalism lost control of its distribution. See, e.g., Emily Bell, "The End of the News as We Know It: How Facebook Swallowed Journalism," *Tow Center,* March 7, 2016, https://medium.com/tow-center /the-end-of-the-news-as-we-know-it-how-facebook-swallowed-journalism-60344fa50962.

15. Amy Webb, "The 'Uber for X' Fad Will Pass Because Only Uber Is Uber," *Wired,* December 9, 2016, www.wired.com/2016/12/uber-x-fad-will-pass-uber-uber/.

16. My first formal research project with media, culture, and communications scholar Luke Stark on Uber commenced in late December 2014, though we began doing background research in June 2014.

17. These are Austin, Texas; Dallas and the Ft. Worth area in Texas; Orlando, Florida; Cambridge and adjoining Boston, Massachusetts; San Francisco, Palo Alto, and Los Angeles, California; New York City and the New Jersey area close to the city; Salt Lake City, Utah; Atlanta, Georgia; New Orleans, Louisiana; Washington, DC; and Montreal, Quebec in Canada.

18. These are Ann Arbor and the Detroit area in Michigan; Denver, Colorado; San Jose, California; Boca Raton and the Miami area, in Florida; Juneau and Anchorage, Alaska; Seattle, Washington; Charleston, South Carolina; Bozeman, Montana; Winnipeg, Manitoba; Vancouver, British Columbia; and Toronto and Ottawa, Ontario. I have conducted phone interviews with people in cities I have done physical fieldwork in, as well as in cities I have not visited, which include: Savannah, Georgia; Baton Rouge, Louisiana; Houston, Texas; and Raleigh, North Carolina.

19. Global News Staff, "Uber Can Now Legally Operate in Quebec," *Global News,* October 22, 2016, http://globalnews.ca/news/3019867/uber-can-now-legally-operate-in-quebec/.

20. Julia Simon-Mischel, "Uber and Lyft: Where Are We Going?" (panel presentation, Continuing Legal Education for the Pennsylvania Bar Institute, November 28, 2017); Training Assocs. Corp. v. Unemployment Comp. Bd. of Review, 101 A.3d 1225, 2014 Pa. Commw. LEXIS 501 (Pa. Commw. Ct. 2014).

21. Thanks to Lisa Conrad for this insight, in an email, August 3, 2017. See, e.g., https://en.wikipedia.org/wiki/How_the_Other_Half_Lives.

22. Outside of Salt Lake City, the majority religion of Utah is Mormonism. See, e.g., Matt Canham, "Salt Lake County Is Becoming Less Mormon—Utah County Is Headed in the Other Direction," *Salt Lake Tribune,* July 16, 2017, http://archive.sltrib.com/article.php?id=5403049&itype=CMSID.

23. U.S. Federal Trade Commission, "Uber Settles FTC Allegations That It Made Deceptive Privacy and Data Security Claims," August 15, 2017, www.ftc.gov/news-events/press-releases/2017/08/uber-settles-ftc-allegations-it-made-deceptive-privacy-data.

24. Sarah Lacy, "Uber Executive Said the Company Would Spend 'A Million Dollars' to Shut Me Up," *Time*, November 14, 2017, http://motto.time.com/5023287/uber-threatened-journalist-sarah-lacy/.

25. Aaron Deliwiche and Jennifer Jacobs Henderson, "What Is Participatory Culture?" in *The Participatory Cultures Handbook*, eds. Aaron Deliwiche and Jennifer Jacobs Henderson (New York: Taylor and Francis, 2013), 4.

26. I found evidence in my research that the number and location of the little black sedans displayed to passengers on the Uber passenger app did not, in fact, resemble the true location and accurate number of Uber cars available in real life.

1. DRIVING AS GLAMOROUS LABOR

1. To read important critiques of the sharing economy movement and its political implications, see Trebor Scholz, *Uberworked and Underpaid: How Workers Are Disrupting the Digital Economy* (Cambridge, UK: Polity, 2016), and Nick Srnicek, *Platform Capitalism* (Cambridge, UK: Polity, 2016).

2. Legal scholar Orly Lobel highlights the fact that there is no firm consensus on the definition of the sharing economy and no phrase "completely captures the entire scope of the paradigmatic shift in the ways we produce, consume, work, finance, and learn." Orly Lobel, "The Law of the Platform," *University of Minnesota Law Review* 101, no. 1 (2016): 87–89; Ryan Calo and Alex Rosenblat, "The Taking Economy: Uber, Information, and Power," *Columbia Law Review* 117, no. 6 (2017), http://columbialawreview.org/content/the-taking-economy-uber-information-and-power/. For a description of the sharing economy as an object of popular thinking and imagination, see Caroline Jack, "Imagining the Sharing Economy," *Points*, November 21, 2016, https://points.datasociety.net/imagining-the-sharing-economy-3a2048469da5.

3. Anne Washington, "A Crisis of Logics: Vocabulary Shifts in 2007–2008 Monetary Policy" (presentation, egos2017, Copenhagen, June 24, 2017).

4. Christine MacDonald and Joel Kurth, "Detroit Backed Off Suing Lenders over Risky Mortgages, Blight," *Detroit News*, June 25, 2015, www.detroitnews.com/story/news/special-reports/2015/06/25/detroit-backed-off-suing-lenders/29289237/.

5. As the economists Barth and colleagues observe, "Employment fell sharply in the Great Recession and increased slowly in the recovery so that in 2015, six years into the recovery, the employment-population ratio was 3.6 points lower than in 2007." See, e.g., Erling Barth, James Davis, Richard

Freeman, and Sari Pekkala Kerr, "Weathering the Great Recession: Variation in Employment Responses, by Establishments and Countries," *Russell Sage Foundation Journal of the Social Sciences* 3, no. 3 (2017): 50–69, www.rsfjournal.org /doi/full/10.7758/RSF.2017.3.3.03.

6. Ann R. Tickamyer, Jennifer Sherman, and Jennifer Warlick, eds., *Rural Poverty in the United States* (New York: Columbia University Press, 2017), 124.

7. Ofer Sharone, *Flawed System/Flawed Self* (Chicago: University of Chicago Press, 2013), 7; the author cites Challenger, Grey, and Christmas, "More on White-Collar Job Loss," October 6, 2009, *Challenger @Work,* http://challenger atworkblog.blogspot.com/2009/10/more-on-white-collar-job-loss.html.

8. Janice Nittoli, "Our Blue-Collar Great Depression," *Wall Street Journal,* August 25, 2010, www.wsj.com/articles/SB10001424052748704023404575429864 088150270.

9. Barth and colleagues note that "in 2015, six years into the recovery, the employment-population ratio was 3.6 points lower than in 2007." See, e.g., Barth, Davis, Freeman, and Kerr, "Weathering the Great Recession," 2; for additional discussions about the persistent impact of the Great Recession on unemployment, see, e.g., Tickamyer, Sherman, and Warlick, *Rural Poverty,* 124.

10. Sasha Ingber, "U.N. Investigator on Extreme Poverty Issues a Grim Report—on the U.S.," *NPR Goats and Soda,* December 21, 2017, www.npr.org /sections/goatsandsoda/2017/12/21/572043850/u-n-investigator-on-extreme-poverty-issues-a-grim-report-on-the-u-s.

11. Wendy Chun, "Proxy Politics as Social Cybernetics" (presentation, Cybernetics Conference, November 18, 2017), webcast by Internet Society, https://livestream.com/accounts/9197973/events/7940973/videos/166218044.

12. See, e.g., John Cassidy, "Does Tackling Inequality Reduce Growth? No," *New Yorker,* February 26, 2014, www.newyorker.com/news/john-cassidy/does-tackling-inequality-reduce-growth-no; and Christian R. Proaño, "A Paradigm Change and the IMF?" *Development and Cooperation,* January 12, 2016, www.dandc .eu/en/article/imf-econmomists-worry-about-growing-inequality.

13. Charlie Savage, "Wells Fargo Will Settle Mortgage Bias Charges," *New York Times,* July 12, 2012, www.nytimes.com/2012/07/13/business/wells-fargo-to-settle-mortgage-discrimination-charges.html.

14. Tressie McMillan Cottom, *Lower Ed: The Troubling Rise of For-Profit Colleges in the New Economy* (New York: New Press, 2017), ch. 9; The Movement for Black Lives, "Platform," n.d., https://policy.m4bl.org/platform/.

15. Chris Hughes, *Fair Shot: Rethinking Inequality and How We Earn* (New York: St. Martin's Press, 2018).

16. Todd Haselton, "Mark Zuckerberg Joins Silicon Valley Bigwigs in Calling for Government to Give Everybody Free Money," *CNBC,* May 25, 2017, www.cnbc.com/2017/05/25/mark-zuckerberg-calls-for-universal-basic-income-at-harvard-speech.html.

17. Eric A. Posner and Glen E. Weyl, "Property Is Only Another Name for Monopoly," *Journal of Legal Analysis* (January 31, 2017), https://ssrn.com/abstract=2818494.

18. Jack, "Imagining the Sharing Economy."

19. Robin Chase, "Bye, Bye Capitalism: We're Entering the Age of Abundance," *Backchannel,* July 16, 2015, https://medium.com/backchannel/see-ya-later-capitalism-the-collaborative-economy-is-taking-over-34a5fc3a37cd. Robin Chase is also the author of *Peers, Inc.,* a book on the sharing economy.

20. Srnicek's work traces platform capitalism's development through economic boom-and-bust cycles and its reemergence as the collaborative economy today.

21. Nick Srnicek, *Platform Capitalism* (Cambridge, UK: Polity, 2016).

22. Jay Shambaugh and Ryan Nunn, "Why Wages Aren't Growing in America," *Harvard Business Review,* October 24, 2017, https://hbr.org/2017/10/why-wages-arent-growing-in-america.

23. Darrell Etherington, "Uber Crosses the 5 Billion Trip Milestone amid Ongoing Issues," *TechCrunch,* June 29, 2017, https://techcrunch.com/2017/06/29/uber-crosses-the-5-billion-trip-milestone-amid-ongoing-issues/.

24. Uber Public Policy, e-mail message to author, March 5, 2018.

25. Pew Research Center, "America's Shrinking Middle Class: A Close Look at Changes within Metropolitan Areas," May 11, 2016, www.pewsocialtrends.org/2016/05/11/americas-shrinking-middle-class-a-close-look-at-changes-within-metropolitan-areas/.

26. As we will see later in the book, these figures conflict with many other reports of actual driver earnings.

27. Studs Turkel, *Working: People Talk about What They Do All Day and How They Feel about What They Do* (New York: New Press, 1997); John Bowe, Marisa Bowe, Sabin Streeter, eds., *Gig* (New York: Three Rivers Press, 2001).

28. Lawrence F. Katz and Alan B. Krueger, "The Rise and Nature of Alternative Work Arrangements in the United States, 1995–2015," National Bureau of Economic Research, June 18, 2017, https://scholar.harvard.edu/files/lkatz/files/katz_krueger_cws_resubmit_clean.pdf.

29. U.S. Bureau of Labor Statistics, "Why This Counts: Measuring 'Gig' Work," March 3, 2016, https://blogs.bls.gov/blog/tag/contingent-workers/.

30. Lauren Weber, "Some of the World's Largest Employers No Longer Sell Things, They Rent Workers," *Wall Street Journal,* December 28, 2017, www.wsj.com/articles/some-of-the-worlds-largest-employers-no-longer-sell-things-they-rent-workers-1514479580.

31. Vili Lehdonvirta, "Considering the Taylor Review: Ways Forward for the Gig Economy," *Policy and Internet Blog,* July 21, 2017, http://blogs.oii.ox.ac.uk/policy/considering-the-taylor-review-ways-forward-for-the-gig-economy/.

32. See, e.g., Barth, Davis, Freeman, and Kerr, "Weathering the Great Recession."

33. Even companies that emerged at about the same time as Uber, like Airbnb, or preceded Uber, like TaskRabbit, are overshadowed by Uber's prominence as the face of the sharing economy. For discussion of the "Uber for X" phenomenon, see Nathan Heller, "Is the Gig Economy Working?" *New Yorker,* May 15, 2017, www.newyorker.com/magazine/2017/05/15/is-the-gig-economy-working.

34. Juggernaut, "11 Uber for X Startups That Failed— Are You Making the Same Mistakes?" April 28, 2015, http://nextjuggernaut.com/blog/11-uber-for-x-startups-that-failed-are-you-making-the-same-mistakes/.

35. Aaron Smith, "Gig Work, Online Selling and Home Sharing," Pew Research Center, November 17, 2016, www.pewinternet.org/2016/11/17/gig-work-online-selling-and-home-sharing/.

36. Sara Ashley O'Brien, "Airbnb's Valuation Soars to $30 Billion," *CNN Tech,* August 8, 2016, http://money.cnn.com/2016/08/08/technology/airbnb-30-billion-valuation/index.html.

37. Vili Lehdonvirta, "The Online Gig Economy Grew 26% over the Past Year," iLabour Project, July 10, 2017, http://ilabour.oii.ox.ac.uk/the-online-gig-economy-grew-26-over-the-past-year/.

38. The terms ascribed to the sharing economy also include the *peer-to-peer economy,* the *collaborative economy,* and others.

39. Uber Under the Hood, "Uber Partners with NAACP to Increase Flexible Work Opportunities," January 5, 2016, https://medium.com/uber-under-the-hood/uber-partners-with-naacp-to-increase-flexible-work-opportunities-78cfc51695b3.

40. Uber, "Uber | MADD," www.uber.com/partner/madd/.

41. See also Gabriel Thompson, "What We Talk about When We Talk about the Gig Economy," *Capital and Main,* July 27, 2017, https://capitalandmain.com/what-we-talk-about-when-we-talk-about-the-gig-economy-0727; on income volatility in the gig economy, see JP Morgan Chase, "Paychecks, Paydays, and the Online Platform Economy Big Data on Income Volatility," February

2016, www.jpmorganchase.com/corporate/institute/report-paychecks-paydays-and-the-online-platform-economy.htm.

42. Amir Efrati, "Investors Rethink Uber's Long-Term Value," *The Information,* December 7, 2017, www.theinformation.com/investors-rethink-ubers-long-term-value.

43. Greg Bensinger, "What Is Uber Really Worth?" *Wall Street Journal,* November 15, 2017, www.wsj.com/articles/with-two-price-tags-from-softbank-what-is-uber-really-worth-1510741802.

44. Harrison Weber, "Uber's Unreal $70 Billion Valuation Really Was Unreal," *Gizmodo,* December 28, 2017, https://gizmodo.com/uber-s-unreal-70-billion-valuation-really-was-unreal-1821633772.

45. Theodore Schleifer, "Uber's Latest Valuation: $72 Billion," *ReCode,* February 9, 2018, www.recode.net/2018/2/9/16996834/uber-latest-valuation-72-billion-waymo-lawsuit-settlement.

46. Valerio de Stefano, "Introduction: Crowdsourcing, the Gig Economy, and the Law," *Comparative Labor Law & Policy Journal* 37, no. 3 (April 24, 2016): 2, https://papers.ssrn.com/sol3/papers.cfm?abstract_id=2767383.

47. The forerunners to the sharing economy model may be franchise operations (like McDonald's or Subway) rather than their respective industry competitors (like taxis). Like ridehail drivers, restaurant franchisees are also required to submit to significant corporate controls on the operations they run as small business entrepreneurs.

48. Platforms in the sharing economy are distinct from networks of independent distributors who sell skin care products, cosmetics, nutritional products, and others distributed by firms like Amway, Mary Kay, Avon, and Herbalife. As Jessica Burch, a professor in the business school at the University of Utah observed to me in an email in January 2018, "Direct sales executives often don't see themselves as part of the sharing economy. Some prefer the term 'freedom economy.' From their point of view, the sharing economy requires one to have a room or car to share but direct selling is open even to those who own nothing. The language of freedom captures the openness of entry but also implies that direct sellers may be 'free' from assets."

49. Juliet B. Schor, "Collaborating and Connecting: The Emergence of the Sharing Economy," in *Handbook on Research and Sustainable Consumption,* ed. Lucia Reisch and John Thogersen (Northampton, MA: Edward Elgar, 2015).

50. Yochai Benkler, "Sharing Nicely: On Shareable Goods and the Emergence of Sharing as a Modality of Economic Production," *Yale Law Journal* 114, no. 2 (November, 2004): 273–358.

51. Alexandra Mateescu, "Who Cares in the Gig Economy?" *Points,* July 12, 2017, https://points.datasociety.net/who-cares-in-the-gig-economy-6d75a079a889. For a description of the sharing economy as a signifier of a constellation of business activities with roots in collaborative commerce, see sociologist Juliet B. Schor, "On the Sharing Economy," *Contexts* 14, no. 1 (2015): 12–19, http://journals .sagepub.com/doi/pdf/10.1177/1536504214567860; see also Edward T. Walker, "Beyond the Rhetoric of the 'Sharing Economy,'" *Contexts* 14, no. 1 (2015): 12–19, http://journals.sagepub.com/doi/pdf/10.1177/1536504214567860; Natasha Singer, "Twisting Words to Make 'Sharing' Apps Seem Selfless," *New York Times,* August 8, 2015; Caroline Jack, "Imagining the Sharing Economy," *Points,* November 21, 2016, https://points.datasociety.net/imagining-the-sharing-economy-3a2048469da5.

52. Axel Bruns, *Blogs, Wikipedia, Second Life, and Beyond: From Production to Produsage* (New York: Peter Lang, 2008), 3, also see chap. 12.

53. Emma Paling, "Wikipedia's Hostility to Women," *Atlantic,* October 21, 2015, www.theatlantic.com/technology/archive/2015/10/how-wikipedia-is-hostile-to-women/411619/; for more on the cultural context of technology and inequities in contributions to Wikipedia by female editors, see Alice Marwick, *Status Update* (New Haven, CT: Yale University Press, 2013), 75; Claudia Wagner et al., "It's a Man's Wikipedia? Assessing Gender Inequality in an Online Encyclopedia," Cornell University Library, January 26, 2015, https://arxiv.org/abs/1501.06307; Lam et al., "WP: Clubhouse? An Exploration of Wikipedia's Gender Imbalance" (presentation at WikiSym'11, Mountain View, California, October 3–5, 2011), http://files.grouplens.org/papers/wp-gender-wikisym2011.pdf.

54. Marwick, *Status Update,* 29–35, 44.

55. Bruns, *Blogs, Wikipedia, Second Life, and Beyond,* 3.

56. Julia Ticona, conversation with the author, August 3, 2017.

57. "Anti-Uber Protests around the World, in Pictures," *Telegraph,* n.d., www.telegraph.co.uk/technology/picture-galleries/11902080/Anti-Uber-protests-around-the-world-in-pictures.html.

58. Labor and employment platforms, like Uber, are generally distinguished from asset-heavy platforms, like Airbnb, where a host needs spare real estate in order to make use of the platform—although drivers generally bring their own, or rental, vehicles to work. Anyone who needed to make ends meet could get a side gig through a smartphone app, such as delivering groceries via Instacart; performing a variety of sundry tasks, from moving to carpentry, via TaskRabbit; supplying cleaning services via Handy; or doing other types of labor via numerous other pop-up shops.

59. Philip M. Napoli and Robyn Caplan, "Why Media Companies Insist They're Not Media Companies, Why They're Wrong, and Why It Matters," *First Monday* 22, no. 5 (May 2017), http://firstmonday.org/ojs/index.php/fm/article/view/7051/6124.

60. Erin Griffith, "Memo to Facebook: How to Tell If You're a Media Company," *Wired,* October 12, 2017, www.wired.com/story/memo-to-facebook-how-to-tell-if-youre-a-media-company/.

61. Julia Tomassetti, "Does Uber Redefine the Firm? The Postindustrial Corporation and Advanced Information Technology," *Hofstra Labor and Employment Law Journal* 34, no. 1 (2016): 8; Calo and Rosenblat, "The Taking Economy."

62. Sharon Terlep, "Millennials as Seen by Corporate America," *Wall Street Journal,* 2017, https://graphics.wsj.com/glider/millennials-c671d444–6267–4e9b-ba6b-384a5b2fdb03.

63. Sometimes, narcissism, as ascribed to millennial women, is a derogatory euphemism for women bent on assertive self-determination.

64. See, e.g., Alison J. Pugh, *The Tumbleweed Society* (Oxford: Oxford University Press, 2015).

65. For ethnographic work on how working-class adults integrate these ideas into their own career and life plans, see Jennifer M. Silva, *Coming Up Short: Working-Class Adulthood in an Age of Uncertainty* (Oxford: Oxford University Press, 2013), particularly pp. 29–31.

66. Jia Tolentino, "The Gig Economy Celebrates Working Yourself to Death," *New Yorker,* March 22, 2017, www.newyorker.com/culture/jia-tolentino/the-gig-economy-celebrates-working-yourself-to-death.

67. Elizabeth Wissinger, "Glamor Labour in the Age of Kardashian," *Critical Studies in Fashion and Beauty* 7, no. 2 (December 2016): 141–152, www.ingentaconnect.com/contentone/intellect/csfb/2016/00000007/00000002/art00002.

68. International Finance Corporation–World Bank, "Driving toward Equality: Women, Ride-Hailing, and the Sharing Economy," March 1, 2018, http://documents.worldbank.org/curated/en/856531520948298389/Driving-toward-equality-women-ride-hailing-and-the-sharing-economy.

69. Kaleigh Rogers, "Love in the Time of Ridesharing," *Motherboard,* May 27, 2016, https://motherboard.vice.com/en_us/article/yp33yg/love-in-the-time-of-ridesharing-uber-lyft-romance-technology.

70. Lobel, "The Law of the Platform"; Calo and Rosenblat, "The Taking Economy."

71. Tressie McMillan Cottom, "Credentials, Jobs and the New Economy," *Inside Higher Ed,* March 2, 2017, www.insidehighered.com/views/2017/03/02/impact-new-economy-profit-colleges-and-their-students-essay.

72. Alex Rosenblat and Luke Stark, "Algorithmic Labor and Information Asymmetries: A Case Study of Uber's Drivers," *International Journal of Communication* 10, no. 27 (2016): 3762, http://ijoc.org/index.php/ijoc/article/view/4892.

73. A portion of my fieldwork cited here and at different points throughout this book has also been used in a joint research project and related publications. See, e.g., Alexandra Mateescu, Alex Rosenblat, and Julia Ticona, "Mapping Inequalities in the On-Demand Economy" (unpublished white paper, New York: Data & Society Research Institute, January 31, 2018).

74. Harry Campbell, who runs a popular and highly informative blog for rideshare drivers, encapsulates the hidden costs of this job here: "The Hidden Costs of Rideshare Driving," *The Rideshare Guy,* January 11, 2017, http://therideshareguy.com/the-hidden-costs-of-rideshare-driving-infographic/.

75. Caroline O'Donavan, "Here's How Much Uber Drivers Make, According to a New Uber Report," *BuzzFeed News,* November 21, 2016, www.buzzfeed.com/carolineodonovan/heres-how-much-uber-drivers-make-according-to-a-new-uber-rep.

76. Alison Griswold, "MIT's Uber Study Couldn't Possibly Have Been Right: It Was Still Important," *Quartz,* March 7, 2018, https://qz.com/1222744/mits-uber-study-couldnt-possibly-have-been-right-it-was-still-important/.

77. Caroline O'Donavan, "No, Uber Drivers Are Probably Not Earning Only $3.37 an Hour," *BuzzFeed News,* March 6, 2018, www.buzzfeed.com/carolineodonovan/uber-driver-earnings-research-mit-dara-khosrowshahi?utm_term=.qdWoE4MJmZ#.glqNagnyYm.

2. MOTIVATIONS TO DRIVE

1. Lyft, email correspondence with the author, December 9, 2017.

2. Uber, email correspondence with the author, March 5, 2018, and May 29, 2018.

3. Cody Cook, Rebecca Diamond, Jonathan Hall, John A. List, and Paul Oyer. "The Gender Earnings Gap in the Gig Economy: Evidence from over a Million Rideshare Drivers," January 2018, 9, https://web.stanford.edu/~diamondr/UberPayGap.pdf, p. 9; Alexandra Mateescu, Alex Rosenblat,

and Julia Ticona, "Mapping Inequalities in the On-Demand Economy" (unpublished white paper, New York: Data & Society Research Institute, January 31, 2018).

4. This book contains excerpts of the following article: Alex Rosenblat, "What Motivates Gig Economy Workers," *Harvard Business Review,* November 17, 2016, https://hbr.org/2016/11/what-motivates-gig-economy-workers. The excerpts appear at different points in the book, and I've cited these in each instance.

5. Jonathan V. Hall and Alan B. Krueger, "An Analysis of the Labor Market for Uber's Driver-Partners in the United States," January 22, 2015, https://s3.amazonaws.com/uber-static/comms/PDF/Uber_Driver-Partners_Hall_Kreuger_2015.pdf. Similarly, a survey of 453 subscribers to Harry Campbell's popular blog for rideshare drivers found that Uber drivers who work twenty hours or less per week (nearly half of them) accounted for about 24 percent of Uber's services and hours worked, whereas a minority (14 percent) of drivers who work full time or more (over forty hours per week) are responsible for providing 31 percent of Uber's services.

6. Lyft, "National Data," 2018 Economic Impact Report, https://take.lyft.com/economic-impact/.

7. James Manyika, Susan Lund, Jacques Bughin, Kelsey Robinson, Jan Mischke, and Deepa Mahajan, "Independent Work: Choice, Necessity, and the Gig Economy," McKinsey & Company, October 2016, www.mckinsey.com/global-themes/employment-and-growth/independent-work-choice-necessity-and-the-gig-economy.

8. Diana Farrell and Fiona Greig, "The Online Platform Economy: Has Growth Peaked?" JP Morgan Chase, November 2016, www.jpmorganchase.com/corporate/institute/document/jpmc-institute-online-platform-econ-brief.pdf; Lyft, "New York City," 2018 Economic Impact Report, https://take.lyft.com/economic-impact/; Rosenblat, "What Motivates Gig Economy Workers."

9. Lyft, "National Data," 2018 Economic Impact Report, https://take.lyft.com/economic-impact/.

10. Sachin Kansal, "Another Step to Prevent Drowsy Driving," *Uber Newsroom,* February 12, 2018, www.uber.com/newsroom/drowsydriving/.

11. Uber policy team, email correspondence with author, February 13, 2018.

12. Office of the Mayor, *For-Hire Vehicle Transportation Study* (New York: Office of the Mayor, January 2016), 9, www1.nyc.gov/assets/operations/downloads/pdf/For-Hire-Vehicle-Transportation-Study.pdf.

13. Lyft, "New York City," 2018 Economic Impact Report, https://take.lyft.com/economic-impact/.

14. Noah Zatz, "Is Uber Wagging the Dog with Its Moonlighting Drivers?" *On Labor,* February 1, 2016, https://onlabor.org/is-uber-wagging-the-dog-with-its-moonlighting-drivers/; Rosenblat, "What Motivates Gig Economy Workers."

15. Rosenblat, "What Motivates Gig Economy Workers."

16. David Gutman, "Judge Dismisses Lawsuit Seeking to Block Seattle Law Allowing Uber and Lyft Drivers to Unionize," *Seattle Times,* August 1, 2017, www.seattletimes.com/seattle-news/transportation/judge-dismisses-lawsuit-seeking-to-block-seattle-law-allowing-uber-and-lyft-drivers-to-unionize/.

17. Seattle.gov, "For-Hire Driver Collective Bargaining," n.d., www.seattle.gov/business-regulations/taxis-for-hires-and-tncs/for-hire-driver-collective-bargaining.

18. Lindsey D. Cameron, "Making Out While Driving: Control, Coordination, and Its Consequences for Algorithmic Labor" (PhD diss., Stephen M. Ross School of Business, 2018).

19. Aaron Smith, "Gig Work, Online Selling and Home Sharing," Pew Research Center, November 17, 2016, www.pewinternet.org/2016/11/17/gig-work-online-selling-and-home-sharing/.

20. Rosenblat, "What Motivates Gig Economy Workers"; Smith, "Gig Work, Online Selling."

21. Rosenblat, "What Motivates Gig Economy Workers."

22. JP Morgan Chase, "Paychecks, Paydays, and the Online Platform Economy Big Data on Income Volatility," February 2016, www.jpmorganchase.com/corporate/institute/report-paychecks-paydays-and-the-online-platform-economy.htm.

23. Hall and Krueger, "Analysis of the Labor Market," 16.

24. Ibid.

25. Step-parenting anecdote, from Alison Pugh, *The Tumbleweed Society: Working and Caring in an Age of Insecurity* (New York: Oxford University Press, 2015), 184.

26. Alex Rosenblat, "The Truth about How Uber's App Manages Drivers," *Harvard Business Review,* April 6, 2016, hbr.org/2016/04/the-truth-about-how-ubers-app-manages-drivers.

27. Douglas MacMillan and Deepa Seetharaman, "Uber Eases Screening Rules in California," *Wall Street Journal,* January 13, 2016, www.wsj.com/articles/uber-eases-screening-rules-in-california-1452668401.

28. This interview and its description are excerpted from Alexandra Mateescu, Alex Rosenblat and Julia Ticona, "Mapping Inequalities in the On-Demand Economy" (working paper, New York: Data & Society Research Institute, March 2018).

29. U.S. Federal Trade Commission, "Uber Agrees to Pay $20 Million to Settle FTC Charges That It Recruited Prospective Drivers with Exaggerated Earnings Claims," January 19, 2017, www.ftc.gov/news-events/press-releases/2017/01/uber-agrees-pay-20-million-settle-ftc-charges-it-recruited.

30. Caroline O'Donovan and Jeremy Singer-Vine, "How Much Uber Drivers Actually Make per Hour," *BuzzFeed News,* June 22, 2016, www.buzzfeed.com/carolineodonovan/internal-uber-driver-pay-numbers.

31. Lawrence Mishel, "Uber and the Labor Market: Uber Drivers' Compensation, Wages, and the Scale of Uber and the Gig Economy," Economic Policy Institute, May 15, 2018, www.epi.org/publication/uber-and-the-labor-market-uber-drivers-compensation-wages-and-the-scale-of-uber-and-the-gig-economy/

32. Kate Conger, "In Letter, Uber Said Drivers Didn't Make Advertised Earnings due to Their 'Choices.'" *Gizmodo,* December 21, 2017, https://gizmodo.com/in-letter-uber-said-drivers-didnt-make-advertised-earn-1820928444.

33. For further research into workplace surveillance and how this dynamic intersects with the work of being an independent driver in the trucking industry, see Karen Levy, "The Automation of Compliance: Techno-Legal Regulation in the United States Trucking Industry" (unpublished manuscript, 2014).

34. David C. Shonka and Katherine Worthman, "Complaint for Permanent Injunction and Other Equitable Relief," Federal Trade Commission v. Uber Technologies, Case 3:17-cv-00261, Filed 1/19/17, United States District Court for the Northeastern District of California, p. 7, www.ftc.gov/system/files/documents/cases/1523082ubercmplt.pdf.

35. Katie Wells, Kafui Attoh, and Declan Cullen, "The Work Lives of Uber Drivers: Worse Than You Think," *Working-Class Perspectives,* July 10, 2017, https://workingclassstudies.wordpress.com/2017/07/10/the-work-lives-of-uber-drivers-worse-than-you-think/; Alison Griswold, "Inside Uber's Unsettling Alliance with Some of New York's Shadiest Car Dealers," *Quartz,* June 27, 2017, https://qz.com/1013882/ubers-rental-and-lease-programs-with-new-york-car-dealers-push-drivers-toward-shady-subprime-contracts/.

36. See, e.g., Griswold, "Inside Uber's Unsettling Alliance."

37. See, e.g., ibid.

38. Michael Lazar, "The Average American Auto Payment Is ... ," *Huffington Post,* December 6, 2017, www.huffingtonpost.com/michael-lazar/the-average-american-auto_b_9405176.html.

39. Lauren Day, "Uber Driver Says Driving Isn't Worth It," *KMIR,* July 19, 2017, www.kmir.com/story/35926469/uber-driver-says-driving-isnt-worth-it.

40. Griswold, "Inside Uber's Unsettling Alliance."

41. Wells, Attoh, and Cullen, "The Work Lives of Uber Drivers."

42. Alex Rosenblat, "How Uber's Alliance with Montréal Drivers Turns Labo[u]r's Tactics On Its Head," *Uber Screeds,* August 4, 2016, https://medium.com/uber-screeds/how-ubers-alliance-with-montr%C3%A9al-drivers-turns-labo-u-r-s-tactics-on-its-head-af490b252dae.

43. Alex Rosenblat, "Is Your Uber/Lyft Driver in Stealth Mode?" *Uber Screeds,* July 19, 2016, https://medium.com/uber-screeds/is-your-uber-driver-in-hiding-484696894139.

44. Mike Isaac, "Uber's C.E.O. Plays with Fire," *New York Times,* April 23, 2017, www.nytimes.com/2017/04/23/technology/travis-kalanick-pushes-uber-and-himself-to-the-precipice.html; Ali Griswold, "Oversharing: Waymo Hits Uber Where It Hurts, Instacart Talks Cash-Flow, and Airbnb Dorm Rooms," Quartz, April 25, 2017.

45. Cook et al., "The Gender Earnings Gap in the Gig Economy," 9.

46. Harry Campbell, "Why Driving for a Car Service Is a Great Side Gig," *The Points Guy,* July 1, 2017, https://thepointsguy.com/2017/07/driving-car-service-uber-lyft/.

3. THE TECHNOLOGY PITCH

1. Uber, "Vehicle Requirements Boston," n.d., www.uber.com/boston-drivers/requirements/vehicle-requirements/.

2. Alex Rosenblat, "What Motivates Gig Economy Workers," *Harvard Business Review,* November 17, 2016, https://hbr.org/2016/11/what-motivates-gig-economy-workers.

3. Ilana Gershon, "The Quitting Economy," *Aeon,* July 26, 2017, https://aeon.co/essays/how-work-changed-to-make-us-all-passionate-quitters.

4. Michael Grothaus, "Uber Will Pay $3 Million to Settle New York Class Action Suit," *Fast Company,* January 10, 2018, www.fastcompany.com/40515514/uber-will-pay-3-million-to-settle-new-york-class-action-suit.

5. This example comes from a description of job fares in Carrie M. Lane, *A Company of One: Insecurity, Independence, and the New World of White-Collar Unemployment* (Ithaca, NY: Cornell University Press, 2011), 3.

6. Alex Rosenblat, "Uber's Drive-By Politics," *Motherboard,* May 27, 2016, https://motherboard.vice.com/en_us/article/gv5jaw/uber-lyft-austin-drive-by-politics.

7. Alex Rosenblat and Luke Stark, "Algorithmic Labor and Information Asymmetries: A Case Study of Uber's Drivers," *International Journal of*

Communication 10, no. 27 (2016): 3763, http://ijoc.org/index.php/ijoc/article/view/4892.

8. Alice Marwick, *Status Update* (New Haven, CT: Yale University Press, 2013), 184.

9. Sarah Lacy (keynote speech at Start-Up Montréal Festival, July 2017).

10. Chuck Collins, *Born on Third Base: A One Percenter Makes the Case for Tackling Inequality, Bringing Home Wealth, and Committing to the Common Good* (White River Junction, VT: Chelsea Green , 2016), audible version, section 1:30.

11. Molly McHugh, "Brake for Bathroom Breaks," *The Ringer,* November 21, 2016, https://theringer.com/brake-for-bathroom-breaks-f65cf6d68aad.

12. In theory, one way that bloggers can game this system is by building up a large audience of drivers and then declaring that everyone should switch to a competitor, which reaps another round of referral-code income. I rarely hear of blogger-driver entrepreneurs becoming the target of that type of suspicion from their audiences of drivers, though.

13. Chris Siron, "Uber Drivers Continue Strike While Awaiting Decision from Company," *Dallas News,* September 2015, www.dallasnews.com/news/transportation/2015/09/18/dozens-of-uber-dallas-drivers-protest-transportation-companys-west-end-offices.

14. As of April 2017, uberBlack drivers earn a base fare of $7.00, $0.35 per minute, and $3.45 per mile, and uberX drivers earn a base fare of $1.00, $0.10 per minute, and $0.85 per mile (in U.S. dollars).

15. Uber specifies which types of cars are eligible for the range of services it offers in each city. For example, a Toyota Camry, a Prius, and other basic four-door sedans are eligible for uberX if they are 2002 models or newer. The same vehicles are eligible for uberXL if they fit six passengers, excluding the driver. UberX is often the cheapest tier of service Uber offers, and it has lower pay rates, while Uber's luxury chauffeur services, like uberBlack and uberSelect, have stricter conditions. To qualify for these categories, a driver must have a four-door luxury sedan with a black interior, such as a Lincoln Town Car, a Range Rover, or an Audi A3, and it must be relatively new—for example, 2013 or newer. Such requirements vary by city.

16. See, e.g., changes to car eligibility for uberX to uberBlack dispatches in New York City.

17. See, e.g., Paolo Verme, "Facts vs. Perception: Understanding Inequality in Egypt," blog post, *The World Bank,* January 24, 2013, http://blogs.worldbank

.org/arabvoices/facts-vs-perceptions-understanding-inequality-egypt; John Cassidy, "Does Tackling Inequality Reduce Growth? No," *New Yorker*, February 26, 2014, www.newyorker.com/news/john-cassidy/does-tackling-inequality-reduce-growth-no; Christian R. Proaño, "A Paradigm Change at the IMF?" Group for Study and Research on Globalizations, December 1, 2016, www.mondialisations.org/php/public/art.php?id=40678&lan=EN.

18. Thanks to Sara Al-Nashar, Amr El-Mougy, and Nora EnCharge for an invigorating discussion on this topic.

19. A classic example of how the competing logics of macro- and microeconomics *feels* conflicting manifests when public services are privatized. Lots of employees might get laid off when a private enterprise takes over a public agency to weed out inefficiencies in its operations, but the overall impact of this activity could spur greater job creation. The specific people who get laid off may, however, remain unemployed.

20. Julia Ticona and Alexandra Mateescu, "Trusted Strangers," *Reshaping Work in the Platform Economy*, October 4, 2017, www.reshaping-work.com/blog8/2017/10/4/trusted-strangers-boundary-work-in-domestic-work-platforms-in-the-on-demand-economy.

21. Mike Isaac, "Uber's C.E.O. Plays with Fire," *New York Times*, April 23, 2017, www.nytimes.com/2017/04/23/technology/travis-kalanick-pushes-uber-and-himself-to-the-precipice.html.

22. Other researchers have found similar speculation among drivers. See, e.g., Mareike Glöss, Moira McGregor, and Barry Brown, "Designing for Labour: Uber and the On-Demand Mobile Workforce" (paper presented at the ACM CHI Conference on Human Factors in Computing Systems, San Jose, CA, 2016), 6, www.mobilelifecentre.org/sites/default/files/uber%20final%20camera%20ready.pdf.

23. Rosanna Smart, Brad Rowe, Angela Hawken, Mark Kleiman, Nate Mladenovic, Peter Gehred, and Clarissa Manning, *Faster and Cheaper: How Ride-Sourcing Fills a Gap in Low-Income Los Angeles Neighborhoods* (Los Angeles: BOTEC Analysis Corporation, July 2015), http://botecanalysis.com/wp-content/uploads/2015/07/LATS-Final-Report.pdf.

24. Rosenblat and Stark, "Algorithmic Labor," 3762.

25. Ibid.

26. Harry Campbell, "How to Take Advantage of Uber's New Acceptance Rate Policy," *The Rideshare Guy*, August 5, 2016, http://therideshareguy.com/how-to-take-advantage-of-ubers-new-acceptance-rate-policy/.

27. Rosenblat and Stark, "Algorithmic Labor," 3762.

28. Benjamin Sachs, "Uber's Passenger Acceptance Rules: More Evidence of Employee Status," *On Labor,* July 14, 2017, https://onlabor.org/ubers-passenger-acceptance-rules-more-evidence-of-employee-status.

29. Mike Isaac, "How Uber Deceives the Authorities Worldwide," *New York Times,* March 3, 2017, www.nytimes.com/2017/03/03/technology/uber-greyball-program-evade-authorities.html.

30. Alex Rosenblat, "Uber's Phantom Cabs," *Motherboard,* July 27, 2015, https://motherboard.vice.com/en_us/article/mgbz5a/ubers-phantom-cabs.

31. Liat Clark, "Uber Denies Researchers' 'Phantom Cars' Map Claim," *Wired,* July 28, 2015, www.wired.co.uk/article/uber-cars-always-in-real-time.

32. "Uber CEO Kalanick Argues with Driver over Falling Fares," YouTube, February 28, 2017, www.youtube.com/watch?v=gTEDYCkNqns; Eric Newcomer, "In Video, Uber CEO Argues with Driver over Falling Fares," February 28, 2017, *Bloomberg Technology,* www.bloomberg.com/news/articles/2017-02-28/in-video-uber-ceo-argues-with-driver-over-falling-fares.

33. The ways that Kalanick was castigated in the press seemed to satisfy a desire to censure the company's aggrandized image, which reminds me of Emmett Penny's article on "lectureporn." Emmett Penny, "Lectureporn: The Vulgar Art of Liberal Narcissism," *Paste,* June 26, 2017, www.pastemagazine.com/articles/2017/06/lectureporn-the-vulgar-art-of-liberal-narcissism.html.

34. Johana Bhuiyan, "A New Video Shows Uber CEO Travis Kalanick arguing with a Driver over Fares," *ReCode,* February 28, 2017, www.recode.net/2017/2/28/14766964/video-uber-travis-kalanick-driver-argument.

35. Julia Carrie Wong, "Uber CEO Travis Kalanick Resigns Following Months of Chaos," *The Guardian,* June 21, 2017, www.theguardian.com/technology/2017/jun/20/uber-ceo-travis-kalanick-resigns.

36. Rosenblat, "What Motivates Gig Economy Workers."

4. THE SHADY MIDDLEMAN

1. Alex Rosenblat, "How Can Wage Theft Emerge in App-Mediated Work?" *The Rideshare Guy,* August 10, 2016, therideshareguy.com/how-can-wage-theft-emerge-in-app-mediated-work/.

2. Eric Newcomer, "Uber Starts Charging What It Thinks You're Willing to Pay," *Bloomberg Technology,* May 19, 2017, www.bloomberg.com/news/articles/2017-05-19/uber-s-future-may-rely-on-predicting-how-much-you-re-willing-to-pay/.

3. Kashmir Hill, "How Facebook Figures Out Everyone You've Ever Met," *Gizmodo*, November 7, 2017, https://gizmodo.com/how-facebook-figures-out-everyone-youve-ever-met-1819822691.

4. Tarleton Gillespie, "Can an Algorithm Be Wrong?" *Limn*, no. 2 (2012), https://escholarship.org/uc/item/0jk9k4hj; see, e.g., Tarleton Gillespie, "The Politics of 'Platforms,'" *New Media & Society* 12, no. 3 (2010): 347–364, http://hdl.handle.net/1813/12774.

5. Siva Vaidhyanathan, *The Googlization of Everything* (Hangzhou, China: Zhejiang People's Publishing House, 2014), 62; danah boyd and Kate Crawford, "Critical Questions for Big Data," *Information, Communications & Society* 15, no. 5 (March 20, 2012): 662–679, www.tandfonline.com/doi/pdf/10.1080/1369118X.2012.678878; Cathy O'Neil, *Weapons of Math Destruction: How Big Data Increases Inequality and Threatens Democracy* (New York: Crown, 2016); Frank Pasquale, *The Black Box Society: The Secret Algorithms That Control Money and Information* (Cambridge, MA: Harvard University Press, 2015).

6. Alexis C. Madrigal, "The False Dream of a Neutral Facebook," *The Atlantic*, September 28, 2017, www.theatlantic.com/technology/archive/2017/09/the-false-dream-of-a-neutral-facebook/541404/.

7. Julia Angwin and Surya Mattu, "Amazon Says It Puts Customers First; But Its Pricing Algorithm Doesn't," *ProPublica*, September 20, 2016, www.propublica.org/article/amazon-says-it-puts-customers-first-but-its-pricing-algorithm-doesnt.

8. Aniko Hannak, Gary Soeller, David Lazer, Alan Mislove, and Christo Wilson, "Measuring Price Discrimination and Steering on E-Commerce Web Sites," *Proceedings of the 2014 Internet Measurement Conference* (New York: ACM, 2014): 305–318, https://dl.acm.org/citation.cfm?id=2663744.

9. See, e.g., Jennifer Valentino-DeVries, Jeremy Singer-Vine, and Ashkan Soltani, "Websites Vary Prices, Deals Based on Users' Information," *Wall Street Journal*, December 24, 2012, www.wsj.com/articles/SB10001424127887323777204578189391813881534; Julia Angwin and Jeff Larson, "The Tiger Mom Tax: Asians Are Nearly Twice as Likely to Get a Higher Price from Princeton Review," *ProPublica*, September 1, 2015, www.propublica.org/article/asians-nearly-twice-as-likely-to-get-higher-price-from-princeton-review.

10. Dana Mattioli, "On Orbitz, Mac Users Steered to Pricier Hotels," *Wall Street Journal*, August 23, 2012, www.wsj.com/articles/SB10001424052702304458604577488822667325882.

11. Uber Team, "Uber's New CEO," *UBER Newsroom*, August 29, 2017, https://newsroom.uber.com/ubers-new-ceo/.

12. Sarah Buhr, "Uber Appoints Former Orbitz CEO Barney Harford as Chief Operating Officer," *Tech Crunch,* December 20, 2017, https://techcrunch .com/2017/12/20/uber-appoints-former-orbitz-ceo-as-chief-operating-officer/.

13. E.H., "How Might Your Choice of Browser Affect Your Job Prospects?" *The Economist,* April 11, 2013, www.economist.com/blogs/economist-explains/2013/04 /economist-explains-how-browser-affects-job-prospects; see, e.g., Alex Rosenblat, Kate Wikelius, danah boyd, Seeta Peña Gangadharan, and Corrine Yu, "Data & Civil Rights: Employment Primer," Data & Society Research Institute, October 30, 2014, www.datacivilrights.org/pubs/2014–1030/Employment.pdf.

14. Mimi Onuoha, "Side-by-Side Images Expose a Glitch in Google's Maps," *Quartz,* June 6, 2017, https://qz.com/982709/google-maps-is-making-entire-communities-invisible-the-consequences-are-worrying/.

15. Latanya Sweeney, "Discrimination in Online Ad Delivery," *Data Privacy Lab,* 2013, https://dataprivacylab.org/projects/onlineads/.

16. Samuel Gibbs, "Women Less Likely to Be Shown Ads for High-Paid Jobs on Google, Study Shows," *The Guardian,* July 8, 2015, www.theguardian.com /technology/2015/jul/08/women-less-likely-ads-high-paid-jobs-google-study; see, e.g., Amit Datta, Michael Carl Tschantz, and Anupam Datta, "Automated Experiments on Ad Privacy Settings: A Tale of Opacity, Choice, and Discrimination," *Proceedings on Privacy Enhancing Technologies,* no. 1 (2015), www.degruyter.com /view/j/popets.2015.1.issue-1/popets-2015–0007/popets-2015–0007.xml.

17. Safiya Umoja Noble, "Google Equates Black Girls with Sex; Why?" *The Root,* March 13, 2013, www.theroot.com/google-equates-black-girls-with-sex-why-1790895563.

18. Hans Rollman, "Don't Google It! How Search Engines Reinforce Racism," *popMatters,* January 30, 2018, www.popmatters.com/algorithms-oppression-safiya-umoja-noble-2529677349.html.

19. Alex Rosenblat, Karen E.C. Levy, Solon Barocas, and Tim Hwang, "Discriminating Tastes: Uber's Customer Ratings as Vehicles for Workplace Discrimination," *Policy & Internet* 9 (2017): 256–279, doi:10.1002/poi3.153.

20. Robinson Meyer, "Everything We Know about Facebook's Secret Mood Manipulation Experiment," *The Atlantic,* June 28, 2014, www.theatlantic .com/technology/archive/2014/06/everything-we-know-about-facebooks-secret-mood-manipulation-experiment/373648/.

21. Adam D.I. Kramer, Jamie E. Guillory, and Jeffrey T. Hancock, "Experimental Evidence of Massive-Scale Emotional Contagion through Social Networks," *Proceedings of the National Academy of Sciences* 111, no. 24 (2014): 8788–8790, doi: 10.1073/pnas.1320040111.

22. Olivia Solon, "Russia-Backed Facebook Posts 'Reached 126m Americans' during US Election," *The Guardian,* October 30, 2017, www.theguardian .com/technology/2017/oct/30/facebook-russia-fake-accounts-126-million.

23. This section is largely excerpted from a blog post titled "How Can Wage Theft Emerge in App-Mediated Work?" that I wrote for Harry Campbell's *The Rideshare Guy,* August 10, 2016, https://therideshareguy.com/how-can-wage-theft-emerge-in-app-mediated-work/.

24. Rasier, LLC, "TECHNOLOGY SERVICES AGREEMENT," https://s3.amazon-aws.com/uber-regulatory-documents/country/united_states/RASIER+Tech nology+Services+Agreement+Decmeber+10+2015.pdf.

25. Josh Constine, "Now Some Ubers Will Only Wait 2 Minutes before Charging You, Not *5*," *TechCrunch,* April 26, 2016, https://techcrunch .com/2016/04/26/no-you-cant-go-to-the-bathroom-first/.

26. Michael Tee in conversation with Harry Campbell, "RSG035: Michael Tee on Launching the App Rideshare Timer," *The Rideshare Guy,* February 29, 2016, https://therideshareguy.com/rsg035-michael-tee-on-launching-the-app-rideshare-timer/.

27. Christian Perea, "Uber's Upfront Pricing Is Secretly Overcharging Passengers without Paying Drivers," *The Rideshare Guy,* September 26, 2016, https://therideshareguy.com/ubers-upfront-pricing-is-secretly-overcharging-passengers-without-paying-drivers/.

28. Alison Griswold, "How to Tell When Uber Is Overcharging You," *Quartz,* April 5, 2017, https://qz.com/948785/how-to-tell-when-ubers-upfront-pricing-is-overcharging-you/.

29. Ibid.

30. Ibid.

31. Sophano Van v. Raiser, LLC, *United States District Court Central District of California,* Case No. 2:17-cv-02550-DMB-JEM, p. 15, https://arstechnica.com /wp-content/uploads/2017/09/uberresponsecheatingsoftwaresuitseptember14 .pdf; David Kravets, "Uber: We Don't Have to Pay Drivers Based on Rider Fares," *Ars Technica,* September 18, 2017, https://arstechnica.com/tech-policy/2017/09/uber-driver-pay-plan-puts-a-significant-risk-on-ride-hailing-service/.

32. Alex Rosenblat, "The Truth about How Uber's App Manages Drivers," *Harvard Business Review,* April 6, 2016, hbr.org/2016/04/the-truth-about-how-ubers-app-manages-drivers.

33. Douglas O'Connor, Thomas Colopy, Matthew Manahan, and Elie Gurfinkel vs. Uber Technologies, Inc., no. C 13–3826 EMC, "Transcript of

Proceedings," p. 59, U.S. District Court, Northern California: January 30, 2015, http://uberlawsuit.com/Uber%20-%20Transcript%20of%20hearing%20on%20 summary%20judgment%20-%201–30–15.pdf.

34. Alex Rosenblat, "How Can Wage Theft Emerge in App-Mediated Work?" *The Rideshare Guy*, August 10, 2016, https://therideshareguy.com/how-can-wage-theft-emerge-in-app-mediated-work/.

35. Julia Carrie Wong, "Uber Admits Underpaying New York City Drivers by Millions of Dollars," *The Guardian*, May 23, 2017, www.theguardian.com /technology/2017/may/23/uber-underpaid-drivers-new-york-city.

36. Liat Clark, "Uber Denies Researchers 'Phantom Cars' Map Claim," *Wired*, July 28, 2015, para. 6, www.wired.co.uk/article/uber-cars-always-in-real-time; Tim Hwang and M.C. Elish, "The Mirage of the Marketplace," *Slate*, July 27, 2015, www.slate.com/articles/technology/future_tense/2015/07 /uber_s_ algorithm_and_the_mirage_of_the_marketplace.html; Alex Rosenblat and Luke Stark, "Algorithmic Labor and Information Asymmetries: A Case Study of Uber's Drivers," *International Journal of Communication* 10, no. 27 (2016): 3768, http://ijoc.org/index.php/ijoc/article/view/4892.

37. See Le Chen, Alan Mislove, and Christo Wilson, "Peeking beneath the Hood of Uber," in *Proceedings of the 2015 Internet Measurement Conference*, Tokyo, October 28–30, 2015 (New York: ACM, 2015), 1, https://dl.acm.org/citation .cfm?id=2815681.

38. Ibid., 2.

39. For example, when a passenger opens the app, Uber's technical system is supposed to figure out what area that person is in and deterministically assign him or her to a specific server in a given area within a grid; everyone in that area is supposed to get that price. However, the system isn't seamless: users in the same general area might be accessing data through different remote servers. Instead of being tied to one server, surge prices are based on requests that are moving across different servers. If they are not seamlessly synchronized, this can result in different prices for different users in the same geographic zone. See ibid., 1–3.

40. Excerpted from Ryan Calo and Alex Rosenblat, "The Taking Economy: Uber, Information, and Power," *Columbia Law Review* 117, no. 6 (2017), http://columbia lawreview.org/content/the-taking-economy-uber-information-and-power/.

41. Rosenblat and Stark, "Algorithmic Labor"; Alex Rosenblat and Tim Hwang, "Wisdom of the Captured," Data & Society Research Institute, September 2016, https://datasociety.net/pubs/ia/Wisdom_of_Captured_09-16.pdf.

42. This section is excerpted in part from Rosenblat and Stark, "Algorithmic Labor," 3770–3771.

43. Angèle Christin, "Algorithms in Practice: Comparing Web Journalism and Criminal Justice," July 16, 2017, *Big Data & Society* 4 (2): 1–14, http://journals.sagepub.com/doi/abs/10.1177/2053951717718855.

44. Rosenblat and Hwang, "Wisdom of the Captured," 4–5.

45. Ibid.

46. Drivers do resist some of Uber's control—for example, by GPS spoofing.

47. Rosenblat and Hwang, "Wisdom of the Captured," 4.

48. Rosenblat and Stark, "Algorithmic Labor," 3768.

49. Ibid., 3766.

50. Cass R. Sunstein, "Misconceptions about Nudges," September 6, 2017, https://papers.ssrn.com/sol3/papers.cfm?abstract_id=3033101.

5. BEHIND THE CURTAIN

1. "New LAX Rule: Taxi Drivers Who Discriminate Will Lose Permits," *CBS Los Angeles,* February 2, 2016, http://losangeles.cbslocal.com/2016/02/02/la-city-council-to-consider-revoking-permits-from-taxi-cab-drivers-who-refuse-service-at-lax/; Yanbo Ge, Christopher R. Knittel, Don MacKenzie, and Stephen Zoepf, "How Apps Like Uber Perpetuate the Cab Industry's Racial Discrimination," *Alternet,* January 6, 2017, www.alternet.org/economy/how-apps-uber-perpetuate-cab-industrys-racial-discrimination.

2. Yanbo Ge, Christopher R. Knittel, Don MacKenzie, and Stephen Zoepf, "Racial and Gender Discrimination in Transportation Network Companies," National Bureau of Economic Research, October 2016, www.nber.org/papers/w22776.

3. Andrew Beinstein and Ted Sumers, "How Uber Engineering Increases Safe Driving with Telematics," *UBER Engineering,* June 29, 2016, https://eng.uber.com/telematics/.

4. In other publicly reported incidents of sexual harassment by passengers, drivers similarly cite weak communications from Uber in responding to their incidents. See, e.g., Cheryl Herd, "San Francisco Uber Driver Sexually Harassed by Passenger on New Year's Eve," *NBC Bay Area,* January 26, 2018, www.nbcbayarea.com/news/local/San-Francisco-Uber-Driver-Sexually-Harrassed-by-Passenger-on-New-Years-Eve-471398763.html.

5. Alex Rosenblat and Tim Hwang, "Wisdom of the Captured," Data & Society Research Institute, September 2016, p. 3, https://datasociety.net/pubs/ia/Wisdom_of_Captured_09–16.pdf.

6. Tarleton Gillespie, "The Relevance of Algorithms," in *Media Technologies,* ed. Tarleton Gillespie, Pablo Boczkowski, and Kristen Foot (Cambridge,

MA: MIT Press, 2014); Angele Christin, "Algorithms in Practice: Comparing Web Journalism and Criminal Justice," *Big Data & Society* (2017): 1–4, http://journals.sagepub.com/doi/pdf/10.1177/2053951717718855.

7. On nudging as "choice architecture," see, e.g., Cass R. Sunstein, "Nudging: A Very Short Guide," *Journal of Consumer Policy* 37, no. 4 (2014): 583–588, doi:10.1007/s10603–014–9273–1.

8. Josh Horwitz, "Uber Customer Complaints from the US Are Increasingly Handled in the Philippines," *Quartz*, July 30, 2015, https://qz.com/465613/uber-customer-complaints-from-the-us-are-increasingly-handled-in-the-philippines/.

9. See, e.g., Heather Timmons, "Uber Explains Why a Search for 'Rape' in Its Customer Support Inbox Gets Thousands of Results," *Quartz*, March 7, 2016, https://qz.com/632440/uber-explains-why-a-search-for-rape-in-its-customer-support-inbox-gets-thousands-of-results/.

10. "180 Days of Change: Building Together in 2018," Uber, December 7, 2017, www.uber.com/blog/180-days-of-change-building-together-in-2018/.

11. Jay Cradeur, "Uber Deactivated My Driver Account for No Reason," *The Rideshare Guy*, December 20, 2017, https://therideshareguy.com/uber-deactivation/.

12. Aaron Sanking, "Senate Report Shows a New Way Wireless Companies Are Ripping You Off," *Daily Dot*, July 31, 2014, www.dailydot.com/layer8/cramming-cellphone-fee-senate-report/.

13. Avi Asher-Schapiro, "As Uber Probes Sexual Harassment at Its Offices, It Overlooks Hundreds of Thousands of Female Drivers," *The Intercept*, May 4, 2017, https://theintercept.com/2017/05/04/as-uber-probes-sexual-harassment-at-its-offices-it-overlooks-hundreds-of-thousands-of-female-drivers/.

14. Harry Braverman, *Labor and Monopoly Capital: The Degradation of Work in the Twentieth Century* (New York: New York University Press, 1974); James R. Beniger, *The Control Revolution: Technological and Economic Origins of the Information Society* (Cambridge, MA: Harvard University Press, 1989); Elia Zureik, "Theorizing Surveillance: The Case of the Workplace," in *Surveillance as Social Sorting: Privacy, Risk and Digital Discrimination,* ed. David Lyon (London, UK: Routledge, 2002): 31–56; Alex Rosenblat and Luke Stark, "Algorithmic Labor and Information Asymmetries: A Case Study of Uber's Drivers," *International Journal of Communication* 10, no. 27 (2016): 3772, http://ijoc.org/index.php/ijoc/article/view/4892.

15. Jessica Bruder, "These Workers Have a New Demand: Stop Watching Us," *The Nation*, May 27, 2015, www.thenation.com/article/these-workers-

have-new-demand-stop-watching-us/; Monique Girard and David Stark, "Distributing Intelligence and Organizing Diversity in New Media Projects," *Environment and Planning A* 34, no. 11 (2002): 1927–1949; Rosenblat and Stark, "Algorithmic Labor," 3772.

16. Linda Fuller and Vicki Smith, "Consumers' Reports: Management by Customers in a Changing Economy," *Work, Employment and Society* 5, no. 1 (1991): 1–16; Luke Stark and Karen E. C. Levy, "The Consumer as Surveillor" (paper presented at the Privacy Law Scholars Conference, Berkeley, CA, June 2015); Manuel Castells, *The Rise of the Network Society* (Oxford, UK: Blackwell, 2002); Rosenblat and Stark, "Algorithmic Labor," 3774.

17. Nikil Saval, *Cubed: A Secret History of the Workplace* (New York: Doubleday, 2014), 297.

18. Harry Campbell, "How to Take Advantage of Uber's New Acceptance Rate Policy," *The Rideshare Guy*, August 6, 2016, https://therideshareguy.com /how-to-take-advantage-of-ubers-new-acceptance-rate-policy/.

19. There's a caveat: drivers' ratings are compared only to those of other drivers in their market. A driver with a rating of 4.6/5 stars in Baton Rouge, Louisiana, is not compared to a driver with a rating of 4.8/5 stars in Los Angeles, California. There's a reason for that: because ratings are locally sourced from passengers, it wouldn't make sense to, for instance, deactivate drivers in a local market where all ratings are a bit lower based on a standard set by drivers and passengers in another market.

20. Rosenblat and Stark, "Algorithmic Labor," 3775–3776.

21. Gina Neff, *Venture Labor: Work and the Burden of Risk in Innovative Industries* (Cambridge, MA: MIT Press., 2012), 28; Rosenblat and Stark, "Algorithmic Labor," 3772.

22. Robin Leidner, "Emotional Labor in Service Work," *Annals of the American Academy of Political and Social Science* 561, no. 1 (1999): 83; Rosenblat and Stark, "Algorithmic Labor," 3772.

23. This emotional-labor role is captured by the phrase *emotional hit man*, which describes the affective harm workers experience from certain oppressive workplace practices: Winifred Poster, "Hidden Side of the Credit Economy: Emotions, Outsourcing, and Indian Call Centers," *International Journal of Comparative Sociology* 54, no. 3 (2013): 225, https://nebula.wsimg.com/bo550d72bc3b5a3 787bee8ob63ob9266?AccessKeyId=BE299D66B75FCD35FBFD&disposition= 0&alloworigin=1.

24. See also Mareike Glöss, Moira McGregor, and Barry Brown, "Designing for Labour: Uber and the On-Demand Mobile Workforce," *Proceedings of*

the 2016 CHI Conference on Human Factors in Computing Systems (New York: ACM, 2016): 1632–1643, http://doi.acm.org/10.1145/2858036.2858476.

25. Noopur Raval and Paul Dourish, "Standing Out from the Crowd: Emotional Labour, Body Labour, and Temporal Labour in Ridesharing," *Proceedings of the 19th ACM Conference on Computer-Supported Cooperative Work and Social Computing* (New York: ACM): 97–107, http://doi.acm.org/10.1145/2818048.2820026.

26. Arlie Russell Hochschild, *The Managed Heart: Commercialization of Human Feeling, Twentieth Anniversary Edition, with a New Afterword,* 2nd ed. (Oakland, CA: University of California Press, 2003), www.jstor.org/stable/10.1525/j.ctt1ppocf.

27. Alison Pullen and Ruth Simpson, "Managing Difference in Feminized Work: Men, Otherness and Social Practice," *Human Relations* 62, no. 4 (2009): 561–587.

28. Among the changes implemented after Uber instituted "180 Days of Change"—a program in which Uber endeavored to make driver-friendly changes to the app to improve its relationship with drivers, beginning in June 2017—Uber started making passengers explain low ratings. See Uber, "180 Days of Change," www.uber.com/c/180-days/.

29. Alex Rosenblat, Karen E.C. Levy, Solon Barocas, and Tim Hwang, "Discriminating Tastes: Uber's Customer Ratings as Vehicles for Workplace Discrimination," *Policy & Internet* 9 (2017): 256–279, doi:10.1002/poi3.153. Thanks to law professor Benjamin G. Edelman for this insightful point.

30. See, e.g., Johnson v. Zema Systems Corp., 170 F. 3d 734—Court of Appeals, 7th Circuit 1999. https://scholar.google.com/scholar_case?case=71980 99510076927053&hl=en&as_sdt=6,33; Fernandez v. Wynn Oil Co., 653 F. 2d 1273—Court of Appeals, 9th Circuit 1981. https://scholar.google.com/scholar_case?case=17090205096023394365&hl=en&as_sdt=6,33.

31. Rosenblat, Levy, Barocas, and Hwang, "Discriminating Tastes."

32. Ibid.

33. Fair Work Commission. Mr. Michael Kaseris v. Raisier Pacific V.O.F. FWC 6610, Melbourne, Australia, December 21, 2017, www.fwc.gov.au/documents/decisionssigned/html/2017fwc6610.htm.

34. Michael Lewis, "Proposed Ontario Class-Action Claims Uber Drivers Are Employees Not Contractors," *The Star,* January 24, 2017, www.thestar.com/business/2017/01/24/proposed-ontario-class-action-claims-uber-drivers-are-employees-not-contractors.html.

35. Employment Appeal Tribunal, Appeal No. UKEAT/0056/17/DA (London, November 10, 2017), https://assets.publishing.service.gov.uk/media/5a046b06e5274a0ee5a1f171/Uber_B.V._and_Others_v_Mr_Y_Aslam_and_Others_UKEAT_0056_17_DA.pdf.

36. "Court: Uber Drivers Are Independent Contractors, Not Employees," *CBS*, February 1, 2017, http://miami.cbslocal.com/2017/02/01/court-uber-drivers-contractors-employees/.

37. Mike Isaac and Natasha Singer, "California Says Uber Driver Is Employee, Not a Contractor," *New York Times*, June 17, 2015, www.nytimes .com/2015/06/18/business/uber-contests-california-labor-ruling-that-says-drivers-should-be-employees.html?mtrref=www.nytimes.com.

38. Quote from Judge Edward M. Chen in Douglas O'Connor, Thomas Colopy, Matthew Manahan, and Elie Gurfinkel vs. Uber Technologies, Inc., No. C 13–3826 EMC, court transcript (U.S. District Court, Northern CA: January 30, 2015), 17.

39. Complaint for Permanent Injunction and Other Equitable Relief at 10–11, FTC v. Uber Techs., Inc., No. 17–261 (N.D. Cal. Jan. 19, 2017); Ryan Calo and Alex Rosenblat, "The Taking Economy: Uber, Information, and Power," *Columbia Law Review* 117, no. 6 (2017), http://columbialawreview.org/content /the-taking-economy-uber-information-and-power/.

40. James Vincent, "Leaked Document Shows How Gig Economy Companies Avoid the Term 'Employee,'" *The Verge*, April 6, 2017, www.theverge .com/2017/4/6/15204098/deliveroo-gig-economy-language-dos-donts-workers.

41. Jordan Pearson, "Uber Is Using AI to Charge People as Much as Possible for a Ride," *Motherboard*, May 19, 2017, https://motherboard.vice.com/en_ us/article/ywmex5/uber-is-using-ai-to-charge-people-as-much-as-possible-for-a-ride.

42. Kara Swisher and Johana Bhuiyan, "A Top Uber Executive, Who Obtained the Medical Records of a Customer Who Was a Rape Victim, Has Been Fired," *ReCode*, June 7, 2017, www.recode.net/2017/6/7/15754316/uber-executive-india-assault-rape-medical-records.

43. Ben Smith, "Uber Executive Suggests Digging Up Dirt on Journalists," *BuzzFeed*, November 18, 2014, www.buzzfeed.com/bensmith/uber-executive-suggests-digging-up-dirt-on-journalists?utm_term=.tieA9mVK54#.qyo-Q7PvoLK; Sarah Lacy, "The Moment I Learned Just How Far Uber Will Go to Silence Journalists and Attack Women," *Pando*, November 17, 2014, https:// pando.com/2014/11/17/the-moment-i-learned-just-how-far-uber-will-go-to-silence-journalists-and-attack-women/.

44. Biz Carson, "Bombshell Letter Exposes Uber's Corporate Spy Tactics," *Forbes*, December 15, 2017, www.forbes.com/sites/bizcarson/2017/12/15 /jacobs-letter-uber-spy-tactics/#697c4817f9f6.

45. Kashmir Hill, "'God View': Uber Allegedly Stalked Users for Party-Goers' Viewing Pleasure (Updated)," *Forbes*, October 3, 2014, www.forbes.com

/sites/kashmirhill/2014/10/03/god-view-uber-allegedly-stalked-users-for-party-goers-viewing-pleasure/#3a9f548c3141.

46. Natasha Singer and Mike Isaac, "Uber Data Collection Changes Should Be Barred, Privacy Group Urges," *New York Times,* June 22, 2015, www.nytimes.com/2015/06/23/technology/uber-data-collection-changes-should-be-barred-privacy-group-urges.html.

47. Woodrow Hartzog (@hartzog), Twitter, August 29, 2017, https://twitter.com/hartzog/status/902639193033240580.

48. Mike Isaac, "Uber's C.E.O. Plays with Fire," *New York Times,* April 23, 2017, www.nytimes.com/2017/04/23/technology/travis-kalanick-pushes-uber-and-himself-to-the-precipice.html.

49. See, e.g., Julie E. Cohen, *Configuring the Networked Self: Law, Code, and Play of Everyday Practice* (New Haven, CT: Yale University Press, 2012); Evan Selinger, Jules Polonetsky, and Omer Tene, eds., *The Cambridge Handbook of Consumer Privacy* (New York: Cambridge University Press, 2018).

50. Jaron Lanier, *Who Owns the Future?* (New York: Simon and Schuster, 2013).

51. Mary L. Gray (@marylgray), Twitter, December 29, 2017, https://twitter.com/marylgray/status/946904792118460416.

52. Portions of this section of the chapter originally appeared as an article I wrote for *Fast Company.* See Alex Rosenblat, "The Network Uber Drivers Built," *Fast Company,* January 9, 2018, www.fastcompany.com/40501439/the-network-uber-drivers-built. This fieldwork also draws on a collaborative project: Alexandra Mateescu, Alex Rosenblat, and Julia Ticona, "Mapping Inequalities in the On-Demand Economy" (unpublished white paper, New York: Data & Society Research Institute, January 31, 2018).

53. Eric Newcomer, "Uber Paid Hackers to Delete Stolen Data on 57 Million People," *Bloomberg Technology,* November 21, 2017, www.bloomberg.com/news/articles/2017-11-21/uber-concealed-cyberattack-that-exposed-57-million-people-s-data.

54. Maureen K. Ohlhaussen and Terrell McSweeny, "Decision and Order in the Matter of Uber Technologies, Inc.," *United States of America before the Federal Trade Commission,* Case No. 1523054, August 15, 2017, www.ftc.gov/system/files/documents/cases/1523054_uber_technologies_decision_and_order.pdf.

55. Derrick Harris, "The One-Night Stand, Quantified by Uber," *GIGAOM,* March 26, 2012, https://gigaom.com/2012/03/26/uber-one-night-stands/.

56. Christian Rudder, "10 Charts about Sex," *OkCupid Blog,* April 18, 2011, https://theblog.okcupid.com/10-charts-about-sex-47e30d9716b0.

57. Damon Beres, "Netflix Pulls Some Big Brother Nonsense with Your Data," *Mashable,* December 11, 2017, http://mashable.com/2017/12/11/netflix-a-christmas-prince-tweet-privacy/.

58. Ibid.

59. Josh Constine, "Facebook Changes Mission Statement to 'Bring the World Closer Together,'" *Tech Crunch,* June 22, 2017, https://techcrunch.com/2017/06/22/bring-the-world-closer-together/.

6. IN THE BIG LEAGUES

1. Caroline O'Donovan, "Uber Bans Racists Too," *Buzzfeed News,* August 14, 2017, www.buzzfeed.com/carolineodonovan/uber-is-also-willing-to-ban-white-supremacists.

2. Christine Hauser, "GoDaddy Severs Ties with Daily Stormer after Charlottesville Article," *New York Times,* August 14, 2017, www.nytimes.com/2017/08/14/us/godaddy-daily-stormer-white-supremacists.html.

3. See, e.g., Alison Pugh, *The Tumbleweed Society: Working and Caring in an Age of Insecurity* (New York: Oxford University Press, 2015). Pugh also discusses the conjoined themes of family and workplace commitment and notes the separation of them for some and the pairing of them for others. Andrew Cherlin discusses marital churn in American society by situating it in the context of a growing dichotomy between individualism and neoliberal autonomy, and marriage as a formal, long-standing commitment, in *The Marriage-Go-Round* (New York: Vintage, 2010).

4. Kirstie S. Ball and Stephen T. Margulis, "Electronic Monitoring and Surveillance in Call Centres: A Framework for Investigation," *New Technology, Work and Employment* 26, no. 2 (2011): 113–126, http://onlinelibrary.wiley.com/doi/10.1111/j.1468–005X.2011.00263.x/abstract.

5. Global News Staff, "Uber Can Now Legally Operate in Quebec," *Global News,* October 22, 2016, http://globalnews.ca/news/3019867/uber-can-now-legally-operate-in-quebec/.

6. Carmel DeAmicis, "HomeJoy Shuts Down after Battling Worker Classification Lawsuits," *ReCode,* July 17, 2015, www.recode.net/2015/7/17/11614814/cleaning-services-startup-homejoy-shuts-down-after-battling-worker.

7. Olivia Solon, "'It's Digital Colonialism': How Facebook's Free Internet Service Has Failed Its Users," *The Guardian,* July 27, 2017, www.theguardian.com/technology/2017/jul/27/facebook-free-basics-developing-markets?CMP=twt_a-technology_b-gdntech.

8. Ziru Li, Yili Hong, and Zhongju Zhang, "Do On-Demand Ride-Sharing Services Affect Traffic Congestion? Evidence from Uber Entry," 2016, https://papers.ssrn.com/sol3/papers.cfm?abstract_id=2838043; Office of the Mayor, *For-Hire Vehicle Transportation Study* (New York: Office of the Mayor, January 2016), www1.nyc.gov/assets/operations/downloads/pdf/For-Hire-Vehicle-Transportation-Study.pdf.

9. Natasha Singer, "How Silicon Valley Pushed Coding into American Classrooms," *New York Times,* June 27, 2017, www.nytimes.com/2017/06/27/technology/education-partovi-computer-science-coding-apple-microsoft.html.

10. Ibid.

11. Amar Toor, "Airbnb Comes under Fire for Tone-Deaf San Francisco Ads," *The Verge,* October 22, 2015, www.theverge.com/2015/10/22/9591596/airbnb-san-francisco-ad-campaign-proposition-f.

12. Ryan Calo and Alex Rosenblat, "The Taking Economy: Uber, Information, and Power," *Columbia Law Review* 117, no. 6 (2017), http://columbialawreview.org/content/the-taking-economy-uber-information-and-power/.

13. For context: Uber provided these comments to me and my coauthor Ryan Calo as part of our fact-checking effort in preparation for our law review article, "The Taking Economy: Uber, Information and Power."

14. Sam Levin, "Uber Admits to Self-Driving Car 'Problem' in Bike Lanes as Safety Concerns Mount," *The Guardian,* December 19, 2016, www.theguardian.com/technology/2016/dec/19/uber-self-driving-cars-bike-lanes-safety-san-francisco.

15. Julia Carrie Wong, "California Threatens Legal Action against Uber Unless It Halts Self-Driving Cars," *The Guardian,* December 16, 2016, www.theguardian.com/technology/2016/dec/16/uber-defies-california-self-driving-cars-san-francisco.

16. Mike Isaac (@Mikeisaac) wrote, "The state attorney generals office is not happy with Uber." Twitter, December 16, 2016, https://twitter.com/MikeIsaac/status/809936567078965248.

17. Marisa Kendall, "Uber Sends Self-Driving Cars to Arizona after Failed San Francisco Pilot," *Mercury News,* December 23, 2016, www.mercurynews.com/2016/12/22/uber-ships-self-driving-cars-to-arizona-after-failed-san-francisco-pilot/.

18. Selena Larson, "Arizona Suspends Uber's Self-Driving Car Tests after Fatal Crash," *CNN Tech,* March 27, 2018, http://money.cnn.com/2018/03/26/technology/arizona-suspends-uber-self-driving-cars/index.html.

19. Oliver Laughland, Jessica Glenza, Steven Thrasher, and Paul Lewis, "'We Can't Breathe': Eric Garner's Last Words Become Protestors' Rallying Cry," *The Guardian*, December 4, 2014, www.theguardian.com/us-news/2014/dec/04/we-cant-breathe-eric-garner-protesters-chant-last-words.

20. Paul Bradley Carr, "Travis Shrugged: The Creepy, Dangerous Ideology behind Silicon Valley's Cult of Disruption," *Pando*, October 24, 2012, https://pando.com/2012/10/24/travis-shrugged/.

21. Sarah Kessler, "The Gig Economy Won't Last Because It's Being Sued to Death," *Fast Company*, February 17, 2015, www.fastcompany.com/3042248/the-gig-economy-wont-last-because-its-being-sued-to-death.

22. DeAmicis, "HomeJoy Shuts Down."

23. Marisa Kendall, "Lyft off the Hook in Driver Case, 3 years and $27 million Later," *Mercury News*, March 16, 2017, www.mercurynews.com/2017/03/16/lyft-off-the-hook-in-driver-case-3-years-and-27-million-later/.

24. Benjamin Peters, *How Not to Network a Nation: The Uneasy History of the Internet* (Cambridge, MA: MIT Press, 2016), 11.

25. Benjamin Edelman, Michael Luca, and Dan Svirsky, "Racial Discrimination in the Sharing Economy: Evidence from a Field Experiment," *American Economic Journal: Applied Economics*, September 16, 2016, www.benedelman.org/publications/airbnb-guest-discrimination-2016-09-16.pdf.

26. Sam Levin, "Airbnb Gives In to Regulator's Demand to Test for Racial Discrimination by Hosts," *The Guardian*, April 27, 2017, www.theguardian.com/technology/2017/apr/27/airbnb-government-housing-test-black-discrimination.

27. Alex Rosenblat, "Uber's Drive-By Politics," *Motherboard*, May 27, 2016, https://motherboard.vice.com/en_us/article/gv5jaw/uber-lyft-austin-drive-by-politics.

28. Michael King, "Lege for Sale?" *Austin Chronicle*, March 14, 2017, www.austinchronicle.com/daily/news/2017-03-14/lege-for-sale/.

29. Texas HB 100, www.capitol.state.tx.us/BillLookup/History.aspx?LegSess=85R&Bill=HB100.

30. Kimberly Reeves, "Uber's Big Win: Texas Ridesharing Rules Bill Passes through Senate," *Austin Business Journal*, May 17, 2017, www.bizjournals.com/austin/news/2017/05/17/ubers-big-win-texas-ridesharing-rules-bill-passes.html.

31. HR 100, 85 Cong. (2017) (enacted), https://legiscan.com/TX/text/HB100/2017.

32. Joy Borkholder, Mariah Montgomery, Miya Saika Chen, and Rebecca Smith, "Uber State Interference: How Transportation Network Companies Buy, Bully, and Bamboozle Their Way to Deregulation," National Employment

Law Project and the Partnership for Working Families, January 2018, www
.forworkingfamilies.org/sites/pwf/files/publications/Uber%20State%20Inter
ference%20Jan%202018.pdf.

33. Rosenblat, "Uber's Drive-By Politics."

34. Mike Ramsey and Douglas MacMillan, "Carnegie Mellon Reels after
Uber Lures away Researchers," *Wall Street Journal,* May 31, 2015, www.wsj.com
/article_email/is-uber-a-friend-or-foe-of-carnegie-mellon-in-robotics-1433084582-
lMyQjAxMTEiMjA5MTUwNzE5Wj.

35. Cecilia Kang, "No Driver? Bring It On: How Pittsburgh Became Uber's
Testing Ground," *New York Times,* September 10, 2016, www.nytimes.com
/2016/09/11/technology/no-driver-bring-it-on-how-pittsburgh-became-ubers-
testing-ground.html.

36. Cecilia Kang, "Pittsburgh Welcomed Uber's Driverless Car Experiment; Not Anymore," *New York Times,* May 21, 2017, www.nytimes.com/2017
/05/21/technology/pittsburgh-ubers-driverless-car-experiment.html.

37. Complaint for Permanent Injunction and Other Equitable Relief at
10–11, FTC v. Uber Techs., Inc., No. 17–261 (N.D. Cal. Jan. 19, 2017); Calo and
Rosenblat, "The Taking Economy."

38. The original blog post was located here: https://newsroom.uber.com
/an-uber-impact-20000-jobs-created-on-the-uber-platformevery-month-2/.
However, it has since been relocated or removed from the company's website.
The official blog post is on file with the author.

39. Caroline O'Donovan, "Uber Rallies Drivers against Teamster Unionization Efforts with Podcasts and Pizza Parties," *Buzzfeed News,* March 9, 2017,
www.buzzfeed.com/carolineodonovan/uber-to-seattle-drivers-protect-your-
freedom-from-the-teamst.

40. Mike Maffie (@maffiemd), a PhD student at Cornell, made a similar
observation: "Seems like a clever way to gauge interest in #rideshare union.
Track who listens and for how long." Twitter, March 15, 2017, https://twitter
.com/maffiemd/status/841999619697573891.

41. Alison Griswold, "Three US States Have Already Blessed Uber's Independent Contractor Employment Model," *Quartz,* December 10, 2015, https://
qz.com/571249/three-us-states-have-already-blessed-ubers-independent-con
tractor-employment-model/; Lisa Nagele-Piazza, "Florida Legislature Approves
Ride-Hailing Driver Bill," Society for Human Management, www.shrm.org
/resourcesandtools/legal-and-compliance/state-and-local-updates/pages/florida-
legislature-approves-ride-hailing-driver-bill.aspx; Dara Kerr, "Uber and Lyft
Messed with Texas—and Won," *CNET,* June 20, 2017, www.cnet.com/news/uber-

lyft-toyed-with-texas-to-get-their-ride-hailing-way/; Kimberly Reeves, "Uber's Big Win: Texas Ridesharing Rules Bill Passes through Senate," *Austin Business Journal,* May 17, 2017, www.bizjournals.com/austin/news/2017/05/17/ubers-big-win-texas-ridesharing-rules-bill-passes.html.

42. Lindsey Hadlock, "Upstate New York Ride-Hailing Drives Gig Economy," Cornell University Media Relations Office, June 29, 2017, http://mediarelations.cornell.edu/2017/06/29/upstate-new-york-ride-hailing-drives-gig-economy/.

43. Safraz Maredia, "Westchester Would Send Anti-business Message by Opting Out from Ride-Hailing: Uber Official," *lohud,* June 25, 2017, www.lohud.com/story/opinion/contributors/2017/06/26/westchester-ride-hailing-uber-view/427351001/.

44. Edward T. Walker, "The Uberization of Activism," *New York Times,* August 6, 2015, www.nytimes.com/2015/08/07/opinion/the-uber-ization-of-activism.html?mcubz=1.

45. Nikil Saval, "Disrupt the Citizen: Against Ride Sharing," *Portside,* July 11, 2017, https://portside.org/2017-07-11/disrupt-citizen-against-ride-sharing.

46. Ibid.; Wolfgang Streenck, "Citizens as Customers," *New Left Review* 76 (2012), https://newleftreview.org/II/76/wolfgang-streeck-citizens-as-customers.

47. Jack Weatherford, *Genghis Khan and the Making of the Modern World* (New York: Broadway Books, 2014).

48. Tom Slee, *What's Yours Is Mine: Against the Sharing Economy* (New York: OR Books, 2016).

49. "Uber, NAACP Create Partnership to Hire Minority Drivers in New Jersey," December 23, 2015, *CBS New York,* http://newyork.cbslocal.com/2015/12/23/new-jersey-minority-uber-drivers-naacp/.

50. An Uber official posted the company's response on Instagram: "Proud to accept this sponsor award for @Uber from the NAACP of NJ. Congrats to Sean Conner on his great work building this partnership and our fantastic counterparts in the organization." Nikolenka, Instagram, June 29, 2017, www.instagram.com/p/BV74IA-g6Pi/.

51. Travis Kalanick, "Record Shouldn't Bar Ex-offenders from Work," *Uber Under The Hood,* October 5, 2016, https://medium.com/@UberPubPolicy/record-shouldnt-bar-ex-offenders-from-work-a42732d2861b.

52. Ashley Nellis, "The Color of Justice: Racial and Ethnic Disparity in State Prisons," *The Sentencing Project,* June 14, 2016, www.sentencingproject.org/publications/color-of-justice-racial-and-ethnic-disparity-in-state-prisons/.

53. Tim Shorrock, "Labor-Clergy Coalition to March on Nissan Plant in Mississippi," *Portside,* March 3, 2017, www.portside.org/2017–03–04/labor-clergy-coalition-march-nissan-plant-mississippi.

54. Nancy MacLean, *Democracy in Chains* (New York: Viking, 2017), 31.

55. Jordan Pearson, "Uber's AI Hub in Pittsburgh Gutted a University Lab—Now It's in Toronto," May 9, 2017, https://motherboard.vice.com/en_us/article/3dxkej/ubers-ai-hub-in-pittsburgh-gutted-a-university-lab-now-its-in-toronto.

56. Calo and Rosenblat, "The Taking Economy."

57. Anne Washington in Skype interview with author, August 5, 2017.

58. Andrew Zimbalist and Roger G. Noll, "Sports, Jobs, and Taxes: Are New Stadiums Worth the Cost?" *Brookings,* June 1, 1997, www.brookings.edu/articles/sports-jobs-taxes-are-new-stadiums-worth-the-cost/; Gregg Easterbrook, "How the NFL Fleeces Taxpayers," *Atlantic,* October 2013, www.theatlantic.com/magazine/archive/2013/10/how-the-nfl-fleeces-taxpayers/309448/; Bret Schrotenboer, "Abandoned NFL Cities Have Old Stadium Debt, New Outlook," *USA Today,* March 31, 2017, www.usatoday.com/story/sports/nfl/2017/03/31/relocation-oakland-raiders-san-diego-chargers-st-louis-rams/99848210/.

59. Alice Marwick, *Status Update* (New Haven, CT: Yale University Press, 2013), ch. 5.

60. UBER, "Uber | MADD," www.uber.com/partner/madd/.

61. "MADD Canada" and "Driving for an Angel: Shelly's Story," Uber passenger app, December 2017, screenshot taken by the author.

62. See, e.g., in Canada, "Don't Drink and Drive: Make DDADD Your Last Call," Designated Drivers Against Drinking Drivers, https://ddadd.ca/; Christina Stevens, "Designated Driver Companies in Durham Say New Municipal Rules Will Kill Industry," *Global News,* December 9, 2015, http://globalnews.ca/news/2391673/designated-driver-companies-in-durham-say-new-municipal-rules-will-kill-industry/; Adam Hunter, "Sask. Company Hoping to Curb Drunk Driving Problem in Province," *CBC News,* September 16, 2016, www.cbc.ca/news/canada/saskatchewan/sask-designated-driving-company-looking-for-support-1.3765611; for the United States, see Scott Koegler, "Free Designated Drivers in 24 Cities in the US," *Exuberation!* http://exuberation.com/regions-and-travels-publisher/326-free-designated-drivers-in-24-cities-in-the-us; DrinkingandDriving.org, "Prevention Tools," www.drinkingand driving.org/designated-driver-services/.

63. Alex Rosenblat, "Is Your Uber/Lyft Driver in Stealth Mode?" *Uber Screeds,* July 19, 2016, https://medium.com/uber-screeds/is-your-uber-driver-in-hiding-484696894139.

64. Judgment of December 20, 2017, Asociación Profesional Élite Taxi v. Uber Systems Spain SL, EU:C:2017:981, http://curia.europa.eu/juris /documents.jsf?num=C-434/15.

65. Charlotte Alter, "UN Women Breaks Off Partnership with Uber," *Time,* March 23, 2015, http://time.com/3754537/un-women-breaks-off-partnership-with-uber/.

66. Susan Fowler, "Reflecting on One Very, Very Strange Year at Uber," *Susan Fowler* (blog), February 19, 2017, www.susanjfowler.com/blog/2017/2/19 /reflecting-on-one-very-strange-year-at-uber.

67. Ibid.

68. Sarah Lacy, "Susan Fowler Did This," *Pando,* June 12, 2017, https:// pando.com/2017/06/12/susan-fowler-did/.

69. Sara Ashley O'Brien, "Backlash Results after Uber Teams Up with Girls Who Code," *CNN Tech,* August 25, 2017, http://money.cnn.com/2017 /08/25/technology/business/uber-girls-who-code-donation-backlash/index .html.

70. Corinne Warnshuis (@corinnepw), Twitter, August 24, 2017, https:// twitter.com/corinnepw/status/900915184960667649.

71. For further reading, the dynamics of masculine toughness mentioned here are explored in the context of low-income fatherhood in Kathryn Edin and Timothy J. Nelson, *Doing the Best I Can: Fatherhood in the Inner City* (Berkeley: University of California Press, 2014).

72. Perri Chase, "My Comments on the Unroll.Me/Uber Situation," *Medium,* April 25, 2017, https://medium.com/@bethebutterfly/i-need-to-say-something-about-the-freak-out-in-response-to-uber-and-unroll-me-f17c42abaaa1.

73. Lucinda Shen, "200,000 Users Have Left Uber in the #DeleteUber Protest," *Fortune,* February 3, 2017, http://fortune.com/2017/02/03/uber-lyft-delete-donald-trump-executive-order/.

74. Alison Griswold, "Uber Did Nothing Wrong, but That Couldn't Stop the Liberal Outrage of #DeleteUber," *Quartz,* January 30, 2017, https://qz .com/898159/why-are-people-deleting-uber-a-trump-backlash-the-company-didnt-deserve/.

75. Sherman Alexie quoted in Anne Helen Petersen, "Sherman Alexie on Not Being 'the Kind of Indian That's Expected,'" *Buzzfeed News,* June 25, 2017, www.buzzfeed.com/annehelenpetersen/sherman-alexie-is-not-the-indian-you-expected.

76. Benjamin Edelman, "Uber Can't Be Fixed—It's Time for Regulators to Shut It Down," *Harvard Business Review,* June 21, 2017, https://hbr.org/2017/06 /uber-cant-be-fixed-its-time-for-regulators-to-shut-it-down.

77. Jim Dwyer, "For Uber and Other Drivers at Kennedy, a Long Wait to Do Their Business," *New York Times,* June 29, 2017, www.nytimes.com/2017/06/29/nyregion/uber-drivers-kennedy-airport-restrooms.html.

78. Noam Scheiber, "Uber to Repay Millions to Drivers, Who Could Be Owed Far More," *New York Times,* May 24, 2017, www.nytimes.com/2017/05/23/business/economy/uber-drivers-tax.html.

79. Alison Griswold, "Inside Uber's Unsettling Alliance with Some of New York's Shadiest Car Dealers," *Quartz,* June 27, 2017, https://qz.com/1013882/ubers-rental-and-lease-programs-with-new-york-car-dealers-push-drivers-toward-shady-subprime-contracts/.

80. See, e.g., Biz Carson, "A Former Uber Driver Who Slept in Her Car Just Won a $15,000 Legal Settlement with Uber," *Business Insider,* January 12, 2016, www.businessinsider.com/uber-driver-slept-with-family-in-vehicle-rented-from-uber-2016-1; Carla Green and Sam Levin, "Homeless, Assaulted, Broke: Drivers Left Behind as Uber Promises Change at the Top," *The Guardian,* June 17, 2017, www.theguardian.com/us-news/2017/jun/17/uber-drivers-homeless-assault-travis-kalanick.

81. Eric Newcomer and Olivia Zaleski, "When Their Shifts End, Uber Drivers Set Up Camp in Parking Lots across the U.S.," *Bloomberg Technology,* January 23, 2017, www.bloomberg.com/news/articles/2017-01-23/when-their-shifts-end-uber-drivers-set-up-camp-in-parking-lots-across-the-u-s.

82. Avi Asher-Schapiro, "As Uber Probes Sexual Harassment at Its Offices, It Overlooks Hundreds of Thousands of Female Drivers," *The Intercept,* May 4, 2017, https://theintercept.com/2017/05/04/as-uber-probes-sexual-harassment-at-its-offices-it-overlooks-hundreds-of-thousands-of-female-drivers/.

83. Douglas MacMillan and Newley Purnell, "Smoke, Then Fire: Uber Knowingly Leased Unsafe Cars to Drivers," *Wall Street Journal,* August 3, 2017, www.wsj.com/articles/smoke-then-fire-uber-knowingly-leased-unsafe-cars-to-drivers-1501786430.

84. Mike Isaac, "Uber's C.E.O. Plays with Fire," *New York Times,* April 23, 2017, www.nytimes.com/2017/04/23/technology/travis-kalanick-pushes-uber-and-himself-to-the-precipice.html.

85. Julia Carrie Wong, "Uber's 'Hustle-Oriented' Culture Becomes a Black Mark on Employees' Résumés," *The Guardian,* March 7, 2017, www.theguardian.com/technology/2017/mar/07/uber-work-culture-travis-kalanick-susan-fowler-controversy.

86. Susan J. Fowler, "Reflecting on One Very, Very Strange Year at Uber," February 19, 2017, *Susan Fowler* (blog), www.susanjfowler.com/blog/2017/2/19/reflecting-on-one-very-strange-year-at-uber.

87. Kara Swisher, "With Her Blog Post about Toxic Bro-Culture at Uber, Susan Fowler Proved That One Person Can Make a Difference," *ReCode,* June 21, 2017, www.recode.net/2017/6/21/15844852/uber-toxic-bro-company-culture-susan-fowler-blog-post.

88. Reuters, "Uber Picks Dallas and Dubai for Its Planned 2020 Flying Taxi Launch," *Fortune,* April 25, 2017, http://fortune.com/2017/04/26/uber-dallas-dubai-2020-flying-taxi-launch/.

89. Tony Romm, "A Powerful Group of Black Lawmakers Is Pressuring Uber to Hire More Diverse Executives," *ReCode,* June 26, 2017, www.recode.net/2017/6/26/15871344/uber-black-lawmakers-hire-diversity-executives-cedric-richmond-congressional-caucus.

CONCLUSION

1. Portions of this section originally appeared as a *Fast Company* article I wrote. See Alex Rosenblat, "The Network Uber Drivers Built," January 9, 2018, *Fast Company,* www.fastcompany.com/40501439/the-network-uber-drivers-built. This fieldwork also draws on a collaborative project: see Alexandra Mateescu, Alex Rosenblat, and Julia Ticona, "Mapping Inequalities in the On-Demand Economy" (unpublished white paper, New York: Data & Society Research Institute, January 31, 2018).

2. V. B. Duval, email correspondence with the author, February 1, 2018.

3. Mateescu, Rosenblat, and Ticona, "Mapping Inequalities."

4. Alison Griswold, "Uber Drivers Are Using This Trick to Make Sure the Company Doesn't Underpay Them," *Quartz,* April 13, 2017, https://qz.com/956139/uber-drivers-are-comparing-fares-with-riders-to-check-their-pay-from-the-company/.

5. Christian Perea, "Uber's Upfront Pricing Is Secretly Overcharging Passengers without Paying Drivers," *The Rideshare Guy,* September 26, 2016, https://therideshareguy.com/ubers-upfront-pricing-is-secretly-overcharging-passengers-without-paying-drivers/.

6. "Workers who provide services through online intermediaries, such as Uber or Task Rabbit, accounted for 0.5 percent of all workers in 2015." Lawrence F. Katz and Alan B. Krueger, "The Rise and Nature of Alternative Work Arrangements in the United States, 1995–2015," working paper 22667, *National Bureau of Economic Research,* September 2016, www.nber.org/papers/w22667.pdf.

7. Noam Scheiber, "How Uber's Tax Calculation May Have Cost Drivers Hundreds of Millions," *New York Times,* July 6, 2017, www.nytimes.com/2017/07/05/business/how-uber-may-have-improperly-taxed-its-drivers.html.

8. Fredrick Kunkle, "Lyft Drivers Call for Investigation into Alleged 'Wage Theft,'" *Washington Post,* May 31, 2017, www.washingtonpost.com/news/tripping /wp/2017/05/31/lyft-drivers-call-for-investigation-into-alleged-wage-theft/.

9. Lawrence F. Katz and Alan B. Krueger, "The Rise and Nature of Alternative Work Arrangements in the United States, 1995–2015," Working Paper 22667, National Bureau of Economic Research, September 2016, www.nber .org/papers/w22667.pdf.

10. Jared Meyer, "By Losing Uber, Austin Is No Longer a Tech Capital," *Forbes,* May 11, 2016, www.forbes.com/sites/jaredmeyer/2016/05/11/by-losing-uber-austin-is-no-longer-a-tech-capital/. Meyer, author of *How Progressive Cities Fight Innovation* (Encounter Books, 2017), has been a strong sharing-economy proponent.

11. In February 2017, Statistics Canada released numbers demonstrating that between November 2015 and October 2016, only 5 percent of Vancouverites had used ridehailing services, in contrast to their peers in Toronto (about 15 percent) and Ottawa-Gatineau (about 18 percent). See Statistics Canada, "Proportion of the Population Aged 18 and Older That Used Peer-to-Peer Ride Services from November 2015 to October 2016, by Selected Census Metropolitan Areas," n.d., www.statcan.gc.ca/daily-quotidien/170228/cg-b002-eng.htm.

12. University of British Columbia, "Why Has Vancouver Been So Slow to Join the Sharing Economy?" n.d., www.alumni.ubc.ca/2017/webcasts/vancouver-slow-join-sharing-economy/.

13. Tracey Read, "Painsville Judge Requiring Drunk Driving Defendants to Download Uber, Lyft on Smartphones," *News-Herald,* June 10, 2017, www .news-herald.com/general-news/20170610/painesville-judge-requiring-drunk-driving-defendants-to-download-uber-lyft-on-smartphones.

14. TOI Staff, "Traffic Jam as Waze Mistakenly Declares J'lem-TA Road Closed," *Times of Israel,* February 22, 2017, www.timesofisrael.com/traffic-snarls-as-waze-mistakenly-declares-main-road-closed/.

15. Tim Wu, "The Tyranny of Convenience," *New York Times,* February 16, 2018, www.nytimes.com/2018/02/16/opinion/sunday/tyranny-convenience.html ?mtrref=www.nytimes.com&assetType=opinion.

APPENDIX 1. METHODOLOGY

1. From our first research study, which began with a grant from Microsoft Research in 2014, my colleague Dr. Luke Stark and I coauthored a journal

article titled "Algorithmic Labor and Information Asymmetries: A Case Study of Uber's Drivers." Our research primarily relied on ethnography in driver forums, but we also interviewed seven drivers as part of our study. It was submitted to the New York University Institutional Review Board, which deemed it exempt from further review. In 2016, I embarked on a second study, on which I am the sole principal investigator, titled "Regional Adaptations: Ridehail Driving." It was overseen by Advarra (formerly Chesapeake Research Review, Institutional Review Board) and partly funded by the John D. and Catherine T. MacArthur Foundation through an initiative at the Data & Society Research Institute titled Intelligence & Autonomy. I submitted a modification to "Regional Adaptations: Ridehail Driving" to the Advarra Institutional Review Board in order to expand its scope and include a focus on health, and it, too, was deemed exempt from further review under the same supervision by Advarra. The results of this modified section of the study were used as part of a comparative project with sociologist Dr. Julia Ticona (the lead principal investigator of this project) and research analyst Alexandra Mateescu. The project was titled "Mapping Inequalities in the On-Demand Economy" and funded by the Robert Wood Johnson Foundation.

APPENDIX 2. RIDEHAILING BEYOND UBER

1. Lyft Blog, "Lyft Is Now Live across 40 States," August 31, 2017, https://blog.lyft.com/posts/live-across-40-states.

2. Darrell Etherington, "Lyft Raises $1 Billion at $11 Billion Valuation Led by Alphabet's CapitalG," *Tech Crunch,* October 19, 2017, https://techcrunch.com/2017/10/19/lyft-raises-1-billion-at-11-billion-valuation-led-by-alphabets-capitalg/.

3. Rani Molla, "Uber's Market Share Has Taken a Big Hit," *Recode,* August 31, 2017, www.recode.net/2017/8/31/16227670/uber-lyft-market-share-deleteuber-decline-users.

4. San Francisco County Transportation Authority, "TNCs Today: A Profile of San Francisco Transportation Network Company Activity," June 2017, www.sfcta.org/sites/default/files/content/Planning/TNCs/TNCs_Today_112917.pdf.

5. Jessica, "New Survey: Drivers Choose Uber for Its Flexibility and Convenience," *Uber Newsroom,* December 7, 2015, https://newsroom.uber.com/driver-partner-survey/.

6. Lyft, "Explore," February 14, 2018, www.lyft.com/.

7. Uber, "Get there," February 14, 2018, www.uber.com/.

8. Harry Campbell, "2018 Uber and Lyft Driver Survey Results—*The Ride-share Guy*," February 26, 2018, *The Rideshare Guy*, https://therideshareguy .com/2018-uber-and-lyft-driver-survey-results-the-rideshare-guy/.

INDEX